THEOLOGY IN TRANSPOSITION

THEOLOGY IN TRANSPOSITION

A CONSTRUCTIVE APPRAISAL OF T. F. TORRANCE

MYK HABETS

Fortress Press
Minneapolis

THEOLOGY IN TRANSPOSITION

A Constructive Appraisal of T. F. Torrance

Copyright © 2013 Fortress Press. All rights reserved. Except for brief quotations in critical articles or reviews, no part of this book may be reproduced in any manner without prior written permission from the publisher. Visit http://www.augsburgfortress.org/copyrights/ or write to Permissions, Augsburg Fortress, Box 1209, Minneapolis, MN 55440.

An alternate version of chapter 4 appeared as "Beyond Henry's Nominalism and Evangelical Foundationalism: Thomas Torrance's Theological Realism," in *Gospel, Truth and Interpretation: Evangelical Identity in Aotearoa New Zealand*, Archer Studies in Pacific Christianity, ed. Tim Meadowcroft and Myk Habets, forewords by Derek Tidball and David Bebbington (Auckland: Archer Press, 2011), 205–40, © used with permission.

An alternate version of chapter 5 appeared as "T. F. Torrance: Mystical Theologian *Sui Generis*," *Princeton Theological Review* 14.2, Issue 39 (Fall 2008): 91–104, © used with permission.

An alternate version of chapter 6 appeared as "How 'Creation is Proleptically Conditioned by Redemption,'" *Colloquium* 41 (2009): 3–21, © used with permission.

Cover design: Alisha Lofgren

Library of Congress Cataloging-in-Publication Data

Print ISBN: 978-0-8006-9994-9

eBook ISBN: 978-1-4514-6529-7

The paper used in this publication meets the minimum requirements of American National Standard for Information Sciences — Permanence of Paper for Printed Library Materials, ANSI Z329.48-1984.

Manufactured in the U.S.A.

This book was produced using PressBooks.com, and PDF rendering was done by PrinceXML.

To Odele, my friend, companion, and wife: the greatest gift the Lord could give; a constant reminder of God's love, mercy, and grace in my life. I am a better person because of you—I love you.

CONTENTS

Acknowledgements ix
Abbreviations xi
Foreword xiii
Introduction 1

Part I. The Architectonic Nature of Torrance's Scientific Christian Dogmatics: Essays on Method

1. Who Is Thomas Forsyth Torrance? 7
2. Scientific Theology 27
   And Theological Science
3. Natural Theology 67
   And a Theology of Nature
4. Realist Theology 95
   And Theological Realism

Part II. Select Themes within Torrance's Theological Oeuvre: Essays on Content

5. Mystical Theology 125
   Reading Torrance as a Mystical Theologian Sui Generis
6. Integrative Theology 145
   God, World, Humanity
7. Christocentric Theology 163
   The Fallen Humanity of the Son of God

Postscript: Torrance for the Twenty-First Century 197
Bibliography 199
Index of Names and Subjects 221

Acknowledgements

Studying the theology of Thomas Torrance has been a fascinating and rewarding journey for me. When I first started doctoral studies I was immersed into the primary and secondary literature on Torrance; his influences, critics, and sources. In addition, the world of Eastern Orthodox theology was opened up to me for the first time in any real depth. I was forced to interact with the theology-science dialogue, something I had avoided for too long, as I read Einstein, Polanyi, Maxwell, and Polkinghorne, among many others. I was enticed into the protracted debates that surround Reformed theology more generally.

One thing I found out very quickly was how enthusiastic and supportive fellow Torrance scholars are, no matter what continent or time zone. My first contact was with Professor Elmer Colyer, Torrance's foremost interpreter. His enthusiasm for my project and his sage advice were welcome words along the scholarly journey. I am grateful for the foreword El most generously provided for this work, and the kind words he offered there. I next met (if cyberspace counts as a "meeting") Professor Alan Torrance, who offered explanations and advice almost as often as I would email him. A visit to St. Andrews in 2004 resulted in a personal meeting over coffee and cake, where I was treated to an impromptu theology lesson replete with napkin-drawn diagrams. The cake and coffee was no match for the conversation and charts. A visit to Oxford also allowed me to talk at some length with Professor Alister McGrath and Father Thomas Weinandy, who both welcomed me graciously and never once looked at their clocks (as far as I am aware). Father Weinandy's knowledge and assistance was very welcome, and Professor McGrath's advice on method encouraged me that I was headed in the right direction in my studies. Of course my doctoral supervisor, colleague, and friend Professor Ivor Davidson was supremely useful in keeping me on track, directing my studies, and critiquing my work. His influence on my work on Torrance is profound, even when I may disagree with him. His regular comment, "Where is the critique?" still rings in my ears. I trust in this work the critique is obvious.

After doctoral studies I had the good fortune to get to know Professor Paul Molnar, first through his publications and then in person as we worked together on a project on Barth's theology. Paul quickly became a friend and has offered many insights into Torrance's theology and its implications, for which I am grateful. He also provided me with a fifteen-page critique of my PhD thesis as part of his external examination of it! Thank you Paul; I appreciate you very much.

This short list could be amplified many times over. Scholars around the world have willingly offered their time and expertise in discussing aspects of Torrance's theology with me, from Professor Bruce McCormack to Torrance blogger Bobby Grow. Thank you all, and I trust I will in turn pass on to others what I have received.

I am grateful to the principal and board of Carey Baptist College for a research sabbatical in the second semester of 2009, which allowed me to complete a first draft of the project, and to SAIACS (Bangalore, India) for the invitation to teach and spend time in researching and writing parts of the manuscript. A second sabbatical and a second trip to SAIACS, along with a fall semester at Princeton Theological Seminary in the second semester of 2012, allowed me to complete the project. I can only echo the words of Princeton's most famous son, Albert Einstein: "I am privileged . . . to live here in Princeton. I feel doubly thankful that there has fallen on my lot a place for work and a scientific atmosphere which could not be better or more harmonious." I am thankful to Dr. Ian Payne, principal of SAIACS, and to Professor Iain Torrance, president of PTS, for invitations to research at their respective institutions, and for the warm welcome my family and I received.

I appreciate the expert assistance provided by Michael Gibson and the team at Fortress Press whose professionalism and efficiency made the task of publication both pleasant and smooth.

Finally, my thanks and love go to my wife Odele and our two children—Sydney and Liam. I am truly blessed by God to have such a wife as Odele whose love and encouragement is unfailing. My heart swells as my daughter Sydney points out "daddy's books" to visitors with great pride, despite the fact that they have no pictures in them. It is to Liam, however, that I offer my final thanks, as it was directly due to his influence that the present volume was conceived very early one morning after one of his restless nights. Thanks, Liam!

Myk Habets
Doctor Serviens Ecclesiae
Princeton, NJ

Abbreviations

ATI American Theological Inquiry
ANF Ante-Nicene Fathers
BibSac Bibliotheca Sacra
BJPS British Journal for the Philosophy of Science
CBQ Catholic Biblical Quarterly
CD Church Dogmatics
CQR Church Quarterly Review
EvQ Evangelical Quarterly
GOTR Greek Orthodox Theological Review
HTR Harvard Theological Review
HeyJ Heythrop Journal
IJST International Journal of Systematic Theology
ITQ Irish Theological Quarterly
JASA Journal of the American Scientific Affiliation
MTSB Moravian Theological Seminary Bulletin
NZST Neue Zeitschrift für systematische Theologie und Religionsphilosophie
NBf New Blackfriars
NPNF² Nicene and Post-Nicene Fathers, Second Series
PSCF Perspectives on Science and Christian Faith
RefR Reformed Review
RelS Religious Studies
SBET Scottish Bulletin of Evangelical Theology
SJT Scottish Journal of Theology
StudBT Studia Biblica Et Theologia
SHPS Studies in History and Philosophy of Science
Them Themelios
TS Theological Studies
TLZ Theologische Literaturzeitung
TT Theology Today
TAD Tradition and Discovery: The Polanyi Society Periodical
TJ Trinity Journal

WTJ *Westminster Theological Journal*
ZDTh *Zeitschrift für dialektische Theologie*
ZdZ *Zweschen den Zeiten*

Foreword

Theology in Transposition is a marvelous and erudite analysis of Thomas F. Torrance's method and theology. This is no small feat, as anyone who wants to grasp Torrance's work is forced into deep dialogue with the history of modern philosophy, natural science, hermeneutics, and theology simply to be able to enter into real conversation with Torrance. Indeed, nearly everyone in the theological world agrees that theological method is one of several areas where Torrance breaks new ground. The sheer depth and breadth of Torrance's awareness of this vast intellectual terrain is virtually unique among theologians.

What is impressive about Myk Habets's work is that he sees the interconnection between the Trinitarian and christological content of Torrance's theology and the whole area of theological method in a manner that few others do. This is not entirely surprising, since Habets has been reading Torrance for a long time, indeed all the way back to his doctoral studies and even before that. His numerous publications on Torrance's theology cover nearly a decade and reveal a prolonged encounter with Torrance's work. This addition to a growing body of secondary literature is crucial reading for anyone interested in Torrance's work on theological method and his theology in general.

The first chapter of *Theology in Transposition* helpfully places Torrance's work within his life and career. Habets then deals with Torrance's methodological commitments in relation to philosophy of science, natural theology, and biblical hermeneutics. Part two illustrates the interconnections between theological content and theological method by examining three key themes in Torrance's theology: mystical theology (what I would call the participatory dimension of Torrance's theology), the integrative character of Torrance's doctrine of creation, and christology, especially the vicarious nature of Christ's assuming our fallen sinful humanity.

Throughout, Habets enters into critical dialogue not only with Torrance, but also with Torrance's interpreters and critics. By the end, one not only has a grasp of Torrance's own position, but that of others who have entered into dialogue with him. This is a masterful work and deserves a careful reading by all those interested in Torrance's theology.

On a personal note, I have known Professor Habets for many years. We have corresponded extensively since his doctoral studies. He is an outstanding scholar and person who has made yet another stunning contribution to Torrance scholarship.

October 5, 2012
Rev. Dr. Elmer M. Colyer
Professor of Systematic Theology
Stanley Professor of Wesley Studies
University of Dubuque Theological Seminary
Dubuque, IA

Introduction

What follows is an exposition of Torrance's theological method and an examination of several key theological themes that model his theological method and provide opportunities to see his theology in a holistic and unified fashion. Part one is a modest attempt to supplement Elmer Colyer's fine *How to Read Thomas Torrance*[1] with a critical and concise overview of Torrance's method and scope—his architectonic scientific Christian dogmatics. It is not an attempt at an intellectual biography as offered by Alister McGrath,[2] nor is it a theological appraisal of how his doctrine of the Trinity structures his entire dogmatics, something ably provided by Paul Molnar.[3] Rather, it is a critical introduction to Torrance's methodological commitments, especially as these relate to the philosophy of science in chapter two and natural theology in chapter three. The former discussion brings Torrance into dialogue with scientists of all stripes, while the latter brings his theology into dialogue with that of Karl Barth and his modern-day interpreters. In chapter four, Torrance's hermeneutic and adoption of a "depth exegesis" is explained and then compared and contrasted with certain features of, and criticism from, fundamentalist evangelicals such as Carl Henry.

Part two examines several areas of Torrance's theology in which he has particularly distinctive emphases and brings him into dialogue with contemporary voices that seek to explicate similar themes, albeit in different ways. Chapter five provides something of a summative evaluation of Torrance's theological approach and brings him into dialogue with the mystical tradition common to the East. Torrance's theology exhibits features not normally associated with Western, Reformed theology, especially the place he affords Christian experience. This approach meant that Torrance made space for themes rather unfamiliar in Western theology, which in turn enabled him to incorporate mystical themes into his scientific dogmatics. I will suggest that precisely because of the presence of these themes, Torrance may be regarded as a theological mystic—but one *sui generis*. This claim runs counter to many

---

1. Elmer M. Colyer, *How To Read T. F. Torrance: Understanding his Trinitarian and Scientific Theology* (Downers Grove, IL: InterVarsity, 2001).
2. Alister E. McGrath, *T. F. Torrance: An Intellectual Biography* (Edinburgh: T&T Clark, 1999).
3. Paul D. Molnar, *Thomas F. Torrance: Theologian of the Trinity* (Surrey: Ashgate, 2009).

voices within Torrance scholarship, and yet best explains the evidence and develops his thought in useful ways.

Chapter six illustrates the systematic, coherent, and comprehensive nature of Torrance's theology of integration by examining an aspect of his doctrine of creation. Central to Torrance's theology is an explanation of how creation is proleptically conditioned by redemption. Here we see how Torrance is able to integrate Christology into his doctrine of creation in ways that are faithful to his epistemic commitments and theological interpretation of Scripture. Into the christologically anemic landscape that characterizes much current discussion on doctrines of creation, these insights of Torrance may take on new life and vigor if they are once again taken up and applied to today's constructive theologies. This chapter shows that Torrance was a truly systematic theologian as well as being a renowned dogmatician.

In chapter seven, Torrance's commitment to explicating the fallen humanity of Christ will be brought into dialogue with recent attempts to both support and critique this theology. It will be argued that Torrance has something significant to add to this discussion, and in fact his articulation of the issue may advance current discussion further than it would go if it continued to ignore his unique contribution. As Christology forms the center of his entire theology on the foundation of the doctrine of the Trinity, this chapter will highlight the coherent, consistent, and comprehensive nature of Torrance's dogmatics and how the reality of Jesus Christ the incarnate Word comes to inform and structure the entire content of a truly Christian dogmatics.

Part one is oriented toward the graduate student who may come to Torrance ill prepared to understand the method or content of his theology. For those familiar with Torrance, these chapters provide a critical evaluation of his theological methodology as it is brought into dialogue with recent critics. In so doing, they offer a unique and critical perspective on these aspects of Torrance's work. Part two is intended to move novices into a deeper engagement with Torrance's Christian dogmatics, thus equipping them to take up Torrance's theology and allow it to aid in enriching the grand march of the Great Tradition as Christian thinkers strive by the Spirit to be faithful to God and God's Holy Word. For seasoned scholars, part two offers perspectives on doing theology in a Torrancean key and thus goes beyond introduction. Instead, it presents a dogmatic vision for the transposition of theology inspired by Torrance's dogmatics.

It is my hope that this modest volume may provide a useful introduction to several key aspects of Torrance's theology so that more people can read his work for themselves and be able to mine them for theological truth and spiritual value. It is also intended to show how one may use Torrance's work and yet work through him, as it were, to one's own conclusions. It has been a privilege for me to work in depth with Torrance's theology for a number of years and to be reminded, again and again, of the wonderful love and constant fellowship of the triune God of Grace that shines forth in the incarnate Son of God and is made known by the Holy Spirit sent from the Father, through the Son. May you, the reader, also experience such blessing.

PART I

The Architectonic Nature of Torrance's Scientific Christian Dogmatics: Essays on Method

1

Who Is Thomas Forsyth Torrance?

Professor Thomas Forsyth Torrance—TF to his students (to distinguish him from his brother JB), or Tom to those who knew him—was a towering figure in twentieth century theology. His prodigious literary output, translation work, edited volumes, international speaking engagements, and ecclesiastical and ecumenical endeavors cast a huge influence over theology and theologians working with him, against him, and after him. Now in the twenty-first century the impact of his work is still being felt as PhDs are completed on his work, monographs roll off the presses detailing and critiquing aspects of his theology, and societies and even entire denominations are established to disseminate central features of his thought.[1] Clearly, the theology of Thomas Torrance, his method and content, continues to be of interest today, and for good reason.

To introduce Torrance (1913–2007), a full biography of the man and his life is not in order. Alister McGrath has done an admirable job in providing the interested reader with an intellectual biography.[2] However, given Torrance's axiom that to know God we must know God in God's act and being, it seems appropriate to apply the same methodology to our exploration of Torrance: to

---

1. I am referring specifically to the Thomas Torrance Theological Fellowship and its theological journal, *Participatio*, and Grace Communion International, formerly the Worldwide Church of God, which has adopted Torrance's Trinitarian theology as the basis of its own theological trajectory.

2. Alister E. McGrath, *T. F. Torrance: An Intellectual Biography* (Edinburgh: T&T Clark, 1999). A very short T. F. Torrance "in a nutshell" can be found in A. G. Marley, *T. F. Torrance: The Rejection of Dualism*, Nutshell Series vol. 4 (Edinburgh: Handsel, 1992). A short biography on the three Torrance brothers (Thomas, James, and David) can be found in J. Stein, "The Legacy of the Gospel," in *A Passion for Christ: Vision that Ignites Ministry*, ed. G. Dawson and J. Stein (Edinburgh: Handsel, 1999), 131–50. A brief biography by Jock Stein and an early account of Torrance's parish ministry can be found in *Gospel, Church, and Ministry*, Thomas F. Torrance Collected Studies 1, ed. Jock Stein (Eugene, OR: Pickwick, 2012), ix–xxxii and 1–49. Autobiographical materials on his boyhood in China, student years, parish ministry, war service, and two visits to China in his later years are also available in The Thomas F. Torrance Manuscript Collection. Special Collections, Princeton Theological Seminary Library, Box 10.

know his theology is to know him, and vice versa. To this end we ask: Who is Thomas Forsyth Torrance?

T. F. Torrance is variously described as "an outstanding churchman and theologian,"[3] "one of the greatest Protestant theologians of our day,"[4] "undoubtedly one of the most significant Christian theologians of the twentieth century,"[5] or as Alister McGrath opens his biography on Torrance, "widely regarded, particularly outside Great Britain, as the most significant British academic theologian of the twentieth century."[6] Donald MacLeod, in a critical assessment of Torrance's work on Scottish theology, refers to him as "among the immortals of Scottish theology, his work on the trinity an enduring and priceless legacy."[7] It is perhaps more appropriate to say, with Torrance's American commentator Elmer Colyer, that "there is a growing consensus that Thomas F. Torrance is one of the premier theologians in the second half of the twentieth century."[8] Personally, I find Torrance to be one of the most stimulating and exacting theologians of the past century. Torrance has been particularly formative for my own theological thinking by forcing me back to the Fathers, into other avenues of scientific enquiry, and in developing the doctrine of the Trinity as the ground and grammar of Christian theology. Torrance is a theologian's theologian, and for that reason alone he rewards his commentators with stimulating and fruitful study.

Torrance was a minister of the Church of Scotland, a distinguished professor of Christian dogmatics, a patristic scholar, the chief interpreter of Barth in the English-speaking world, a faithful husband, devoted father, Christian scientist, ecumenical leader, preacher of the gospel, and son of a missionary with an intense missionary fervor himself.[9] Perhaps the greatest

---

3. Daniel W. Hardy, "Thomas F. Torrance," in *The Modern Theologians: An Introduction*, vol. 1, ed. D. F. Ford (Oxford: Blackwell, 1989), 71.

4. Derek Michaud, "Thomas Torrance," in the *Boston Collaborative Dictionary of Western Theology*, http://people.bu.edu/wwildman/bce/torrance.htm, par. 28.

5. Brian Hebblethwaite, "Review of T. F. Torrance: An Intellectual Biography," *SJT* 53 (2000): 239–40.

6. McGrath, *T. F. Torrance*, xi.

7. Donald Macleod, "Dr. T. F. Torrance and Scottish Theology: A Review Article [on his *Scottish Theology from John Knox to John McLeod Campbell*]," *EvQ* 72 (2000): 72.

8. Elmer M. Colyer, *How To Read T. F. Torrance: Understanding His Trinitarian and Scientific Theology* (Downers Grove, IL: InterVarsity, 2001), 11.

9. Iain Mackenzie describes Torrance as "a wild preacher, whose heart and voice sang with a love for a wild Christ." I. Mackenzie, "Let the Brain Take the Strain (or: The Hail in this Tale Falls Mainly on the Gael)," in *St. Andrews Rock*, ed. S. Lamont (London: Bellew, 1992), 82. Interestingly, Mackenzie was referring as much to Torrance's lectures as to his preaching. Early in life Torrance wanted to be a

accolade one could pay Torrance that he himself would welcome is that he was a Christian and one who was utterly persuaded by the truth of the gospel and sought to persuade others of this same truth. He once described himself to his Beechgrove congregation as "a servant of Christ's Word [here] to introduce you to the Saviour, and to help you enter into the fullness of the Christian life."[10]

Family History

Torrance was born in Chengdu, in the province of Sichuan, West China, to missionary parents on August 30, 1913.[11] He is the second-born of six children, three males and three females.[12] Somewhat remarkably, T. F. Torrance's two brothers, James Bruce Torrance and David Wishart Torrance, went on to be theologically educated and ordained as ministers of the Church of Scotland.[13] All three also studied at one time or another under Karl Barth in Basel. The three daughters married ordained ministers of the Church of Scotland. Adding to this already impressive family are two more ministers of the Church of Scotland and professors of theology: Iain, the son of T. F. Torrance,[14] and Alan,

---

missionary "with Tibet in mind." The Thomas F. Torrance Manuscript Collection, Special Collections, Princeton Theological Seminary Library, Box 10, "Student Years– Edinburgh to Basel. 1934–1938," 1.

10. The Thomas F. Torrance Manuscript Collection, Special Collections, Princeton Theological Seminary Library, Box 20, "Beechgrove Church Publications. April 1949," 3, col. 2.

11. His father, Thomas Torrance (1871–1959), was a Presbyterian Scot; his mother, Annie Elizabeth Sharpe (1833–1929), was an Anglican Brit. Both, incidentally, were published authors. Annie ("Betty") Torrance published *How Shall We Train the Child?* and Thomas senior published *China's First Missionaries*.

12. Alister McGrath provides a good overview of Torrance's childhood in Sichuan in McGrath, *T. F. Torrance: An Intellectual Biography* (Edinburgh: T&T Clark, 1999), 3–18, based upon the autobiographical material found in The Thomas F. Torrance Manuscript Collection. Special Collections, Princeton Theological Seminary Library, Box 10, "My Boyhood in China 1913-1927." The three girls are Mary (b. 1912), Grace (b. 1915), and Margaret (b. 1917); the boys are Thomas (b. 1913), James (b. 1923), and David (b. 1924).

13. James Bruce Torrance (1923–2003) was Professor of Systematic Theology at the University of Aberdeen in Scotland. He also served as a parish minister at Invergowrie (Dundee, Scotland), and as a lecturer at New College, University of Edinburgh. For a brief biographical sketch, see A. E. Heron, "James Torrance: An Appreciation," in *Christ in Our Place: The Humanity of God in Christ for the Reconciliation of the World: Essays Presented to Professor James Torrance*, ed. T. A. Hart and D. P. Thimell (Exeter: Paternoster, 1981), 1–8. David Wishart Torrance (1924–), also a brilliant student (like his elder brothers, he too was awarded the Senior Cunningham Fellowship, effectively becoming Dux of New College, Edinburgh), committed himself to parish ministry. Between 1955 to his retirement in 1991 he held three charges: Livingston in West Lothian, Summerhill in Aberdeen, and Earlston in the Borders.

14. Torrance was married to Margaret Spear, an Anglican, in 1946. All three Torrance brothers married into the medical profession: Thomas to a nurse; James to a doctor, Mary Aitken; and David to a doctor, Elizabeth Barton.

the son of J. B. Torrance.[15] It is no wonder that the Torrance clan is sometimes referred to as a theological dynasty![16] Tongue firmly in cheek, Ian Mackenzie comments that Torrance's brain is "in a class of its own." Elaborating further, tongue not so firmly in cheek, he comments, "The Torrance brain is, of course, a reproductive brain, reproducing other Torrance brains in due season, but so far Godfather Torrance is not intellectually threatened by junior members of the neo-orthodox Mafia littered elegantly around the theological colleges of Scotland."[17] In a similar vein, Duncan Forrester once remarked, "And what of Tom the person? We all know him as a bonny fechter [fighter]. He does not cease from mental fight, nor does his sword sleep in his hand. He is the chieftain and patriarch of a remarkable theological clan."[18]

Prior to teaching, T. F. Torrance spent ten years in the ministry of the Church of Scotland, both before and after the Second World War,[19] and later served as Moderator of the General Assembly (1976–77). During the Second World War, Torrance was an army chaplain for the Church of Scotland's Huts and Canteens Committee in the Middle East and then with the Tenth Indian Division in Italy as the Church of Scotland chaplain to one of the battalions, mostly an English battalion—The King's Own Royal Rifles.[20] Torrance's service

---

15. Iain Torrance (1949–) was Professor of Theology at the University of Aberdeen, Scotland, and Moderator of the General Assembly of the Church of Scotland, 2003–4. Since 2001 he has been Chaplain to Her Majesty the Queen of England in Scotland, and has been the co-editor of the *Scottish Journal of Theology* since 1982. From July 2004 to December 2012 he was the president of Princeton Theological Seminary. Alan Torrance is currently Professor of Systematic Theology at St. Andrews University, Scotland, and has taught in Erlangen, Aberdeen, Dunedin, and King's College London as director of the Research Institute in Systematic Theology.

16. The word "dynasty" is used by Alasdair I. Heron, "T. F. Torrance In Relation to Reformed Theology," in *The Promise of Trinitarian Theology: Theologians in Dialogue with T. F. Torrance,* ed. E. M. Colyer (Lanham, MD: Rowman & Littlefield, 2001), 48, n. 25. Several of T. F. Torrance's grandchildren have also engaged in higher theological study (at Cambridge University and the University of Otago).

17. I. Mackenzie, "Let the Brain Take the Strain (or: The Hail in this Tale Falls Mainly on the Gael)," in *St. Andrews Rock*, ed. S. Lamont (London: Bellew, 1992), 76–77.

18. The Thomas F. Torrance Manuscript Collection, Special Collections, Princeton Theological Seminary Library, Box 15, "Speech by Duncan Forrester on the occasion of the unveiling of Thomas F. Torrance's portrait by Geoffrey Squire, New College, Edinburgh. October 3, 1991," 2.

19. In Alyth (1940–43; 45–47) and Aberdeen (1947–50), Scotland. Torrance says of his time as minister of the parish in Alyth that "it was one of the happiest times of my life in the ministry." I. J. Hesselink, "A Pilgrimage in the School of Christ—An Interview with T. F. Torrance," in *RefR* 38 (1984): 55.

20. Hesselink, "A Pilgrimage in the School of Christ," 56, and David W. Torrance, "Thomas Forsyth Torrance: Minister of the Gospel, Pastor, and Evangelical Theologian," in *The Promise of Trinitarian Theology*, 16–17.

in the army was recognized in his 1944 reception of the MBE (Member of the British Empire) for bravery.[21]

EDUCATION

At the University of Edinburgh Torrance studied classics and philosophy, winning various scholarships and awards. It was at this period that he also showed an interest in the philosophy of science. In 1934, after gaining his MA in Classical Languages and Philosophy, Torrance switched to New College and in 1937 gained the BD degree in theology with distinction.[22]

Various teachers in the divinity faculty exercised a lasting influence over Torrance. His interest in Christianity and science was further enhanced as Daniel Lamont introduced Torrance to the work of the scientist Karl Heim of Tübingen. Years later, Torrance would become a member of the Karl Heim *Gesellschaft*. From Hugh Ross Mackintosh Torrance learned the supreme importance of the centrality of Christ, the atonement and the missionary cause. Mackintosh also prompted his interest in the work of Karl Barth,[23] an acquaintance his mother had enhanced when she gave her son a copy of Barth's *Credo* when he entered the Faculty of Divinity at New College. It was this interest and admiration for Barth that prompted Torrance to study under him at Basel in 1937–38 as a member of Barth's little *Sozietät*.[24] Torrance's love for

---

21. Hesselink, "A Pilgrimage in the School of Christ," 56.

22. His BD specialized in systematic theology. Alister E. McGrath, "Profile: Thomas F. Torrance," *Epworth Review* 27 (2000): 11.

23. Thomas F. Torrance, "My Interaction with Karl Barth," in *How Karl Barth Changed My Mind*, ed. D. K. McKim (Grand Rapids: Eerdmans, 1986), 52. Hugh Ross Mackintosh (1870–1936) was Professor of Systematic Theology and then Church Dogmatics at Edinburgh from 1904 to 1936. Torrance regards him as one of his most formative influences and often mentions him in his work. See the memorial essay, T. F. Torrance, "Hugh Ross Mackintosh: Theologian of the Cross," *SBET* 5 (1987): 160–73.

24. Barth never thought that a student was truly theologically qualified unless he understood Latin and could read it proficiently. He set his students a test in translating a Latin text and prescribed an essay to estimate their theological acumen and ability. From them he selected a smaller group to form a more intimate seminar (the *Sozietät*), which met in his own house once a week. In a letter to his friend Eduard Thurneysen, Barth expressed his approval of "der Schotlander." David W. Torrance, "Thomas Forsyth Torrance: Minister of the Gospel, Pastor, and Evangelical Theologian," in *The Promise of Trinitarian Theology: Theologians in Dialogue with T. F. Torrance,* ed. E. M. Colyer (Lanham, MD: Rowman & Littlefield), 9. Incidentally, both of T. F. Torrance's brothers, James and David, were also part of the *Sozietät* in their respective years spent studying with Karl Barth. A firsthand account of Torrance's experiences can be found in The Thomas F. Torrance Manuscript Collection, Special Collections, Princeton Theological Seminary Library, Box 10, "Student Years—Edinburgh to Basel. 1934–1938," where Torrance calls his participation in the group "a priceless privilege" (13). In Torrance's two

and respect of Barth's theology never waned. In one sense his entire writing career has been an attempt to critically explicate the central concerns of Barth's theological method.[25] Torrance would go on to oversee the translation of the *Kirchliche Dogmatik* into English,[26] in addition to devoting several monographs to Barth's life and work.[27]

One should not take from this, however, that Torrance is a Barthian pure and simple. He has always rejected the title and was an appreciative critic of Barth's work, going back to his year studying with Barth in Basel. In a letter to his sister Grace in 1937 he wrote: "I am rereading just now a little book of Barth's on predestination, and so far I don't think he has got to the root of the matter. I have been reading a lot of Barth this summer, and I have been growing rather critical of some things—he lacks the missionary note and the evangelistic note rather sadly. I can't quite make it out, but it is due to his idea of preaching. Barthians are not good preachers. But I will write later about this when I have thought it out more."[28] In a letter to his brother-in-law Ronnie Wallace around the same time Torrance wrote: "'Barth' in German means a beard. Leitzman remarked that one had to be careful and not let one's 'barth' grow too long! I must tell Prin. Curits that when I write him: it will tickle him no end."[29] It obviously amused Torrance too!

---

semesters at Basel the group studied Wolleb's *Compendium Theologiae*, particularly the doctrine of election.

25. Alister E. McGrath, *T. F. Torrance: An Intellectual Biography*(Edinburgh: T&T Clark, 1999), 113–45.

26. T. F. Torrance co-edited and translated the *Church Dogmatics*with Geoffrey Bromiley of Fuller Theological Seminary. See T. F. Torrance, "Preface to New Edition," in *Karl Barth: An Introduction to His Early Theology 1910–1931*(Edinburgh: T&T Clark, 2000), 10.

27. See his various works: *Karl Barth: An Introduction to His Early Theology 1910–1931*; "Karl Barth and the Latin Heresy," *SJT* 39 (1986): 461–82; "My Interaction with Karl Barth," 52–64; and *Karl Barth: Biblical and Evangelical Theologian* (Edinburgh: T&T Clark, 1990). Torrance's correspondence with Barth can be found in The Thomas F. Torrance Manuscript Collection, Special Collections, Princeton Theological Seminary Library, Box 19.

28. Letter to Grace dated October 26, 1937, from Theologisches Alumneum, Basel, in The Thomas F. Torrance Manuscript Collection, Special Collections, Princeton Theological Seminary Library, Box 11, "Letters from Thomas F. Torrance to his parents and siblings, from Basel, Switzerland and Berlin, Germany. 1937–1938," 2 (slightly altered). This should perhaps be balanced with his comments 24 years later when in a personal letter to Barth he noted: "There is little doubt that what Augustine did for centuries and centuries of the Church's thought and preaching, your Church Dogmatics promises to do for the Church of the future, shaping and directing its preaching of the Gospel. It is after all in the service of the Gospels, as you have taught us, that theology has its true place." The Thomas F. Torrance Manuscript Collection, Special Collections, Princeton Theological Seminary Library, Box 19, "Letter from Torrance to Barth dated January 7, 1961," 1–2.

Significant Influences

Throughout Torrance's life and career a constant refrain was the various influences on his spirituality and theology, most notably Athanasius, John Calvin, and Karl Barth in theology,[30] and John Philoponos, Albert Einstein, and Michael Polanyi in the philosophy of science.[31]

Torrance was trained in classics and was a patristic scholar of some renown; his theology is richly steeped in the patristic tradition. His main patristic mentor was Athanasius the bishop of Alexandria.[32] As one of the main shapers of Nicene theology, Athanasius is returned to time and time again in Torrance's corpus for insight and perspective on a range of Trinitarian, christological, and soteriological issues. From Athanasius Torrance adopts the use of the *homoousion* as a heuristic device in which to navigate the epistemological waters of Trinitarian theology.

Torrance wrote theology from a broad and generous Reformed Protestant background. Throughout his life and writings he especially showed an admiration for and reliance upon the theology of John Calvin. Many concepts employed by Calvin were adopted into his own Trinitarian theology. However, while adopting much of Calvin's theological thought, Torrance was scathingly critical of the way Calvin was systematized in later Calvinism, particularly by the seventeenth-century Protestant scholastics.[33] Out of scholasticism (and Enlightenment science) have arisen a number of dualisms that, according to Torrance, threaten to derail or at least sidetrack much contemporary theological

---

29. Letter to Ronnie Wallace dated June 9, 1937 in The Thomas F. Torrance Manuscript Collection, Special Collections, Princeton Theological Seminary Library, Box 11, "Letters from Thomas F. Torrance to his parents and siblings, from Basel, Switzerland and Berlin, Germany. 1937–1938," 1.

30. Other theological influences would include Hilary of Poitiers, Gregory of Nazianzus, Anselm of Canterbury, Richard of St. Victor, John Duns Scotus, John Major, and H. R. Mackintosh. In terms of his patristic influences, Del Colle can correctly speak of Torrance plotting "his own course through the Greek Fathers, a Nicene-Athanasian-Nazianzen-Epiphanian-Cyriline axis to be exact." Ralph Del Colle, "'Person' and 'Being' in John Zizioluas' Trinitarian Theology: Conversations with Thomas F. Torrance and Thomas Aquinas," *SJT* 54 (2001): 77.

31. Other philosophical and scientific mentors include Søren Kierkegaard (a relatively unexamined influence behind Torrance's thought), Karl Heim, and James Clerk Maxwell, among others. Torrance once commented that in his study he has hung on the wall "a line portrait of Einstein . . . looking across to the desk where I work, but I also have in my study portraits of Michael Polanyi and James Clerk Maxwell, from whom I have learned so much." "Thomas Torrance Responds," in *The Promise of Trinitarian Theology: Theologians in Dialogue with T. F. Torrance,* ed. E. M. Colyer (Lanham, MD: Rowman & Littlefield, 2001), 333.

32. Torrance wrote in his little work *Christ's Words* (Jedburgh: The Unity Press, 1980), 4, that Athanasius is "my favourite theologian." There is scarcely a single publication of Torrance's in which the insights of Athanasius are not brought out either implicitly or more often than not, explicitly.

(and scientific) endeavor.³⁴ In Torrance's own work he set himself the task of removing all *a priori* dualisms that have crept into contemporary theology.³⁵

Torrance saw Karl Barth as the most faithful advocate of Calvin's theology and of the orthodox faith in general. As such, Barth's doctrine of God was one of the most influential on Torrance's own exposition of the Christian doctrine of God. Like Barth, Torrance believed that nothing is or can be known of God but that which comes by God's active self-revelation. Torrance took up and consistently developed Barth's claim that what God is in God's revelation, God is antecedently and eternally in Godself (*in se*).³⁶ It is for this reason that Torrance is above all a theologian of the doctrine of the knowledge of God. This knowledge of God is available in a "scientific manner," which leads us into Torrance's "scientific theology."

Beginning in his undergraduate days, progressing through his doctoral studies, and then into his own publications Torrance consistently sought to work out a *scientific* theology. He learned this methodology from several key influences, most notably John Philoponos, Albert Einstein, and Michael Polanyi, and it was modeled for him by Anselm of Canterbury and Karl Barth. Given Torrance's epistemology of self-revelation, he argued it is only natural that this be termed a "scientific theology." Theology for Torrance is always *a posteriori*: first we encounter the active self-presentation of reality that is before us, then we press deeper to understand the order and connectedness of deeper structures of reality. In theological terms, this is a consistent and considered outworking of Anselm's *fides quarens intellectum* tradition of theological enquiry, a methodology that Torrance argues is proper to all scientific investigation, not simply to theology alone. The difference between the various disciplines of theology is, in Derek Michaud's words, that "the nature of the object prescribes

---

33. Something his brother J. B. Torrance is equally concerned about. For a constructive attempt to continue this tradition, see *Evangelical Calvinism: Essays Resourcing the Continuing Reformation of the Church,* ed. Myk Habets and Robert Grow (Eugene, OR: Pickwick, 2012).

34. At this point I am thinking of the theological dualism between *de Deo uno* from *de Deo trino*, something Karl Rahner and Torrance are equally opposed to.

35. See the little work by A. G. Marley, *T. F. Torrance: The Rejection of Dualism,* Nutshell Series vol. 4 (Edinburgh: Handsel, 1992).

36. Barth regarded Torrance as a faithful expositor of his ideas. In 1959, Barth presented Torrance with a copy of *Der Gefangenen Befreiung!* in which he had inscribed the words "Mit herzlichen Dank für viel Treue!" ("with cordial thanks for much loyalty"). Torrance, *Karl Barth: An Introduction to His Early Theology 1910–1931*(Edinburgh: T&T Clark, 2000), 9. In the preface to his work *Karl Barth: Biblical and Evangelical Theologian* (Edinburgh: T&T Clark, 1990), Torrance returned the compliment (xii).

the mode of rationality proper to its investigation."³⁷ We shall consider these issues in more depth in the next chapter.

ACHIEVEMENTS

Torrance earned a doctorate (Dr.Theol.) from Basel in 1946, where he studied under Karl Barth for a year (1937–38),³⁸ and a DLitt (Edinburgh) in 1970.³⁹ He was also awarded eight honorary doctorates,⁴⁰ the Templeton Prize for Progress in Religion (1978), and the Collins Award in Britain for the best work in theology, ethics, and sociology relevant for Christianity for his book *Theological Science*(1967–69). Torrance taught theology at Auburn Seminary, New York for a year (1938–39) before returning to Edinburgh.⁴¹ After two years as Professor of Church History (1950–52), Torrance held the position of Professor of Christian Dogmatics at New College, the University of Edinburgh, for 29 years (1952–79), after which he retired following the conferral of the Templeton Prize in Religion (1978). Torrance started the *Scottish Journal of Theology*, which he co-edited for over thirty years, founded the Scottish Church Theology Society, and served as moderator of the General Assembly of the Church of Scotland in 1976–77. In 1969 he became a member, and from 1972 to 1981 president, of the *Académie Internationale des Sciences Religieuses*. In 1973 he was a founding member, and from 1976 to 1977 president, of the Institute of Religion and Theology of Great Britain and Ireland, and in 1976 a member

---

37. Derek Michaud, "Thomas Torrance," in the *Boston Collaborative Dictionary of Western Theology*, http://people.bu.edu/wwildman/bce/torrance.htm.

38. Torrance returned to Basel to finish his thesis, *Grace in the Apostolic Fathers*(published as *The Doctrine of Grace in the Apostolic Fathers*[Edinburgh: Oliver and Boyd, 1948]), and sit the *Rigorosum* in 1946 after studying at Oriel College, Oxford in 1939–40. The years after 1937–38 at Basel were spent as follows: 1938–39 lecturing at Auburn Seminary, 1939–40 studying at Oxford University, 1940–43 minister at Alyth Parish, 1943–45 war service (including the reception of an MBE in 1944), 1945–47 back to Alyth Parish, 1947–50 minister at Beechgrove Parish.

39. The DLitt was awarded by Edinburgh University on submission of five published works on theological method.

40. Degrees *honoris causa*: DD, 1950: Presbyterian College, Montreal; Dr.Theol., 1959: University of Geneva; D.Théol., 1959: Faculté Libre, Paris; DD, 1960: St. Andrews University; Dr.Theol., 1961: Oslo University; D.Sc., 1983: Heriot-Watt University, Edinburgh; Dr.Th., 1988: Reformed College, Debrecen; and DD, 1997: Edinburgh University. See Alister E. McGrath, *T. F. Torrance: An Intellectual Biography*(Edinburgh: T&T Clark, 1999), 244.

41. The theology component of the Auburn lectures are published as T. F. Torrance, *The Doctrine of Jesus Christ: Auburn Lectures 1938–39*(Eugene, OR: Wipf and Stock, 2002). A full collection of lecture notes, lectures, and other Auburn correspondence is contained in The Thomas F. Torrance Manuscript Collection, Special Collections, Princeton Theological Seminary Library, Boxes 21–23.

of the *Académie Internationale de Philosophie des Sciences*. Beginning in 1979 he was a fellow of the Royal Society of Edinburgh and beginning in 1982 a fellow of the British Academy in London.[42] His work on the interface of science and theology earned him international prestige.

Torrance wrote over thirty books and well over five hundred articles. McGrath has calculated that "Torrance's list of published works contain roughly 320 works which originated during his twenty-nine year period as a professor at Edinburgh. Since retiring from that position in 1979, he has added a further 260 items, including some of his most significant works."[43]

In his various sojourns to the East[44] as part of his scholarship in preparation for his BD degree, Torrance had his first encounters with Eastern Orthodoxy. This relationship would last for the rest of his life as he worked, throughout his teaching and writing career, to form theological bridges between the World Alliance of Reformed Churches and the Eastern Orthodox Churches.[45] In 1954 Torrance called for discussions within the Orthodox Communion between Chalcedonian and non-Chalcedonian "monophysite" traditions. Agreement between them was eventually reached in 1973. Torrance was then invited to Addis Ababa by Methodius, the Greek archbishop of Axum, the see in Ethiopia founded by Athanasius, and was consecrated as a presbyter of the Greek Orthodox Church and given the honorary title of protopresbyter. In 1970, at a session of the General Assembly in Edinburgh, the Patriarch of Alexandria conferred on Torrance the Cross of Saint Mark, which was followed in 1977 by his being given the Cross of Thyateira by the Greek Orthodox archbishop in London. Later Torrance proposed that the Reformed and Eastern

---

42. For a full curriculum vitae see The Thomas F. Torrance Manuscript Collection, Special Collections, Princeton Theological Seminary Library, Box 14, "Thomas F. Torrance—Curricula vitae and bibliography (to 1993)."

43. McGrath, *T. F. Torrance*, 107. The most complete bibliography of T. F. Torrance's works can be found in McGrath, *T. F. Torrance*, 249–96, in which 633 published works from 1941–99 are recorded. Since that time a few additions to the bibliography can be noted, especially the publication of the Auburn Lectures as *The Doctrine of Jesus Christ: Auburn Lectures 1938–39*; and the posthumously published lectures on Christology originally delivered at New College, Edinburgh, from 1952 to 1978: *The Incarnation: The Person and Life of Christ*, ed. Robert T Walker (Downers Grove, IL: IVP Academic, 2008); and *The Atonement: The Person and Work of Christ*, ed. Robert T. Walker (Downers Grove, IL: IVP Academic, 2009).

44. The John Stuart Blackie Fellowship enabled Torrance to travel for three months to the Middle East and a further three months to Greece.

45. Torrance has also been instrumental in ecumenical discussions with the Church of England (1950–58), and the Faith and Order movement (1952–62). See Thomas F. Torrance, *Conflict and Agreement in the Church*, 2 vols. (London: Lutterworth, 1959–60).

Orthodox communions should enter into dialogue, seeking theological consensus on the doctrine of the Trinity, for agreement there would influence all further discussions. The Ecumenical Patriarch and other patriarchs of the Greek Orthodox Church responded favorably, and by 1983 all fourteen Orthodox churches were involved. Between 1986 and 1990 discussions took place resulting in the "Agreed Statement on the Doctrine of the Holy Trinity," reached at Geneva on March 13, 1991.[46] Torrance considered this one of the most important achievements of his lifetime.[47]

Later in life, Torrance returned to China twice and met with the survivors of those churches founded by his father many years earlier. He first visited in October 1984, by way of Hong Kong, the churches of the Upper Min valley. He then returned to the towns of Chengdu and Wenchuan in April–June, 1994. He carried with him a money belt bearing 11,200 yuan, part of a larger gift of money for rebuilding churches destroyed by the communist takeover in 1935.[48] Mention of these visits of Torrance to China, in his seventies and eighties, provides a fitting reminder that he was, first and foremost, a theologian of the church and for the church.

Torrance died on December 2, 2007. Since that time a number of his works have been published, including the two-volume Edinburgh Dogmatics Christology lectures on incarnation and atonement. In addition, the Scottish Journal of Theology Lectures, held annually at the University of Aberdeen, have been renamed the T. F. Torrance Lectures in his honor. Various conferences, themed journal volumes, edited works, theses, and monographs have also been held, completed, and published. The Thomas F. Torrance Theological Fellowship also boasts a healthy and growing membership and the associated journal, *Participatio,*consistently produces volumes of high academic standard and wide interest. His work is still the cause of lively interest and

---

46. Thomas F. Torrance, ed., *Theological Dialogue Between Orthodox and Reformed Churches,*vols. 1 & 2 (Edinburgh: Scottish Academic, 1985, 1993). For the agreed statement see ibid., 2:219–26. Cf. Thomas F. Torrance, *Trinitarian Perspectives: Toward Doctrinal Agreement* (Edinburgh: T&T Clark, 1994).

47. For an analysis and critique of the *filioque* see Myk Habets, "*Filioque? Nein.* A Proposal for Coherent Coinherence," in *Trinitarian Theology After Barth,*ed. Myk Habets and Phillip Tolliday (Eugene, OR: Pickwick, 2011), 161–202.

48. We know these details from the personal unpublished diaries Torrance kept. See Thomas F. Torrance, "The Visit by Thomas F. Torrance to Chengdu, the Capital of Sichuan, and to Weichou and Chiang Villages in Wenchuan County, the Upper Min Valley, Sichuan (October 4–18, 1986)," and "Journal of My Visit to Hong Kong, Chengdu and Wenchuan (April 22–June 3, 1994)," in The Thomas F. Torrance Manuscript Collection, Special Collections, Princeton Theological Seminary Library, Box 10.

considerable debate, and his influence has cast a long shadow over subsequent dogmatics.

Missionary, scholar, world traveler, soldier, pastor, professor, husband, father, and renaissance man—from this briefest of biographies it is evident that Torrance lived a full and exciting life; a life, we may say, worthy of a spot in one of the once popular *Boy's Own Annuals* featuring the exciting lives and daring pursuits of men in the world.[49]

CORE EMPHASES OF TORRANCE'S DOGMATIC THEOLOGY

Torrance's theology has several key components that together comprise his Christian dogmatics. One commentator lists fifteen basic characteristics of his theology: Reformed, Nicene, scientific, realist, relational, systematic, rational, conceptual, personal, doxological, dialogical, ecumenical, christological, Trinitarian, and biblical.[50] It is not germane to our study to comment on all of these areas, but some of the more distinctive aspects will provide a suitable introduction to his theological work, specifically how his theology is at once Reformed, biblical, catholic, ecumenical, christological, and Trinitarian.

REFORMED-BIBLICAL THEOLOGY

Torrance's theology is thoroughly and self-consciously Reformed.[51] As an ordained minister in the Church of Scotland, an authority on John Calvin, a key representative of the World Alliance of Reformed Churches in ecumenical activity, and a pupil of Karl Barth's, Torrance and his theology stand squarely within the Reformed heritage.[52] While Torrance viewed himself as thoroughly

---

49. One wishes he had published his twenty-one-page memoir of his time in the Middle East, as it is a raucous tale of bravery, stupidity, attempted murder, and naïve adventure. During this time Torrance acted as a temporary policeman, was befriended by Nazis, sentenced to death in an Arab court, and propositioned by a woman in one hotel room and a man in another in Athens! See The Thomas F. Torrance Manuscript Collection, Special Collections, Princeton Theological Seminary Library, Box 10, "Memoir of Visit to Palestine and the Middle East in the Spring."

50. Colin Weightman, *Theology in a Polanyian Universe: The Theology of Thomas Torrance*(New York: Peter Lang, 1994), 150, and elaborated on through 155.

51. Torrance's three most important shorter writings on his relation to Reformed theology and what "Reformed theology" itself means are found in "The Deposit of Faith," *SJT* 36 (1983): 1–28; "'The Substance of the Faith': A Clarification of the Concept in the Church of Scotland," *SJT* 36 (1983): 327–38; and "The Distinctive Character of the Reformed Tradition," in *Incarnational Ministry: Essays in Honor of Ray S. Anderson,*ed. C. H. Kettler and T. H. Speidell (Colorado Springs: Helmers and Howard, 1990), 2–15.

52. Despite the criticism of S. Rehnman, "Barthian Epigoni: Thomas F. Torrance's Barth-Reception," *WTJ* 60 (1998): 271–96. See the more conciliatory article by Alasdair I. Heron, "T. F. Torrance in

Reformed, he was a vigorous opponent of Calvin*ism*, that brand of Puritan Calvinism that resulted in the rise of Federal/Westminster Theology, or what has been termed Calvinist scholasticism.[53] As such, Torrance's Reformed theology and vision are what we may call catholic, broad, and generous.

Torrance believed that a genuinely Reformed theology is one in which obedience to Jesus Christ the eternal Word of God as witnessed to through the Word of God written is uppermost. The Reformed *church* is reformed according to the Word of God, and Reformed *theology* is reformed according to the Word of God.[54] As a direct consequence of this feature is its corollary: for Torrance all Christian theology must be biblical. While Torrance's doctrine of Scripture will be analyzed in a subsequent chapter, we can note here his commitment to Scripture as being the Word of God to humanity, the normative realization of God's revelation in Christ.[55] Through the Bible God continues to make Godself known to us in the articulate form of human words. As with Barth, so with Torrance, Scripture is not seen as the revelation of propositional truths than can be adopted as doctrines *simpliciter*. Rather, Scripture does not stand in isolation from Christ *the*Word who speaks through the Word written.[56] For Torrance, as for Barth before him, the Bible constitutes revelation in the sense that through it there is a communication of divine truth in concrete form. In simple terms, Torrance explains that "we do not believe in Jesus Christ because we believe in the Bible, we believe in the Bible because in and through the Bible we meet and know Jesus Christ."[57]

Relation to Reformed Theology," in *The Promise of Trinitarian Theology: Theologians in Dialogue with T. F. Torrance*, ed. E. M. Colyer (Lanham, MD: Rowman & Littlefield, 2001), 31–49.

53. See Thomas F. Torrance, *Scottish Theology from John Knox to John McLeod Campbell* (Edinburgh: T&T Clark, 1996). A histology and evaluation of the diversity that exists within Westminster Calvinism can be found in J. K. Jeon, *Covenant Theology: John Murray's and Meredith Kline's Response to the Historical Development of Federal Theology in Reformed Thought* (Lanham. MD: University Press of America, 1999). For a creative representation of the sort of Reformed trajectory Torrance stood within, see *Evangelical Calvinism: Essays Resourcing the Continuing Reformation of the Church*, ed. Myk Habets and Robert Grow (Eugene, OR: Pickwick, 2012).

54. Thomas F. Torrance, "What Is the Reformed Church?" *Biblical Theology* 9 (1959): 51.

55. See a discussion of Torrance's doctrine of Scripture in chapter four.

56. Torrance, *Theology in Reconstruction*(Eugene, OR: Wipf and Stock, 1996), 134–40.

57. Thomas F. Torrance, "'The Historical Jesus': From the Perspective of a Theologian," in *The New Testament Age: Essays in Honor of Bo Reicke*, vol. 2, ed. W.C. Weinrich (Macon, GA.: Mercer University Press, 1984), 525.

CATHOLIC-ECUMENICAL THEOLOGY

Not only is Torrance's theology Reformed and biblical, it is also catholic. By catholic I mean universally orthodox, grounded in the Great Tradition, and consciously founded on the creeds of Christendom, especially Nicaea and Chalcedon. Indeed, Torrance characterizes his own theology as "deeply Nicene."[58] By "Nicene," Torrance refers to the theologians of the Nicene era, especially Athanasius and Cyril of Alexandria, his two main patristic mentors. It is to these two theologians particularly that Torrance attributes the foundational place of the Trinity in Christian theology as built upon the doctrine of the *homoousion* of Christ (and Spirit) with God the Father.

It is this commitment to a catholic theology that has expressed itself in ecumenical activity and enabled Torrance to interact so productively with the Eastern Orthodox communion along with the Anglican and Roman Catholic traditions. Throughout his ecumenical endeavors the pro-Nicene doctrines of Christology, pneumatology, and Trinity occupied center stage, for Torrance believed that if agreement can be made on those points, then the heart of Christian theology is affirmed and further agreement can be reached in the future on other topics.[59]

TRINITARIAN-CHRISTOLOGICAL THEOLOGY

It naturally follows from the above emphases of Torrance's theology that the doctrines of Theology Proper–God and Christology should come to the fore. Throughout Torrance's life and work these doctrines formed the heart of his theological program. As a lifelong student of Barth, a reader of the Fathers—especially Athanasius—and a Calvin scholar, the doctrine of the Trinity forms the very *ground and grammar* of Torrance's entire theology. Such is the controlling doctrine of the Trinity in his theology that Paul Molnar simply describes Torrance as the "theologian of the Trinity."[60] Torrance's commitment to Trinitarian and Christological theology will become apparent in subsequent chapters.

---

58. R. D. Kernohan, "Tom Torrance: The Man and the Reputation," *Life and Work* 32 (1976): 14.

59. See Thomas F. Torrance, *The School of Faith: The Catechisms of the Reformed Church,* trans. and ed. with introduction by T. F. Torrance (London: James Clarke, 1959), lxviii; "Introduction," in *The Incarnation: Ecumenical Studies in the Nicene-Constantinopolitan Creed A.D. 381,*ed. T. F. Torrance (Edinburgh: Handsel, 1981), xi–xxii; and *Theology in Reconciliation: Essays Towards Evangelical and Catholic Unity in East and West*(reprint, Eugene, OR: Wipf and Stock, 1997), especially "The Agreed Statement on the Holy Trinity," 115–22.

60. Paul D. Molnar, *Thomas F. Torrance: Theologian of the Trinity* (Surrey: Ashgate, 2009).

SCIENTIFIC AND METHODOLOGICAL

Torrance's academic career was almost entirely absorbed by concerns over methodology, to the point that one might suggest all his career might be seen as an attempt at a prolegomena, a clearing of the epistemological ground for a starting point in theological discourse. On more than one occasion Torrance stated that his work was an attempt to clear the way for an explicitly Christian epistemology, one that took seriously the starting point for all knowledge of God in Christology, mediated by the Word written through the Holy Spirit. It was this epistemic concern that led Torrance into his interaction with the sciences—especially physics—and into a concentrated study of hermeneutics.

Torrance sought in the sciences what he sought in theological method—a common starting point. Such a starting point is the awareness of a commitment to a realistic view of the world and then the adoption of a methodology in conformity with the nature of the object under study. Torrance calls this a *kata physic* ("according to the nature of the object") form of scientific inquiry. It is this scientific approach to reality that Torrance saw exemplified in modern scientists such as James Clerk Maxwell and Albert Einstein, to name but two. Maxwell (1831–1879) is generally considered one of the greatest scientists of the modern era and the father of modern physics. Maxwell's experiments led to his discovery of the theory of electromagnetism. Einstein himself credited Maxwell's discoveries as the origins of his own theory of relativity. Torrance looked to the example of Maxwell and his discoveries as a conceptual basis for his own theological methodology, one that stresses continuous fields of relations over and against any mechanical system, for example. Torrance also took note of Maxwell's belief in God and how that influenced his scientific thought. It was on the basis of his Christian beliefs that Maxwell was able to move beyond the accepted scientific theories of his own day in order to develop a fundamentally different concept, which in turn helped him discover the properties of an electromagnetic field of force (what Thomas Kuhn would call a "paradigm shift"). The fact that Maxwell hailed from Edinburgh, Torrance's "home town" would also not be lost on Torrance!

For similar reasons Torrance was enamored with the thought and influence of Albert Einstein (1879–1955), the greatest scientist of them all, according to Torrance. Einstein, like Maxwell, achieved a paradigm shift in physics, but in Einstein's case it effected a revolution. Torrance repeatedly appealed to Einstein as *the* exemplar of a truly scientific method that allows the nature of the object to dictate the appropriate methods for its study. For Einstein this led to the general and special theory of relativity, as well as other things. As a lay scientist, Torrance quickly saw in Einstein's work a *method* (not basis!) for discerning the nature of reality complementary to that of Christian theology. From Einstein's reflections on science and religion Torrance drew much inspiration for his own project in dogmatics.

In 1983 at the conferment of an honorary doctorate in science, Professor S. D. Smith, then Dean of the Faculty of Science at Heriot-Watt University, justified Torrance's suitability for the conferral by likening him to Einstein. In a creative rhetorical flourish, Smith said, "I am required to show, sir, why we in this university and in particular in this Faculty, should add confusion to this obviously already well-known situation. It would seem to be because [Torrance] has dared to tread in the ground between theology and science and been awarded the Templeton Prize to boot."[61] He went on to speak of Torrance's time as Moderator of the Church of Scotland:

> To the physicist . . . a Moderator is a lump of graphite or a tank of heavy water found in a nuclear reactor capable of removing excess energy from over-energetic neutrons. We seek, therefore, analogies between a neutron (a sub-atomic particle) and a minister of the Church of Scotland to understand the properties of a Moderator. I have, sir, therefore, identified our particle. He is simply a stone. In fact, better expressed in the German language—"ein Stein"—the Einstein of theological science: much for the mystic, abundantly for practical theology. So, as with Einstein in physics, for our graduand's contribution to the understanding of the relationship between science and theology, I ask you, Chancellor, by the authority of the Senate, to confer on Thomas Forsyth Torrance the degree of Doctor of Science.[62]

Focusing specifically upon dogmatics, Torrance produced a number of articles on hermeneutics and in 1995 collated a number of these into one volume entitled *Divine Meaning: Studies in Patristic Hermeneutics*.[63] It was Torrance's intent to produce a three-volume work on hermeneutics; however this never eventuated. The Princeton Special Collections contain a number of unpublished articles on hermeneutics that would have formed the basis of the

---

61. The Thomas F. Torrance Manuscript Collection, Special Collections, Princeton Theological Seminary Library, Box 15, "Program and laureation address from the conferment of the Honorary Doctor of Science to Thomas F. Torrance, Heriot-Watt University. November 12, 1983," 1.

62. "Program and laureation address," 2–3.

63. Thomas F. Torrance, *Divine Meaning: Studies in Patristic Hermeneutics* (Edinburgh: T&T Clark, 1995).

other two volumes, in addition to several previous published works.[64] More on Torrance's scientific theology is developed in the next chapter.

MISSIONAL AND EVANGELISTIC

Another feature of Torrance's theology is its missional and evangelistic emphasis. Torrance continually reminded his audiences in person and in print that he was a missionary at heart and that his theology was an attempt to evangelize the scientific culture of his day. He often said that he was as much a missionary to modern theologians as he was to anyone else. Born in China to missionary parents, and originally thinking he would himself be a foreign missionary, his call to the ministry of Word and sacrament, and after this to the academy, was not seen by Torrance as a rejection of his felt call to mission. It was, rather, a channeling of such a call into a more specific context. In an unpublished autobiographical reflection possibly written in the 1990s, Torrance asserts, "I cannot remember ever having had any doubts about God."[65] On his vocation as missionary we read: "This orientation to mission was built into the fabric of my mind, and has never faded—by its essential nature Christian theology has always had for me an evangelistic thrust."[66]

The missional and evangelistic impetus behind Torrance's work is not always evident to the uninitiated in his more academic writings, but the impetus was there nonetheless. This accounts in part for Torrance's consistent focus on Christ as the center of dogmatic inquiry as Christ is the heart of faith. In an early unpublished piece Torrance remarks:

> Surely the uniqueness of the preaching of Jesus demands a correspondingly special form of transmission and surely that is what we do have. That preaching cannot be handed on by mere reporters of history, for the latter cannot see the decisive factor that this

---

64. See The Thomas F. Torrance Manuscript Collection, Special Collections, Princeton Theological Seminary Library, Boxes 30–35. Proposed volumes would focus on biblical hermeneutics, patristic hermeneutics, and Reformation hermeneutics. See also Thomas F. Torrance, *The Hermeneutics of John Calvin*, Monograph Supplements to the SJT (Edinburgh: Scottish Academic, 1988). Also see the forthcoming work Thomas F. Torrance, *The Bible and Its Interpreters*, Thomas F. Torrance Collected Studies vol. 2, ed. Adam Nigh (Eugene, OR: Wipf and Stock, forthcoming). This work collects material that would have formed part of the proposed second volume of Torrance's *Divine Meanings* studies in medieval, Reformation, and modern hermeneutics.

65. The Thomas F. Torrance Manuscript Collection, Special Collections, Princeton Theological Seminary Library, Box 10, "T. F. Torrance, 'Itinerarium Mentis in Deum: My Theological Development,'" 68.

66. "Itinerarium Mentis in Deum," 69.

Jesus discloses and authenticates Himself as the Christ—and what they can see—the Rabbi and exorcist who failed—they will hardly consider worth reporting. But in actual fact the oldest strata of the synoptic Gospels contain no mere historical reports, but reproduce the message and proclamation of Jesus Himself in the form of new preaching. The whole history of the Gospel transmission is to be understood as an evangelistic transmission of the preaching and self-discloser of Jesus, that others may believe.[67]

So insistent was Torrance on the centrality of mission that he often identified true belief with the impetus to mission. While a young minister at the Barony Church, Alyth, Scotland, Torrance could preach a sermon on foreign missions and a call to the Kirk to get back to Christ, which means back to missions. Here he speaks of Christ as the basis of missions:

The second thing I want you to think about this morning is the universalism of Jesus Christ. Just because Jesus Christ is the propitiation for sins, He is not only the propitiation for our sins but the sins of the whole world. Now that is about the most important thing about the Gospel. "Behold the Lamb of God which taketh away the sins of the world." "Thou hast redeemed us to God by Thy blood out of every kindred and tongue and people and nation." You cannot believe in Jesus Christ and have the forgiveness of sins, without believing in Foreign Missions. If you don't believe in Foreign Missions, you simply don't believe in Jesus Christ. The Cross of Christ was so big and stupendous an event that it necessarily has the universe for its correlative . . . . Unless you believe that Christ came to die for the sins of the world, as well as for your own, you don't believe in Him at all.[68]

Torrance was one such believer who, through his academic pursuits, attempted to persuade others of this same truth.

---

67. The Thomas F. Torrance Manuscript Collection, Special Collections, Princeton Theological Seminary Library, Box 16, "The Historical and the Theological Approach to Jesus Christ who is Self-Disclosed in His Preaching," 1.

68. The Thomas F. Torrance Manuscript Collection, Special Collections, Princeton Theological Seminary Library, Box 47, "Sermon on Hebrews 2.2: Alyth December 1940," 6.

ACADEMIC AND PASTORAL

A final feature of Torrance's theology is the academic and pastoral nature of his work. Perhaps it would be better to say the "pastorally academic" nature of his work, for Torrance always intended his work as a product of dogmatics, not, strictly speaking, systematic theology. Dogmatics is a more disciplined and focused study of the Christian faith: centered on Christ, conducted by a believer, for the church. As Barth called his great work of dogmatics *Church Dogmatics,* so too Torrance's work was produced within the context of the church and for the church. Torrance was a church theologian, not a public theologian as such. His audience was those the Holy Scriptures call "sons and daughters of God," and he wrote as one brother in Christ to others. Dogmatics is thus the faithful witness to the reality of the triune God as disclosed in Christ by the Holy Spirit by means of the Word written, as the church gathers around the Word in faithful obedience to listen, to receive, and to perform the faith. Dogmatics is thus grounded in worship and issues into worship. It is, as Rom. 12:1 says, a form of *logike latreia*—logical worship.

In a passage highlighted later I note that, according to Torrance, theological thinking ends with our participation in the life of the Trinity as the Holy Spirit unites us to the humanity of the incarnate Christ. Ultimately, "It is as our communion with God the Father through Christ and in the Spirit is founded in and shares in the inner Trinitarian consubstantial or *homoousial* communion of the Father, Son and Holy Spirit, that the subjectively-given pole of conceptuality is constantly purified and refined under the searching light and quickening power of the objectively-given pole in divine revelation. Within that polarity Christian theology becomes what it essentially is and ought always to be, *logike latreia*, rational worship of God."[69]

When the pastoral intent and context of Torrance's work is not kept in mind, his work is misunderstood as overly academic and unnecessarily dense. Within this context, however, one can keep an eye on the goal of Torrance's dogmatic interests and see how each piece of his *oeuvre* contributes to and helps construct a rigorously faithful path to true knowledge of God in which we think out of a center in God and not out of a center in the self. Such knowledge issues in true worship as we participate in Christ's worship of, and obedience to, the Father.

---

69. Thomas F. Torrance, "Theological Realism," in *The Philosophical Frontiers of Christian Theology: Essays Presented to D. M. MacKinnon,* ed. B. Hebblethwaite and S. Sutherland (Cambridge: Cambridge University Press, 1982), 193.

Conclusion

There is more that can be said in regard to the nature and scope of Torrance's dogmatics, but I trust enough has been outlined here to give the reader an informed entrée into the thinking, backgrounds, influences, and directions that were at play in Torrance's work. It has rightly been said that to understand one area of Torrance's thought requires familiarity with every area of his thought. His aversion to scholasticism and certain forms of systematic theology means that his works are often not as perspicuous or as analytic as they otherwise would have been, nor are they as concise as others writing in the field—although with Barth as a model, brevity was never going to be one of his virtues! However, understanding the context of his work and a number of its key themes allows the reader to more quickly imbibe Torrance's unique thought-world in order to better understand its content and intent.

The subsequent chapters each take a key theme of Torrance's work and interrogate it according to Torrance's own stated methods. Then they develop these ideas in order to retrieve aspects of his theology for contemporary theological discourse. Unless this is done, Torrance's work will only occasion dismay and disagreement, rather than critical and appreciative interaction.

2

Scientific Theology
And Theological Science

The theological corpus of Thomas Forsyth Torrance is unique in that throughout his many published works, spanning over fifty years, a consistent methodology has been employed, which each monograph, article, lecture, and address develops and explicates. This makes the reading of Torrance's work both diverse—considering the many spheres of interest he has—but also unified in terms of form, content, and method. Torrance is convinced there is a right way to *do* Christian theology, or as he preferred, dogmatics, and this right way is a *scientific* one. Given the scientific nature of Christian theology a certain form and method must be adhered to if Christian theology is to be faithful to its object of study (God's very self). This chapter examines the architectonic nature of Torrance's Christian dogmatics and provides a way into an accurate reading of his theology as a whole. While the Eastern Orthodox tradition centers the epistemological foundation for theology on its distinctive apophatic theology,[1] Torrance prefers to construct his epistemological foundation on what he terms *true science*.

Torrance's response to reading Schleiermacher's *The Christian Faith* as an undergraduate at the University of Edinburgh was both positive and negative. Writing about that experience, Torrance comments that he was:

> [C]aptivated by the architectonic form and beauty of Schleiermacher's method . . . . But it was clear to me that the

---

1. Apophaticism is a common epistemological commitment among all Eastern Orthodox writers both ancient and modern, although to differing degrees. Among the various forms of apophaticism Bartos identifies a strict or radical approach and a relative approach as the two most obvious forms. Emil Bartos, *Deification in Eastern Orthodoxy: An Evaluation and Critique of the Theology of Dumitru Stăniloae*(Carlisle: Paternoster, 1999), 25.

whole concept was wrong. Due to its fundamental presuppositions Schleiermacher's approach did not match up to the nature or content of the Christian gospel, while the propositional structure he imposed upon the Christian consciousness lacked any realist scientific objectivity. Another, more adequate way of doing what Schleiermacher had attempted was needed and I was determined from then on to make it one of my primary objectives.[2]

Torrance was also impressed with the works of Augustine and especially Barth, but for various reasons sought to move beyond what he saw as weaknesses in their respective systems. In the theology of Augustine Torrance saw "an even greater beauty and symmetry of theological form," yet "the powerful neo-Platonic ingredients of St. Augustine's thought [and the] controlling presuppositions basically similar to those in Schleiermacher" led Torrance to reject that "system" as well.[3] From Barth Torrance took his Trinitarian "ground and grammar," the self-revelation of God and the crucial role of the incarnation in this self-revelation of the triune God into his own "system" or architectonic structure. Indeed, Torrance made this his primary objective, as his many publications show.

Torrance's initial thesis proposal to Barth involved the working out of a "scientific account" of Christian dogmatics "from its Christological and soteriological center and in the light of its constitutive Trinitarian structure."[4] While Barth considered this too ambitious (!) and Torrance ended up writing his doctorate on grace in the Apostolic Fathers,[5] we can see that from the beginning of his career Torrance sought to construct such a scientific architectonic structure within which the various *loci* of systematic theology "fit." This may even prove to be Torrance's greatest contribution to the Great Tradition.

In discussing what Barth meant to him, Torrance made it very clear that he pursued the development of a clear, scientific structure from his earliest days as an undergraduate in Edinburgh, through his year in Basel with Barth, and

---

2. Thomas F. Torrance, "My Interaction with Karl Barth," in *How Karl Barth Changed My Mind*, ed. D. K. McKim (Grand Rapids: Eerdmans, 1986), 52. Cf. J. I. Hesselink, "A Pilgrimage in the School of Christ: An Interview with T. F. Torrance," *RefR* 38 (1984): 53.

3. Torrance, "My Interaction with Karl Barth," 52–53.

4. Ibid., 54. Cf. Hesselink, "A Pilgrimage in the School of Christ," 52–53.

5. Published as Thomas F. Torrance, *The Doctrine of Grace in the Apostolic Fathers* (Edinburgh: Oliver and Boyd, 1948).

continuing over his long career.⁶ Torrance described his quest as seeking to work out more fully "the scientific substructure of Christian dogmatics."⁷

In order for Torrance to do this he organized his theological *oeuvre* around five main areas: epistemology and methodology; the interaction between theology and natural science; the triunity of God; Christology; and soteriology. Importantly, but not as exhaustively, Torrance also dealt considerably with ecumenical interests and the missionary task.⁸ While each of these themes is distinct, for Torrance they are never completely separate. Like the identity and mission of Jesus Christ, these various *loci* of Torrance's theology are interdependent and constitutive of each other.

Levels of Theologizing

As a consequence of a sustained reading of Einstein and thinking through the implications of his scientific method on all true scientific thinking, Torrance noted that in *all* science there are levels or layers of meaning, not just in *theological* science.⁹ Torrance dealt with this specifically in his lecture "The Stratification of Truth."¹⁰ Rejecting a purely phenomenalist approach to knowledge in favor of a critical realist one, Torrance explains: "We start with

---

6. Torrance, "My Interaction with Karl Barth," 52–64.

7. Ibid., 55.

8. According to John D. Morrison, *Knowledge of the Self-Revealing God in the Thought of Thomas Forsyth Torrance,* Issues in Systematic Theology, vol. 2 (New York: Peter Lang, 1997), 24: "While Torrance's theological interests, concerns and engagements are many, they might be brought under four related headings. These are theological science and methodology (or philosophy of theology, prolegomena); ecumenism or the need to work toward Christian theological unity by bringing positions into engagement with the objective self-revelation of God in Christ; the need for dialogue between theology and the natural sciences; and the missionary task." See pages 24–34 for his survey of these four themes.

9. It should be noted that while Torrance borrows this method significantly from Einstein, he also acknowledges the crucial role played by Maxwell and especially Polanyi in natural science as well as theologians such as Anselm and his *ratio veritatis,* and Karl Barth, especially his *Anselm: Fides Quarens Intellectum: Anselm's Proof of the Existence of God in the Context of his Theological Scheme,* trans. I. W. Robertson (London: SCM, 1960). See Thomas F. Torrance, *Reality and Scientific Theology* (Edinburgh: Scottish Academic, 1985), 131–59, for his treatment of these levels with specific reference to natural science. A. G. Marley, in *T. F. Torrance: The Rejection of Dualism,* Nutshell Series, vol. 4 (Edinburgh: Handsel, 1992), 7–9, explains Torrance's reading of Polanyi at this point in a succinct but helpful way. For a broader examination consult J. H-K. Yeung, *Being and Knowing: An Examination of T. F. Torrance's Christological Science* (Hong Kong: China Alliance, 1996), 46–59.

10. Torrance, "The Stratification of Truth," in *Reality and Scientific Theology,* 131–59, but he mentions the concept at various points of his *oeuvre*.

our ordinary experience in which we operate already with some sort of order in our thought which is essential for our understanding of the world around us and for rational behaviour within it. We assume that the world is intelligible and accessible to rational knowledge, for otherwise our thoughts and experiences could not be coordinated. And so we operate on the assumption that by means of thought we can understand in some real measure the relations between events and grasp their orderly and consistent structure."[11]

This orderly and consistent structure is then the point of contact for a more in-depth and rigorous investigation by which the successive layers of truth are uncovered:

> What we are concerned with in science, however, is to deepen our grasp of that orderly structure. We select a few basic concepts in our experience and apprehension of the world, try to work out their interconnections, and organize them into a coherent system of thought through which like a lens we can gain a more accurate picture of the hidden patterns and coherences embedded in the world. We carry out this activity in other fields of investigation and try to connect together the various structures we discover latent in them, thus widening and at the same time unifying the progress of our science. But all the time we penetrate more and more deeply through different systems and levels of rational complexity that arise in the course of our inquiries as nature manifests itself to us and even discloses to us objective structures that are inherently non-observable but which constitute, so to speak, the invariant back-side of reality.[12]

When this scientific method is rigorously applied to theological science, as Torrance contends, then "without doubt the rehabilitation of a realist approach to knowledge which gives priority to the truth of being over truths of signification and statement opens the way for considerable clarification and simplification by making them point beyond themselves to a unifying ontological ground. This is bound to undermine a nominalist approach to knowledge."[13] When Torrance applies this stratification of truth to theology proper he sees three distinct categories or levels, which will be reviewed below.[14]

---

11. Ibid., 147.
12. Ibid.
13. Ibid., 153.

THE EVANGELICAL AND DOXOLOGICAL LEVEL: EXPERIENCE

The first level is the *evangelical and doxological level*, the most basic level of experience and worship, in which we encounter God's revealing and reconciling activity in the gospel. Its focal point is the encounter with Jesus Christ. This is the level of "experiential apprehension." The object of focus at this level is "God's revealing and saving activity in the Gospel" and our "commitment to faith in Jesus Christ whom God in his love has given to the world as its Saviour."[15] This "experiential apprehension" is not a totally private affair but one that takes place within the context of the daily life and activity of the church, that is, in community.

As the natural scientist discerns patterns of order and regularity within nature, so in theology one is apprehended by the intuitive apprehension of the ordering of the Christian *kerygma* and *didache* of the New Testament: "Our minds apprehend this evangelical Trinity intuitively, and, as a whole, without engaging in analytical or logical process of thought, which we are constrained through faith in Christ to relate to the Mystery of God's inmost Life and Being. Thereby we gain the basic undefined cognition which informally shapes our faith and regulates our trinitarian understanding of God."[16]

Here we are introduced to one of Torrance's distinctive epistemic commitments: our intuitive apprehension of God's self-revelation. This is not to suggest, as others have mistakenly done,[17] that Torrance equates revelation and

---

14. Torrance deals with these levels of meaning specifically in theology in Thomas F. Torrance, *The Christian Doctrine of God: One Being Three Persons*(Edinburgh: T&T Clark, 1996), 88–111. See a discussion of these levels in Elmer M. Colyer, *The Nature of Doctrine in T. F. Torrance's Theology*(Eugene, OR: Wipf and Stock, 2001), 181–87. See an overview in Marley, *T. F. Torrance*, 15–16, and Benjamin Myers, "The Stratification of Knowledge in the Thought of T. F. Torrance," *SJT* 61 (2008): 1–15.

15. Thomas F. Torrance, *The Christian Doctrine of God: One Being Three Persons*(Edinburgh: T&T Clark, 1996), 88. As Torrance states, "Its focal point is personal encounter with Jesus Christ within the structures of our historical existence in space and time."

16. Torrance, *The Christian Doctrine of God*, 89.

17. Here I am referring to Ronald Thiemann's critique of Torrance's doctrine of revelation in his *Revelation and Theology: The Gospel as Narrated Promise*(Notre Dame: University of Notre Dame Press, 1985), 32–45. Thiemann charges Torrance with being a "foundationalist," the very thing Torrance wishes to expunge from all theology! Torrance is not a foundationalist in the sense Thiemann believes he is. By his use of "intuition" and of "indwelling" the story, Torrance draws on and applies these terms in an Einsteinian and Polanyian sense in which this tacit (Polanyi) dimension is open to critical modification as inquiry proceeds. Colyer believes Torrance can thus be termed a "soft-foundationalist" only; see Elmer M. Colyer, *The Nature of Doctrine in T. F. Torrance's Theology*(Eugene, OR: Wipf and Stock, 2001), 50, n.109. For a concentrated discussion on this theme see Myk Habets, "Theological Interpretation of Scripture in Sermonic Mode: The Case of T. F. Torrance," in *Ears That Hear:*

intuition, but rather that this level can be characterized as *incipient theology*.[18] This corresponds to what Polanyi termed "tacit knowledge."[19] As Torrance explains it, "We become spiritually and intellectually implicated in patterns of divine order that are beyond our powers fully to articulate in explicit terms, but we are aware of being apprehended by divine Truth as it is in Jesus which steadily presses for increasing realisation in our understanding, articulation and confession of faith. That is how theology gains its initial impetus, and is then reinforced through constant reading and study of the Bible within the community of the faithful."[20]

This *evangelical and doxological level* is regarded as the essential foundation for the process of theological reflection that will follow; it is "the *sine qua non* of the other levels of doctrinal formulation developed from it."[21] It is also the point to which the Christian disciple repeatedly returns as she ascends and descends the various levels of truth and reality.

THE THEOLOGICAL LEVEL: THE ECONOMIC TRINITY

The second level is the *theological level*, in which the economic Trinitarian relations are explored.[22] This economic level is concerned with the act of God in God's being, with the personal acts of God in God's personal reality as Father, Son, and Holy Spirit. As Torrance expresses it:

Explorations in Theological Interpretation of the Bible, ed. Joel Green and Tim Meadowcroft (Sheffield: Sheffield Phoenix, 2013), 44–71.

18. Torrance, *The Christian Doctrine of God*, 89.

19. Michael Polanyi, *Personal Knowledge: Towards a Post-Critical Philosophy* (Chicago: University of Chicago Press, 1958). See Thomas F. Torrance, "The Framework of Belief," in *Belief in Science and in Christian Life: The Relevance of Michael Polanyi's Thought for Christian Faith and Life*, ed. T. F. Torrance (Edinburgh: Handsel, 1980), 1–27, "The Place of Michael Polanyi in the Modern Philosophy of Science," *Ethics in Science and Medicine* 7 (1980): 57–95; and the secondary literature on Torrance's use of Polanyi: Colin Weightman, *Theology in a Polanyian Universe: The Theology of Thomas Torrance* (New York: Peter Lang, 1994); J.V. Apczynski, "Torrance on Polanyi and Polanyi on God: Comments on Weightman's Criticisms—A Review Essay [*Theology in a Polanyian Universe: The Theology of Thomas Torrance*, by C. Weightman, 1994; reply, C. Weightman, pp. 35–38]," *TAD* 24 (1997–98): 32–34; and John D. Morrison, *Knowledge of the Self-Revealing God in the Thought of Thomas Forsyth Torrance*, Issues in Systematic Theology, vol. 2 (New York: Peter Lang, 1997).

20. Torrance, *The Christian Doctrine of God*, 89.

21. Ibid., 90.

22. At this level we are "concerned with expressing doctrinal knowledge of the Holy Trinity in which our thought moves on from the intuitive incipient form of an understanding of the Trinity to conceptions of what is called the economic Trinity." Thomas F. Torrance, *The Christian Doctrine of God: One Being Three Persons* (Edinburgh: T&T Clark, 1996), 92.

> By forming appropriate intellectual instruments with which to lay bare the underlying epistemological pattern of thought, and by tracing the chains of connection throughout the coherent body of theological truths, they feel their way forward to a deeper and more precise knowledge of what God has revealed of himself, even to the extent of reaching a reverent and humble insight into the inner personal relations of his Being. Our concern at this secondary level, however, while distinctly theological, is not primarily with the organic body of theological knowledge, but with penetrating through it to apprehend more fully the economic and ontological and trinitarian structure of God's revealing and saving acts in Jesus Christ as they are presented to us in the Gospel.[23]

The move from the lower level to this economic level involves moving from the Christian *experience* of God to an *apprehension* of the general theological structures that underlie such experience. While this applies to all of the theological *loci*, Torrance works out this method with regard to the triune being of God in particular; and it is an apt illustration and application of the methodology.[24]

In the first level we experience the Father, the Son, and the Holy Spirit; at the theological level we ask how these three are one: "As we direct our inquiries in the field of evangelical and doxological experience, we reflect on the fact that God reveals his one Being to us as God the Father, God the Son, and God the Holy Spirit, in a three-fold *self*-giving in which revelatory and ontological factors are indivisibly integrated."[25] The *theological* level is equivalent to what the Fathers termed the *oikonomia*. At this level the focus is on the self-revelation of God in history: "It is at this level that the inchoate form of the doctrine of the Holy Trinity latent in the triadic structure of God's redemptive revelation of himself through himself, and in the trinitarian understanding of God implicit in the mind and worship of the God's people [*sic*], evident in the various New Testament formulae which bring the Father, the Son and the Holy Spirit together in the Name of God, is given explicit formulation as the doctrine of the Holy Trinity that underlies and gives coherent structure to all Christian dogmatics."[26]

---

23. Ibid., 91.
24. Ibid., 91–98.
25. Ibid., 92.
26. Ibid., 92.

The heuristic device that enables the movement from the first to the second level is that of the *homoousion* as initially developed during the Nicene period. According to Torrance, the pro-Nicene theologians used the doctrine of the *homoousion* as applied to both the Son and later the Holy Spirit as a heuristic device[27] to move from the *evangelical and doxological level* up to the *theological level*. The *homoousion* affirmed and explicated the oneness in being and act between Christ and the Father upon which the reality and validity of the gospel of revelation and reconciliation depends. Apart from the oneness in being between Jesus Christ and the Father, there is no real mediator between God and humankind, and the identity of Jesus Christ has nothing to do with any *self*-revealing and *self*-giving on the part of the eternal God for the salvation of humankind. As such the *homoousion* is the "ontological and epistemological linchpin of Christian theology."[28]

A direct consequence of the *homoousion* doctrine is the cognate conception of the hypostatic union—the union of God and humankind in the one person of Christ. This moves our thought from the doxological level of intuitive experience (Polanyi) to the explicitly theological level in which we understand the self-revelation of God as Father, Son, and Holy Spirit—not just in terms of God's economic relations toward us but also in terms of what God is antecedently and eternally in God's self. The theological level compels us to

---

27. In a theological lexicon attached to the end of *Belief in Science and in Christian Life: The Relevance of Michael Polanyi's Thought for Christian Faith and Life*, ed. T. F. Torrance (Edinburgh: Handsel, 1980), 138, "heuristics" is defined as follows: "(from the Greek *heuriskein*, to find out, discover or invent)—a heuristic act is a fresh movement of thought serving the art of discovery or the solution of a problem; heuristic power is the capacity of some form or instrument of thought to give rise to additional knowledge. In heuristic activity the mind through an intuitive leap of insight and imagination crosses a 'logical gap' separating it from a hidden reality. This is an unaccountable act but it is not a blind leap, for it takes its rise from an element of foreknowledge which guides it. While heuristic activity operates from an anticipatory frame of thought it is an activity of discovery breaking out of it which involves an irreversible modification of prior knowledge." Neidhardt agrees with Torrance's elevation of the *homoousion* doctrine to the status of being a fundamental heuristic device that acts like Einstein's formula E=MC2 does in physics. In this way, Neidhardt sees Torrance's work as a clarification of the complementarity that exists between natural and theological science. W. J. Neidhardt, "Thomas F. Torrance's Integration of Judeo-Christian Theology and Natural Science: Some Key Themes," *PSCF* 41 (1989): 87–98; "Introduction to T. F. Torrance," in *The Christian Frame of Mind: Order and Openness in Theology and Natural Science,* 2nd ed. (Colorado Springs: Helmers & Howard, 1989), xv-xx.

28. Torrance, *The Christian Doctrine of God*, 95. In addition to Athanasius, it would appear that Torrance developed his own commitment to the *homoousion* from Hugh Ross Mackintosh initially, and then from Karl Barth. See Thomas F. Torrance, "Hugh Ross Mackintosh: Theologian of the Cross," *SBET* 5 (1987): 163–64.

think of God as God is in God's very self—the ontological Trinity—and as such points one upwards to the third level. This is a self-conscious repetition of the patristic move from *oikonomia* to *theologia*. In this movement we see that "Jesus Christ [is] the incarnate Son [and] is one in Being and Act with God the Father. What Jesus Christ does for us and to us, and what the Holy Spirit does in us, is what God himself does for us, to us and in us."[29]

At this second level we do not "take off into a speculative movement of thought" that leaves behind the evangelical and doxological experience encountered in the first level. Rather, we affirm the oneness in being and act between Jesus Christ and God the Father, and between the Holy Spirit and God the Father, as expressed in the doctrine of the *homoousion*. This level thus gives rise to the third and final level of theologizing.

THE HIGHER THEOLOGICAL LEVEL: THE ONTOLOGICAL TRINITY

The third and highest level of theologizing for Torrance is the *higher theological and scientific level*, in which the ontological Trinity is penetrated into more deeply. It is at this level that we discern the Trinitarian relations immanent in God's very self that lie behind, and are the ground of, the economic Trinity.[30]

Moving from the most basic or doxological level to the highest, the ontological level, constitutes the decisive point for theological science, according to Torrance.[31] At this ontological level we have to do with "the objective structures of reality."[32] "[I]n advancing from the second to the third epistemological level, we move from an ordered account of the economic activity of God toward us as Father, Son and Holy Spirit, to an ultimate set of fundamental concepts and relations whereby we seek to formulate in forms of thought and speech the hypostatic, homoousial and perichoretic relations in the eternal dynamic Communion in loving and being loved of the three Divine Persons which God is."[33]

---

29. Torrance, *The Christian Doctrine of God*, 95 (slightly altered).

30. Thomas F. Torrance, *The Ground and Grammar of Theology* (Charlottesville: University of Virginia Press, 1980), 157–58.

31. Ibid., 159.

32. Thomas F. Torrance, *Reality and Scientific Theology* (Edinburgh: Scottish Academic, 1985), 144–47, where Torrance distinguishes between several levels of truth and gives examples from the natural sciences.

33. Thomas F. Torrance, *The Christian Doctrine of God: One Being Three Persons* (Edinburgh: T&T Clark, 1996), 109. The provenance of using the word *homoousios/n* in the form of *homoousial/ly* is highly disputed and yet it is a characteristic of Torrance's usage and one which, following him, I employ throughout the discussion of his theology.

It is at this ontological or *higher theological level* that the great theologians of the early church such as Athanasius, Gregory of Nazianzus, and Cyril of Alexandria identified with the subject matter of theology *par excellence*. Torrance himself liked to think of the doctrine of the Trinity "as the *ultimate ground* of theological knowledge of God, the *basic grammar* of theology, for it is there that we find our knowledge of God reposing upon the final Reality of God himself, grounded in the ultimate relations intrinsic to God's own Being, which govern and control all true knowledge of him from beginning to end."[34]

Three important concepts are specifically related to this third level for Torrance: *homoousion*, not surprisingly; *perichoresis*, another key patristic term; and one of Torrance's own linguistic conventions, *onto-relations*. We have already looked at the role the *homoousion* plays in Torrance's second level, at this third level the *homoousion* takes on a "critical edge" in that it only works one way. The *homoousion* allows us to know the triune God in God's being and act for us in Jesus Christ and the Holy Spirit as God is in God's own being inherently and eternally, but it does not allow us to indiscriminately read back into God what is human and finite. This critical edge stops us from developing a mythological vision of God that would confound God revealed to us with our deficient knowing of God.[35] This applies to the *homoousial* nature of the Son and the Holy Spirit equally, but in distinctive ways. The *homoousion* of the Son is linked with the hypostatic union; the Spirit is not, according to Torrance, knowable in its own distinctive person or *hypostasis* in the same way, for the Spirit is not embodied like the incarnate Son. The Spirit is known indirectly through the Son, with whom the Spirit is one being as the Son is with the Father. "It is through holding constantly in our thought the inseparable unity between the economic activity of God in the Spirit and the economic activity of God in the Son that we may be prevented from reading back into God himself the material or creaturely images . . . that rise out of the reciprocity he has established with us through the incarnation of his Son in space and time as one with us and one of us."[36] By the application of the *homoousion* in these distinct ways appropriate to both Son and Spirit our thought is lifted up from the level of the economic Trinity to the level of the ontological Trinity, "and we reach the supreme point in the knowledge of God in his internal intelligible relations."[37]

---

34. Torrance, The *Ground and Grammar of Theology*, 158–59.
35. Torrance, *The Christian Doctrine of God*, 99.
36. Ibid., 101.
37. Ibid., 102.

As the doctrine of the *homoousion* was central to the second *theological level* the doctrine of *perichoresis* is central to the third *higher theological and scientific level*. *Perichoresis*, the mutual or coinherent co-indwelling of the three divine persons in the eternal communion of their one being, enables us to recognize that the coinherent relations of the Father, Son, and Holy Spirit, revealed in the saving acts of God through Christ and in the Spirit, are not temporary manifestations of God's nature. Instead, they are eternally grounded in the intrinsic and completely reciprocal relations of the Holy Trinity.[38] The doctrine of *perichoresis* is a way to hold together in the doctrine of the Trinity the identity of the divine being and the intrinsic unity of the three divine persons.[39]

As a direct consequence of both the *homoousion* and *perichoresis* Torrance has developed what he terms an *onto-relational* concept of the divine persons. By onto-relational Torrance implies an understanding of the three divine persons in the one God in which the ontic relations between them belong to what they essentially are in themselves in their distinctive *hypostaseis*. In short, onto-relations are being-constituting relations. The differing relations between the Father, Son, and Holy Spirit belong to what they are as Father, Son, and Holy Spirit, so the *homoousial* relations between the three divine persons belong to what they are in themselves as persons and in their communion with one another.[40] In summary, the divine being and the divine communion are to be understood wholly in terms of one another. This onto-relational understanding of person defined as person-in-relationship is also applicable to inter-human relations, but in a created way reflecting the uncreated way in which it applies to the Trinitarian relations in God.[41] *Perichoresis* and onto-relations are thus only applicable to human relationships by analogy and in limited creaturely ways.

The three levels of Torrance's theological method or epistemology are mutually correlated and must never be seen as entirely separate categories. One gives rise to the other necessarily and in moving from one level to the next the "lower" level is never really left behind. Torrance makes this point clear when he writes: "It cannot be sufficiently emphasised, that the theological or

---

38. Thomas F. Torrance, *The Trinitarian Faith: The Evangelical Theology of the Ancient Catholic Church* (Edinburgh: T&T Clark, 1995), 234.

39. Torrance, *The Christian Doctrine of God*, 102.

40. Ibid., 102–3.

41. We can also see in this redefinition of "person" how the scientific method that Torrance borrowed from Maxwell, Einstein, and Polanyi in terms of field theory and relativity is having a direct bearing on theological science, especially here in the realm of anthropology as it relates to Being and personal being (Heidegger). Torrance sees the Fathers as working under the same scientific method and coming to the same theological conclusions. See his discussion of "person," and "being" in ibid., 103–5.

ontological Trinity remains *evangelical*, not only because it is coordinated with the evangelical revelation of God as Father, Son and Holy Spirit, but because it is essentially and intrinsically evangelical. This should be clear even from an examination of the structure of the Nicene-Constantinopolitan Creed in which the clauses devoted to the incarnate Son and his saving activity are placed in the very centre of confession of faith in the Father, Son and Holy Spirit."[42]

Not only is the *higher theological and scientific level* evangelical, by which Torrance means biblical, in itself but it never leaves the doxological element out. When the higher scientific level of theologizing leaves behind its doxological foundation, theology flies off into the realms of speculation and mythology. Torrance counsels us to "keep a constant check on these refined theological concepts and relations," keeping "our feet on the concrete ground of God's actual revelation to us in the incarnation and atonement" so that the "immanent relations in God on which his self-revelation to us is grounded do not detract from the economic relations in which God has actually made himself known to us" in the saving activity of Christ.[43]

By means of this necessary hierarchical coordination of different levels of truth, theological knowledge is concentrated upon the one objective center and content of God's self-revelation in Christ, which is identical with the Truth that God eternally is in the mystery of God's triune being. By utilizing the doctrine of the *homoousion* and *perichoresis* we are moved (epistemologically) from the experience of God (level one) to the theological level (the economic Trinity), finally to the deep theological and scientific structures upon which the first two levels rest (the ontological Trinity).

Corresponding to this *epistemic* movement is the corresponding *theological* movement downwards: working from the fundamental truth of God's triune being (the ontological Trinity) we are able to discern the acts of God that reveal God's being (the economic Trinity), and worship and adore the center of God's self-revealing act and being—the Lord Jesus Christ as made known through the Spirit of the Son and the Father. Torrance concludes his discussion of this very point with the words of his patristic mentor Athanasius, "There is one eternal godhead in Trinity and there is one Glory of the Holy trinity . . . . If theological truth is now perfect in Trinity, this is the true and only divine worship, and this is its beauty and truth, it must have been always so."[44]

---

42. Ibid., 108.
43. Ibid., 109.
44. Ibid., 111. Torrance also includes John 1:14, 18: "The Word was made flesh, and dwelt among us, and we beheld his glory, the glory of the only begotten of the Father, full of grace and truth . . . . No one has seen God at any time; the only Son who is in the bosom of the Father, he has made him known."

From the above discussion we can see that Torrance has exhaustively thought through the basic epistemological and theological foundations upon which a Christian scientific theology must be grounded. From this methodology Torrance proceeds to work through the various *loci* of dogmatic theology in true systematic fashion, but it is not a systematic theology whereby some alien philosophical system is imposed upon or over the top of revelation. Rather, it is a systematic (rational and ordered) witness to God's self-revelation in the Son and through the Spirit. This is why Torrance prefers to speak of Christian dogmatics over systematic theology. While Torrance does not confuse the various *loci* of theology, he does see them as united and thus forming a comprehensive and coherent architectonic Christian scientific theology, the nature of which we examine next.

SCIENTIFIC THEOLOGY

Having outlined Torrance's levels of theologizing, it is now appropriate to further that exploration through a deeper survey of Torrance's contributions to the discussion of the interaction between Christian theology and the natural sciences. Torrance's published works indicate that a central concern of his is to explicate the deep interrelation between Christian theology and the natural sciences.[45] In 1978, Torrance was awarded the prestigious Templeton Foundation Prize for Progress in Religion on account of his contributions to the discussion between these two disciplines. As far as Torrance is concerned, all theological exploration is a *scientific* endeavor, and so it is bound by a common *scientific* methodology. What Torrance is most concerned with in this regard is to expound the right methodology and epistemology by which a truly Christian *scientific*dogmatics operates.[46] While Torrance followed his mentor

---

45. Among his major writings to deal with this theme, the following are widely regarded as being of particular significance: Thomas F. Torrance, *Theological Science*(reprint, Edinburgh: T&T Clark, 1996); *Divine and Contingent Order*(reprint, Edinburgh: T&T Clark, 1998); *Christian Theology and Scientific Culture* (New York: Oxford University Press, 1981); *Transformation and Convergence in the Frame of Knowledge: Explorations in the Interrelations of Scientific and Theological Enterprise* (Grand Rapids: Eerdmans, 1984); *Reality and Scientific Theology*(Edinburgh: Scottish Academic, 1985); *The Christian Frame of Mind: Order and Openness in Theology and Natural Science*, 2nd ed. (Colorado Springs: Helmers & Howard, 1989); and *The Ground and Grammar of Theology*(Charlottesville: University of Virginia Press, 1980). See Eric L. Mascall, *Theology and the Gospel of Christ: An Essay in Reorientation*(London: SPCK, 1977), 25.

46. When we understand Torrance's scientific theology in terms of its form, content, and method we will be able to comprehend his theological statements. Elmer M. Colyer, *The Nature of Doctrine in T. F. Torrance's Theology*(Eugene, OR: Wipf and Stock, 2001), 79. Mascall wrote that Torrance is "one of the

Karl Barth to some extent here, he did not follow Barth's reticence regarding the interaction between theology and natural science. In fact, Torrance's position is significantly different from Barth's and is perhaps to be regarded, as McGrath does, as his most significant point of difference from Barth.[47] In this area Torrance has leaned more heavily on his minor mentors such as Daniel Lamont[48] and natural scientists such as Einstein than he has on his major influences such as Karl Barth.[49]

Barth treats Christian theology and the natural sciences as non-interactive disciplines, and repeatedly turned down invitations to interact with natural scientists such as Max Planck, Günter Howe, and Karl Heim.[50] According to Andrew Louth, this reticence on Barth's part was more than simple disinterest in natural science but actually indicated dis-ease. Barth was adamant that theology does not learn its content from the natural sciences nor is it dependent upon them for its method. Louth considers Torrance to have misunderstood, or at the very least illegitimately adopted, Barth as his sponsor for the interaction between theology and science. For Barth, Louth points out, *science* is the translation of *Wissenschaft*, the German word having a much broader meaning than the English word *science*. "To say that theology is a science means for Barth that it is a "human effort after truth" [*Church Dogmatics* I/1, 10]. . . . Barth is not at all interested in pursuing analogies that might exist between theology and any other sciences; theology "cannot allow itself to be taught by them the concrete meaning which that involves in its own case. As regards method it has nothing to learn from their school" [*Church Dogmatics* I/1, 7]."[51]

---

very few British theologians of recent years who have seriously enquired into the nature of the discipline to which they are committed." *Theology and the Gospel of Christ*, 46.

47. Alister E. McGrath, *T. F. Torrance: An Intellectual Biography*(Edinburgh: T&T Clark, 1999), 197. See R. J. Palma, "Thomas F. Torrance's Reformed Theology," *RefR* 38 (1984): 24.

48. Especially Lamont's work *Christ and the World of Thought* (1934). McGrath, *T. F. Torrance*, 204, rightly discerns the influence of Lamont in Torrance's Auburn Lectures on theology and science in 1938–39. This is a legitimate claim, as much of the content of the Auburn Lectures merely repeated teaching Torrance had learnt from others, being as it was so early in his academic career.

49. This is a contested claim and will be dealt with in more detail in chapter three, when we look at the concept of natural theology in Torrance's work.

50. See G. Howe, *Die Christenheit im Atomzeitalter: Vortlage und Studien* (Stuttgart: Klett, 1970); and L. Gilkey, *Nature, Reality and the Sacred: The Nexus of Science and Religion* (Minneapolis: Fortress, 1993), idem., *Religion and the Scientific Future: Reflections in Myth, Science and Theology*(New York: Harper & Row, 1970), 26–29, and H. Nebelsick, *Theology and Science in Mutual Modification* (Belfast: Christian Journals, 1981), 159–66.

51. Andrew Louth, "Science and Mystery," in *Discerning the Mystery: An Essay on the Nature of Theology* (Oxford: Clarendon, 1983), 51.

Does this mean Torrance's work on science and theology, as derived from his (mis)reading of Barth, is worthless? Not according to his critic, Louth: "If this reading of Torrance's position is accepted, then it must mean that Torrance is mistaken in the fundamental thrust of his enterprise [that is, that theology is a "science" rather than one of the humanities]. But it does not mean there is not much to be learnt from the kind of considerations he raises in the course of his books."[52]

Louth's reading of Torrance is clearly an overstatement. While we don't have to rehearse the contours of the debate here, it is now established that Barth's reticence to deal with the scientists of his day was not due to the reasons Louth adduces above, but rather to the fact that Barth had other, more pressing concerns that occupied his attention. Clearly, it will not be necessary to the objectives of this work to offer a comprehensive analysis and critique of Torrance's interaction with Barth over this issue, or with the natural sciences more generally, as has been attempted numerous times elsewhere. Nevertheless, a brief overview is required in order to understand how Torrance's theology fits within this broader epistemological scheme.

Torrance's approach to scientific theology has five central concerns that will be examined here in part.[53] The first major point Torrance makes in his various writings is that the natural sciences and theology share common points in their view of the universe, the most fundamental of which is that the universe is ordered. The second major point for Torrance is that all sciences share one common methodological dictum—what Torrance calls the *kataphysic* nature of scientific enquiry. Third, Torrance has adopted and adapted a particular epistemology known as "critical realism," which he shares in common with many natural scientists. He has sought to work out his own theological enterprise consistently in accord with this epistemology. It will be seen that this is not an *a priori* philosophy imposed on science or theology, but rather one that recognizes the *a posteriori* nature of knowledge. As a result of this critical realism, we shall look at the fourth feature of Torrance's work in this area, that of his relation to various philosophers of science that he consistently and repeatedly draws upon, most notably Michael Polanyi. Finally, we shall be in a position in the next chapter to see what place natural theology plays

---

52. Ibid., 53. Louth specifically mentions the analysis of the notions of space-time.

53. In an appreciative article, Palma presents four areas in which he believes Torrance has made the most significant contributions to theology: 1) theological discipline through obedient listening; 2) theological integrity through real integration; 3) theological advance through scientific understanding; and 4) theological relevance through real relations. Palma, "Thomas F. Torrance's Reformed Theology," 2–46. The third of his points is what interests us at this part of the study.

within Torrance's theology and in what ways this was dependent on and a development from his mentor Karl Barth. As such, chapter three extends the discussion initiated here.

I. AN ORDERED UNIVERSE

Torrance reads the history of scientific endeavor through the lens of an inherent and ingrained cosmological and epistemological dualism, especially cemented by the Copernican-Newtonian revolution. [54] This form of dualism took its definitive shape, argues Torrance, through the thought of Kant and Descartes and of Newton and Galileo,[55] but goes back to the foundations of classical Western culture in Greece, as found in the philosophy and cosmology of both Plato and Aristotle.[56] After these thinkers introduced various dualisms—such as the empirical and the theoretical, the physical and the spiritual, the temporary and the eternal, the mortal and the divine—what resulted was the solidified system of the Ptolemaic cosmology with its dualism between the supralunar and infralunar realms. According to Torrance, this "inevitably affected all life and thought within its framework right up to the scientific revolution associated with Copernicus and Galileo."[57] In response to this dualistic nature of science and knowing, Torrance reacted strongly in favor of a unitary frame of knowing.[58]

---

54. *Dualism* is an important concept for Torrance, and is defined in a theological lexicon attached to the end of *Belief in Science and in Christian Life: The Relevance of Michael Polanyi's Thought for Christian Faith and Life*, ed. T. F. Torrance (Edinburgh: Handsel, 1980), 136, as "the division of reality into two incompatible spheres of being. This may be cosmological, in the dualism between a sensible and an intelligible realm, neither of which can be reduced to the other. It may also be epistemological, in which the empirical and theoretical aspects of reality are separated from one another, thereby giving rise to the extremes of empiricism and rationalism. It may also be anthropological, in a dualism between the mind and the body, in which a physical and a mental substance are conceived as either interacting with one another or as running a parallel course without affecting one another. In the Judeo-Christian tradition man is regarded as an integrated whole, who is soul of his body and body of his soul."

55. According to Torrance, Descartes' *cogito ergo sum* in part produced the epistemological separation of subject from object; Newton's rigid, mathematical system of cause and effect resulted in a mechanistic scientific methodology bringing about the separation of absolute mathematical space and time from relative space and time; and Kant's synthesis of rationalism and empiricism was effected at the cost of the bifurcation formed between the noumenal and the phenomenological. See the overview of Torrance's critique of dualism in John D. Morrison, *Knowledge of the Self-Revealing God in the Thought of Thomas Forsyth Torrance*, Issues in Systematic Theology, vol. 2 (New York: Peter Lang, 1997), 48–51.

56. Thomas F. Torrance, *The Ground and Grammar of Theology* (Charlottesville: University of Virginia Press, 1980), 21.

57. Ibid.

In applying this dualism to the realm of theology, Torrance sees the most damaging effects. When dualisms were adopted into Christian thinking, Neoplatonic Hellenism prevailed and found its most enduring expression in the Augustinianism of Western Christendom.[59] Here the dualism is between God and the world, the eternal and the temporal, heaven and earth.[60] When these dualisms were felt to threaten knowledge of God, a failed attempt was made to unite them with the help of a resurrected Aristotelian philosophy and science (Aquinas). Not surprisingly, this did not achieve the goal of unity but simply introduced a modified form of the old dualisms.[61]

Locke, Descartes, and Newton introduced the "massive dualism between absolute mathematical time and space and relative apparent time and space that was to become programmatic for all modern science and cosmology up to Einstein."[62] Torrance sees this development giving rise to deism as the cleavage or dualism between God and the world was seen to be so immense that it could not logically be crossed.

But it is for Kant that Torrance reserves his most scathing critique, for his introduction of "the synthetic *a priori*"[63] in which Kant combined sense experience, not with innate ideas, but with built-in structures of the consciousness through which the human knower imposed conceptual order on all he perceived, so that it was impossible for him to ever penetrate behind

---

58. For an endorsement of Torrance's unitary approach to knowledge related to natural scientific claims, see W. J. Neidhardt, "Thomas F. Torrance's Integration of Judeo-Christian Theology and Natural Science: Some Key Themes," *PSCF* 41 (1989): 87–98.

59. Dualist ways of thinking are not exclusive to the West but are also found in Byzantine Christianity. Torrance, *The Ground and Grammar of Theology*, 60–61.

60. Other consequences of dualist ways of thinking mentioned by Torrance include Gnosticism with its bifurcation between two widely disparate realms: a suprasensual, utterly transcendental realm of eternal and divine realities, and an earthly, material realm of transient existence. The gap between them was so wide that it had to be spanned through mythological hierarchies of semi-divine beings. The other form of dualism was found in the Arian movement, according to which the disparate realms of the uncreated and divine and of the creaturely and human touched each other only tangentially at the point of Jesus Christ. See Torrance, *The Ground and Grammar of Theology*, 37–39.

61. Ibid., 22. In reciting this history of dualism, Torrance is providing his own interpretive perspective on what Barth and others spoke of when they called for a Christianity that was built upon the self-revelation of God and not upon alien philosophical presuppositions such as those provided by Platonism or Aristotelianism. While others look specifically to philosophers (Plato, Aristotle, Boethius, etc.) and philosophical theologians (Thomas Aquinas) for the root cause of these alien philosophical notions of Absolute Being, etc., Torrance also looks to scientists and philosophers of science for the root cause of such dualisms. This makes his work an advance on Barth at this point and not a mere repetition.

62. Ibid., 23.

63. Ibid., 25.

his cognitive activity to what things are in themselves, independent of his perceiving and conceiving.[64] The resultant Kantian epistemology involved a rejection of the possibility of any knowledge of things in themselves, limiting knowledge of them to what we can make out from their appearances. It demanded a bifurcation between unknowable "things in themselves," to be treated as no more than hypothetical entities, and what is scientifically knowable, namely, completely determined and necessary objects. More generally, Kant established a dualism between the realm of noumenal essences and ideas and the realm of phenomenal objects and events.[65] The result for Christian theology was that "Kant severed the connection between science and faith, depriving faith of any objective or ontological reference and emptying it of any real cognitive content."[66]

The way beyond this scientific impasse is to turn to thinkers both old and new: first, to notice how the early Christian thinkers, notably Athanasius, rigorously applied their Christian theology to all the realms of knowing. Then, within the field of the natural sciences, look to James Clerk Maxwell, Albert Einstein, and Michael Polanyi above all others. Torrance argues forcefully and repeatedly that Christian theology and natural science must move from a dualist to a unitary outlook.[67] According to Torrance, a "unitary outlook upon the universe" collapses these "pseudo-interpretations" and "pseudo-theologies."[68]

It was long held that the basis to all scientific methodology was the application of *a priori* dictums to everyday knowledge. However, Torrance seeks to work within the post-Newtonian, post-Einsteinian scientific climate of today to construct and be true to a *scientific* theology. J. D. Morrison defines what Torrance means by *science*:

> By 'science', then, Torrance refers neither to the 'natural' sciences necessarily nor to some supposed 'scientific' method as abstracted from one particular discipline to then be imposed upon another science. 'Science' refers rather to appropriate procedures which each science has developed and must develop in relation to the rationality of its own proper object in which 'it has solved its own inductive problem of how to arrive at a general conclusion from a limited set of particular observations.' There occurs then critical and controlled

---

64. Ibid., 25–26.
65. Ibid., 26–27.
66. Ibid., 27.
67. Ibid., 15.
68. Ibid., 27.

extension of ordinary ways of knowing for the goal of real, positive knowledge of the object. The outcome of true science is knowledge of the proper object which is 'transcendent' to the self, but in strict accordance with the object's actual nature as it has disclosed itself to be in itself. Therefore, the appropriate mode of rationality and inquiry will be 'dictated' by the object in the process of 'questioning.'[69]

In case Torrance is misunderstood to be saying that theology must be built upon the methodological dictates of science, which would simply impose upon it a new *a priori,* Torrance clarifies: "What am I saying here? Not that theology today must be grounded upon the new science, but rather that this science, in point of fact, rests upon foundational ideas that science did not and could not have produced on its own, ideas that derive from the Christian understanding of the relation of God to the universe."[70] Torrance reiterates the point that "science as we understand it in the modern world rests upon the basic ideas produced by Christian theology."[71] By this means Torrance retains what is a foundational principle in his theology, the fact that knowledge of God is derived from God's self-revelation, not by forming any logical bridge between the world and God.[72] In other words, epistemology is founded upon ontology.

---

69. Morrison, *Knowledge of the Self-Revealing God*, 105, with a citation from Thomas F. Torrance, *Theological Science* (reprint, Edinburgh: T&T Clark, 1996), 106.

70. Torrance, *The Ground and Grammar of Theology*, 73.

71. Ibid., 110. This point is illustrated in the analysis of Colin Weightman, *Theology in a Polanyian Universe: The Theology of Thomas Torrance* (New York: Peter Lang, 1994), 181–201. As Weightman makes clear on page 194: "Torrance is not arguing from science to God here, though it might appear so. The position which Torrance holds is that the relational, non-dualistic Trinitarian theology of the early Church *stands behind* the relational non-dualistic cosmology of Einstein and so, by the nature of the case, Einsteinian science is compatible with the pre-Augustinian theology of the Greek fathers since its own existence and character is dependent on this relational and on-dualistic theology." This is an important point. Torrance is well aware that it would be foolish to rely too heavily on contemporary scientific theories to build a theology on, a practice entertained by certain eighteenth-century British theologians. See J. Gascoigne, "From Bentley to the Victorians: the Rise and Fall of British Newtonian Natural Theology," *Science in Context* 2 (1988): 219–56. McGrath provides a helpful warning against this practice in his lecture, "Scientific Method and the Reconstruction of Theology: Introducing 'A Scientific Theology'," Lecture for the John Templeton Oxford Seminars on Science and Christianity, Harris Manchester College (July 24, 2003), http://www.metanexus.net/archives/message_fs.asp?ARCHIVEID=8363, para. 34.

72. In the Auburn lectures of 1938–39 this idea was already established in Torrance's Christology and science. See Torrance, *The Doctrine of Jesus Christ: Auburn Lectures 1938–39* (Eugene, OR: Wipf and

This point shall be made again later in this section, especially when we come to consider Torrance's position on the place and role of natural theology.

II. THE KATAPHYSIC NATURE OF SCIENCE

The point was made above that epistemology is founded on or correlated with ontology.[73] This holds true throughout Torrance's method and theology. Like Barth before him, Torrance holds that the distinctive nature of theology is determined by its object, which is defined as God revealed in Jesus Christ. Hence theology, and any and every other true science, is under an intrinsic obligation to give account of reality according to its distinct nature, that is, *kata physin*("according to or after the object under study").[74] The fundamental axiom that Torrance develops throughout his theological exploration is, "We know things in accordance with their natures, or what they are in themselves; and so we let the nature of what we know determine for us the content and form of our knowledge."[75] That is, *kata physin*. He goes on to argue that "science, in every field of our human experience, is only the rigorous extension of that basic way of thinking and behaving."[76] By natural extension, "all this applies as much in our relations with God as in our relations with nature or with one another. There is no secret way of knowing either in science or theology, but there is

---

Stock, 2002), 74, and McGrath, "The Auburn Lectures on Science and Theology," in *T. F. Torrance: An Intellectual Biography*(Edinburgh: T&T Clark, 1999), 199–205.

73. A point made forcefully in Thomas F. Torrance, *Preaching Christ Today*(Grand Rapids: Eerdmans, 1994), 44, with reference to Einstein, Polanyi, and Karl Popper.

74. Thomas F. Torrance, *Theological Science*(reprint, Edinburgh: T&T Clark, 1996), 10. The *kata physic* nature of Torrance's theology is derived from that of Karl Barth in theology (who in turn derived this from his own reading of Anselm, albeit with a rigorous Christological orientation), and Torrance's reading of Einstein in science. Torrance's reading of Barth on *ratio* (rationality and method) is most clearly developed in Torrance, *Karl Barth: An Introduction to His Early Theology 1910–1931*(Edinburgh: T&T Clark, 2000), 180–98. Torrance summarizes the method of the *Church Dogmatics* as follows: "We may express this otherwise by saying that in scientific theological activity the reason is unconditionally bound to its object and determined by it, and that the nature of the object must prescribe the specific mode of the activity of the reason." Ibid.,192. For a concise summary of how Torrance views scientific method see Torrance, *Preaching Christ Today*, 45–49. Beyond Barth and Einstein, Torrance credits John Philoponos with being one of the first to work with a consistent *kata physic* method in science. This is most obvious throughout the various essays comprising Thomas F. Torrance, *Theological and Natural Science* (Eugene, OR: Wipf and Stock, 2002).

75. Thomas F. Torrance, *The Ground and Grammar of Theology*(Charlottesville: University of Virginia Press, 1980), 8. Torrance develops this with especial force in his *Theological Science*(reprint, Edinburgh: T&T Clark, 1996).

76. Ibid.

only one basic way of knowing, which naturally develops different modes of rationality in natural science and in theological science because the nature of what we seek to know in each is different."[77]

The final application of this principle is expounded by Torrance in the following way: "In each field of inquiry, then, we must be faithful to the reality we seek to know and must act and think always in a relation of relentless fidelity to that reality."[78] In this way Torrance has expressed a fundamental and unifying method for all scientific investigation, not least of which includes scientific theology.

As we have seen, Torrance is critical of the use of *a priori* notions in both science and theology, believing that both should respond to the objective reality with which they are confronted, and that they are required to describe.[79] Theology, like the natural sciences, is to be seen as an *a posteriori* activity, conditioned by what is given. In this Torrance is remaining consistent with what he developed in his discussion of the stratification of knowledge.

Working under this "new science," the question has to be asked as to the nature of both Christian theology (dogmatics) and science itself. Torrance defines *dogmatics* as "the pure science of theology: not some system of ideas laid down on the ground of external preconceptions and authorities, not some useless, abstract stuff concerned with detached, merely academic questions, nor again some man-centred ideology that we think up for ourselves out of our socio-political involvements with one another, but the actual knowledge of the living God as he is disclosed to us through his interaction with us in our

---

77. Ibid., 9.
78. Ibid., 10. Torrance attributes this insight to Karl Barth in Torrance, *Karl Barth: Biblical and Evangelical Theologian* (Edinburgh: T&T Clark, 1990), 67–68, when he writes: "All scientific activity is one in which the reason acts strictly and precisely in accordance with the nature of its object, and so lets the object prescribe for it both the limits within which it may be known and the mode of rationality that is to be adopted toward it . . . this is precisely the procedure which Barth adopted in scientific dogmatics—as we can see very clearly in his brilliant interpretation of Anselm's theological method, and in the way in which he has worked out his own epistemology in strict obedience to the nature of the concrete object of theological knowledge, God come to us in Jesus Christ . . . . The procedure common to theological science and all other genuine science is one in which the mind of the knower acts in strict conformity to the nature of what is given, and refuses to take up a standing in regard to it prior to actual knowledge or in abstraction from actual knowledge."
79. Torrance describes four main changes in scientific method that correspond to this unitary way of knowing: 1) it has shed its abstractive character, 2) atomistic thinking is replaced by relational thinking or "fields of force" (Einstein), 3) science is applied to open as opposed to closed systems (Prigogine), 4) "depth dimensions" inherent to the universe are recognized (Polanyi). See Torrance, *The Ground and Grammar of Theology*, 10–13.

world of space and time—knowledge of God that is ultimately controlled by the nature of God as he is in himself."[80] Torrance traces the term *dogmatics* back to philosophers of the first two centuries before and after Christ who devoted themselves to questions yielding positive answers, as opposed to New Academy philosophers, the skeptics who simply asked questions that do not yield the kind of answers that commit one to decision and change. "Thus the 'dogmatic' person turns out to be, not a philosopher, but a scientist who thinks only as he is compelled to think by the objective and intrinsic structures of nature."[81] Torrance stands self-consciously in the long line of what Cyril of Alexandria called *dogmatike episteme*, "dogmatic science."[82] Torrance once defined the task of dogmatics as follows:

> As Mackintosh used to teach us, dogmatics is not the systematic study of the sanctioned dogmas of the Church, but the elucidation of the full content of revelation, of the Word of God as contained in Scripture, and as such is concerned with the intrinsic and permanent truth which church doctrine in every age is meant to express. It is 'systematic' only on the sense that every part of Christian truth is vitally connected with every other part. No doctrine can be admitted that does not bring to expression some aspect of the redemption that is in Christ. Thus for Mackintosh as for Barth it is in Christ alone that the truth of dogmatics finds it organic unity.[83]

We can see in these definitions elements of a *kataphysic* nature. God is revealed in Jesus Christ and so our theology of God is *a posteriori*. In and through Jesus Christ God has made space for Godself to be known and for humanity to respond in a certain way. And so we are under an obligation to respond in faith in accordance with God's self-revelation.

In a similar way to his definition of dogmatics, Torrance defines science for the most part as "natural science in its pure rather than in its applied forms: that is, not something worked up in accordance with *a priori* assumptions and imposed as law upon nature nor merely convenient arrangements of observational data that we can put to practical use in our human attempts to triumph over nature, but rather the knowledge we reach of things in any field

---

80. Ibid., 15–16.
81. Ibid., 49–50.
82. Ibid., 50–52. For the same thought see Torrance, *Preaching Christ Today*, 45–48, where he compares the scientific work of scientists and theologians "working within the same room," as it were.
83. Thomas F. Torrance, "Hugh Ross Mackintosh: Theologian of the Cross," *SBET* 5 (1987): 161.

under the compulsion of their independent reality, in controlled reference to their inherent nature, and formulated in the light of their internal relations."[84] From both definitions we can see how Torrance works as a theologian within the field of science—theological and natural. Torrance's ultimate concern is to provide a *scientific* explanation for the knowledge of God. This cannot be achieved logically or directly from the phenomenological to the noumenal, but rather more in accordance with the nature of the object being studied—in this case, God. Knowledge of God must be revealed by God. This knowledge of God is given, according to Torrance and the Christian tradition, in diverse ways but ultimately through the Person of the Son, Jesus Christ.

> In the face of that dualist outlook in religion and thought invading the Church from the surrounding culture of the ancient world, what line did classical Christian theology take? It was committed to the Gospel of the incarnation of the Son of God, the Word made flesh, and was concerned with a way of believing and thinking imposed upon it by the sheer fact of Christ, in accordance with which it was held that this world of ours in space and time is actually intersected and overlapped, so to speak, by the divine world in the *parousia*, or advent and presence, of Jesus Christ. He was acknowledged and adored, therefore, as one who is God of God and yet man of man, who in his own being belongs both to the eternal world of divine reality and to the historical world of contingent realities.[85]

The essential formulation of this belief was given in the great ecumenical creed of Christendom at Nicea and Constantinople, formalized in what Torrance describes as the "linchpin of this theology,"[86] the *homoousion*, the confession that Jesus Christ the incarnate Son is of one being or of one substance with God the Father. Why is this so crucial to a truly scientific Christian theology? The answer for Torrance is because this provides the realist basis for knowledge of

---

84. Torrance, *The Ground and Grammar of Theology*, 16. Torrance is clearly siding here with Karl Barth in the debate between Barth and Heinrich Sholz and also against the definition of science proposed later by Wolfhart Pannenberg. See Thomas F. Torrance, *Space, Time and Resurrection*(Edinburgh: Handsel, 1976), xi–x; H. Sholz, "Wie ist eine evangelische Theologie als Wisseschaft moglich?" *ZdZ* 9 (1931): 8–53; A. L. Molendijk, "Henirich Sholz-Karl Barth: Ein discussie over de wetenschappelijkheid van de theologie," *Nederlands Theologisch Tijdschrift* 39 (1985): 295–313; and W. Pannenberg in *Theology and the Philosophy of Science*, trans. F. McDonagh (London: Darton, Longman and Todd, 1976), especially 269–76.

85. Torrance, *The Ground and Grammar of Theology*, 39.

86. Ibid.

God. Because Jesus Christ is God of God and man of man in himself, in or through Jesus Christ we who are creatures of this world may truly know God in such a way that our knowledge of God (the object) rests upon the reality of God in God's self. It is not simply a phenomenological phantom or a mythological projection into God, but is grounded and controlled by what God is in God's very self.[87]

Nicene theology thus gave basic shape to the doctrine of the Trinity that was found to belong to the essential structure of faith in God and to the intrinsic grammar of Christian thought. In this way, Torrance moves from a treatment of method or epistemology to his more doctrinal material specifically relating to the doctrine of the triune God. In Jesus Christ is revealed Very God of Very God. God is in God's own being what Christ is as God's revealing Word and saving act toward us. Through Christ and the Spirit we are given access to God as God is in God's self. This access to God is, in part, in the form of knowledge of God, in God's internal relations as Father, Son, and Holy Spirit. The epistemological strength of the *homoousion* works here with full force, for it represents the consubstantial relation between Jesus Christ the Word made flesh and God. As *the* Image of God, identical with God's reality, knowledge of the incarnate Son through the Holy Spirit has a unique and controlling finality in our knowledge of God.[88]

By this means, according to Torrance, the theology of the early church challenged the dualistic foundations of ancient Greek and Roman culture in philosophy, science, and religion.[89] This challenge, if Torrance's position is accepted, must be the work of theologians today as well:

> What, then, is the task of Christian theology today? It must be the same as that of Christian theology in the early centuries when it undertook this reconstruction of the basis of Greek culture as part of the evangelizing activity of the Church, with the hope that Christianity would take root in a developing Christian culture. Today we live in a world being changed by science, which is far more congenial to Christian theology than any period in the history of Western civilization. Here the task of Christian theology must be the recovery of the doctrines of creation and incarnation in such a way that we think through their interrelations more rigorously than

---

87. Ibid., 40.
88. Ibid.
89. Ibid., 44–74.

ever before, and on that ground engage in constant dialogue with the new science, which can only be to the benefit of both.[90]

III. CRITICAL REALISM

Given the fact of an ordered universe and a *kataphysic* way of studying any object we turn now to what is one of the most important scientific and methodological points germane to the architectonic nature of Torrance's theology and his interaction with science: his critical realism. Theologian-scientist Alister McGrath claims that "Torrance is widely credited with having formulated 'the most highly developed version of realism' available in modern theology."[91] For Torrance, the truth can be known and apprehended by the human person, and this knowledge represents a genuine disclosure of that which is real. Christian theology and natural science operate with an understanding of knowledge that has its "ontological foundations in objective reality." Torrance develops his critical realism in two directions: first, from natural science, especially in the work of John Philoponos, James Clerk Maxwell, Albert Einstein, and Michael Polanyi; and second, from theology, especially in the work of Athanasius, Anselm, and Barth.[92] Torrance argues that theology and the sciences share a common commitment to a realist epistemology (given an ordered universe), with both responding appropriately

---

90. Ibid., 74.
91. The quote comes from Alister E. McGrath, *T. F. Torrance: An Intellectual Biography* (Edinburgh: T&T Clark, 1999), 211, who is in turn quoting from Daniel W. Hardy, "Thomas F. Torrance," in *The Modern Theologians: An Introduction*, vol. 1, ed. D. F. Ford (Oxford: Blackwell, 1989), 87. McGrath has himself adopted and developed a commitment to critical realism; see his *The Genesis of Doctrine: A Study in the Foundations of Doctrinal Criticism* (Oxford: Blackwell, 1990), 1–80; *The Foundations of Dialogue in Science and Religion* (Oxford: Blackwell, 1998), 140–64; *A Scientific Theology, vol. 1: Nature* (Grand Rapids: Eerdmans, 2001), 71–78; and especially throughout *A Scientific Theology, vol. 2: Reality* (Grand Rapids: Eerdmans, 2002). McGrath's critical realism draws heavily on the work of Roy Bhaskar. For a critical comparison of the methodology and epistemology of Lindbeck, McGrath, and Torrance in which critical realism is treated in some detail, see the fine but often overlooked work of Elmer M. Colyer, *The Nature of Doctrine in T. F. Torrance's Theology* (Eugene, OR: Wipf and Stock, 2001).
92. We could also include, albeit on a reduced level, the influence of John Duns Scotus and John Major. In a work on Calvin, Torrance wrote: "I write this preface a mile from where John Major was born, at Glegornie, in East Lothian, where I have steeped myself in his thought, and found a remarkable continuity between his critical realism and that of John Duns Scotus, on the one hand, and that of the so-called 'common-sense' philosophy which used to flourish in Scottish Universities, on the other hand." Thomas F. Torrance, *The Hermeneutics of John Calvin* (Edinburgh: Scottish Academic, 1988), viii. Torrance's conviction that Calvin was directly influenced by John Major and had read his works, incidentally, has been convincingly overturned by the work of, among others, Anthony N. S. Lane, *John Calvin: Student of the Church Fathers* (Edinburgh: T&T Clark, 1999), 8–10.

to their respective objects of study (*kata physin*). Each of these disciplines recognizes

> the impossibility of separating out the way in which knowledge arises from the actual knowledge that it attains. Thus in theology the canons of inquiry that are discerned in the process of knowing are not separable from the body of actual knowledge out of which they arise. In the nature of the case a true and adequate account of theological epistemology cannot be gained apart from substantial exposition of the content of the knowledge of God, and of the knowledge of man and the world as creatures of God . . . this means that all through theological inquiry we must operate with an *open* epistemology in which we allow the way of our knowing to be clarified and modified *pari passu* with advance in deeper and fuller knowledge of the object, and that we will be unable to set forth an account of that way of knowing in advance but only by looking back from what has been established as knowledge.[93]

In regard to natural science, Torrance repeatedly turns to the realist approaches of James Clerk Maxwell and Albert Einstein, both of whom he sees as standing at the end of a long line of scientific development spanning the second to the twentieth centuries.[94] In conjunction with the rise of an adoption of dualistic ways of thinking in science and philosophy, not to mention in theology, Torrance sees the history of scientific thought revolving around three main paradigm shifts.[95] The first transition or paradigm shift occurred between the

---

93. Thomas F. Torrance, *Theological Science*(reprint, Edinburgh: T&T Clark, 1996), 10.

94. This is a repeated theme of Torrance's. See his various works: *Theology in Reconciliation: Essays Towards Evangelical and Catholic Unity in East and West* (reprint, Eugene, OR: Wipf and Stock, 1997), 62–78; *God and Rationality*(London: Oxford University Press, 1971), 29–31; and *Reality and Scientific Theology*(Edinburgh: Scottish Academic, 1985), 1–31.

95. Torrance is here echoing the sense of *paradigm shifts* articulated by Thomas S. Kuhn, *The Structure of Scientific Revolutions* (Chicago: The University of Chicago Press, 1962). According to Kuhn's theory, new hypotheses and theories in natural science do not simply emerge by verification or falsification, nor do they evolve naturally. Rather, one paradigm comes to replace an existing one in what can only be termed a "revolution." See T. F. Torrance, "The Integration of Form in Natural and in Theological Science," in *Transformation and Convergence in the Frame of Knowledge: Explorations in the Interrelations of Scientific and Theological Enterprise* (Grand Rapids: Eerdmans, 1984), 71. Maxwell and Einstein are the two scientists Torrance turns to most often to illustrate revolutionary paradigm shifts in addition to Polanyi, whom Thomas Kuhn admitted he had taken the concept of paradigm from! See Thomas F. Torrance, "Michael Polanyi and the Christian Faith—A Personal Report," *TAD* 27 (2000–2001): 31. Torrance does

second and fourth centuries and involved a move from a primitive Hellenistic cosmology, characterized by a thorough dualism, to a Ptolemaic cosmology. As Christianity grew, it was influenced by a Ptolemaic cosmological synthesis that worked its way into Christian theology, most notably in the philosophically defined attributes of God such as aseity and impassibility. Torrance singles out Augustine and his Aristotelian theological/philosophical tradition as canonizing this approach in Christian theology for centuries to come.[96]

The second transition occurred between the sixteenth and seventeenth centuries, from a Ptolemaic to a Copernican and Newtonian cosmology. The Newtonian cosmology resulted in a mechanistic worldview that effectively sidelined God from the world by negating divine involvement or interaction with the world. Torrance views this as a modified form of dualism, a transition from an Augustinian-Aristotelian to an Augustinian-Newtonian dualism.

The third transition occurred in the twentieth century with the profound Maxwellian-Einsteinian revolution that replaced the dualist frames of thinking in favor of a unitary approach based on the notion of continuous fields.[97] What happened in the science of Einstein, Torrance maintains, also happened in the theology of Karl Barth, the demonstration and construction of a unitary approach to reality.[98]

---

not accept or endorse Kuhn's theory completely. In addition to Kuhn's theory of paradigm shifts, Torrance also imports Polanyi's theory of communication in scientific controversy into theological communication, especially apologetics. See Polanyi, *Personal Knowledge: Towards a Post-Critical Philosophy* (Chicago: University of Chicago Press, 1958), 150–60. The little essay "Theological Education Today," in *Theology in Reconstruction*(Eugene, OR: Wipf and Stock, 1996), 13–29, provides a succinct overview of Torrance's views in this regard. Kuhn's theory of scientific revolutions has engendered much criticism, with which Torrance shows no interest in engaging. See P. Hoyningen-Huene, "Kuhn's Conception of Incommensurability," *SHPS*53 (1980): 481–92; M. W. Poirier, "A Comment on Polanyi and Kuhn," *The Thomist*53 (1989): 259–79; and C. Strug, "Kuhn's Paradigm Thesis: A Two-Edged Sword for the Philosophy of Religion," *RelS* 20 (1984): 269–79. See further McGrath, "Scientific Method and the Reconstruction of Theology: Introducing 'A Scientific Theology,'" Lecture for the John Templeton Oxford Seminars on Science and Christianity, Harris Manchester College (July 24, 2003), http://www.metanexus.net/archives/message_fs.asp?ARCHIVEID=8363, para. 35, n. 15.

96. See especially Torrance, *Theology in Reconciliation*, 27–28; 62–78; 267–68.

97. Torrance, *Theology in Reconciliation*, 77. In *Reality and Scientific Theology*, 72, Torrance also includes Michael Faraday as a key scientist in this shift. Reflecting on Torrance's adoption of unitary, relational thinking and "field" patterns as basic to scientific thinking, Palma sees Torrance as moving to a higher plane and a higher unitary theology than the Nicene and Reformed (including Barth) heritage within which Torrance worked. R. J. Palma, "Thomas F. Torrance's Reformed Theology," *RefR* 38 (1984): 24–25. For a study that seeks to elucidate the connection between science and theology within Torrance's dogmatics, see J. H-K. Yeung, *Being and Knowing: An Examination of T. F. Torrance's Christological Science*(Hong Kong: China Alliance, 1996), especially 45–72.

Torrance had a particularly high regard for the work of Einstein and often returned to his scientific insights as illustrations of a realist epistemology in practice.[99] From Einstein's "scientific realism" Torrance sees great application for theology through the means of a critical realism.[100] Torrance is not alone in associating the natural sciences with a realist epistemology. Indeed, a realist epistemology is thought to be the very basis of the ability of the natural sciences to explain the world. "And what more effective explanation may be offered for this success than the simple assertion that what scientific theories describe is really present?"[101] Accepting the legitimate status of epistemic realism, what is the nature of correspondence between reality and our understanding of it? The question of correspondence theories of truth is of great importance to our discussion of science in general and Torrance's theological method in particular.[102]

---

98. Not that Barth was consciously aware of this fact. When Torrance discussed the links between what he saw in Einsteinian science and in Barth's own theology it is reported that Barth responded with appreciation and general agreement. See Torrance, *Transformation and Convergence*, ix.

99. A. Fine, *The Shaky Game: Einstein, Realism and the Quantum Theory* (Chicago: University of Chicago Press, 1986), 86–111, argues for another understanding of Einstein's realism than the one Torrance presents. This has forced one Torrance commentator to conclude that "Torrance's reading of Einstein's realism is not correct." Colin Weightman, *Theology in a Polanyian Universe: The Theology of Thomas Torrance* (New York: Peter Lang, 1994), 193. For other works on Einstein's "realism," see A. Polikarov, "On the Nature of Einstein's Realism," *Epistemologia* 12 (1980): 277–304; F. Laudisa, "Einstein, Bell and Nonseparable Realism," *BJPS* 46 (1995): 309–29. Even if Torrance's reading of Einstein's realism is not correct, and this point is still debatable as the works in the following footnote indicate, the central tenets of his own realism are still valid and operate consistently within his own theological *oeuvre*; Einstein is *illuminative* for Torrance's theology, not *foundational* (as is also the case with Polanyi).

100. Einstein's realism has endeared itself to other theological-scientific scholars. See the other works in the Theology at the Frontiers of Knowledge series published by Scottish Academic Press of Edinburgh and edited by Torrance, such as I. Paul, *Science and Theology in Einstein's Perspective* (Edinburgh: Scottish Academic, 1986); idem., *Science, Theology and Einstein*(New York: Oxford University Press, 1981); R. G. Mitchell, *Einstein and Christ: A New Approach to the Defence of the Christian Religion* (Edinburgh: Scottish Academic, 1987); and W. P. Carvin, *Creation and Scientific Explanation* (Edinburgh: Scottish Academic, 1988).

101. McGrath, *T. F. Torrance*, 215. See further in M. Devitt, *Realism and Truth* (Oxford: Blackwell, 1984); and J. Leplin, ed., *Scientific Realism* (Berkeley: University of California Press, 1984), especially 41–82.

102. See the discussion of Torrance's christocentric analogy in regard to a "created correspondence" in Roland Spjuth, *Creation, Contingency and Divine Presence: In the Theologies of Thomas F. Torrance and Eberhard Jüngel*(Lund: Lund University Press, 1995), 47–57.

Torrance is a realist, not a positivist; thus he does not advocate a scientific positivism that argues for a direct correspondence between concepts and experience. He made this clear when he wrote:

> The fundamental difficulty with abstractive and positivist science . . . is that it operates with a logical bridge between concepts and experience, both at the start and the finish, that is, in the derivation of concepts from the universe as we experience it and in the verificatory procedures relating concepts back to experience. . . . This is not only a difficulty, but an impossibility, for this is not and cannot be any logical bridge between ideas and existence. There is indeed a deep and wonderful correlation between concepts and experience, and science operates with that correlation everywhere, but since there is no logical bridge the scientist does not work with rules for inductive procedures, and cannot finally verify his claims to have discovered the structures of reality by logical means.[103]

Torrance also rejects a "naïve realism" in which there is a direct correspondence between knowledge and reality.[104]

What Torrance does advocate is, in a formal sense, "critical realism."[105] Perhaps one of the better-known advocates of critical realism in biblical theology today is N. T. Wright. He defines critical realism as follows:

> This is a way of describing the process of 'knowing' that acknowledges the *reality of the thing known, as something other than the knower* (hence 'realism'), while also fully acknowledging that the only access we have to this reality lies along the spiralling path of *appropriate dialogue or conversation between the knower and the thing known* (hence 'critical'). This path leads to critical reflection on the

---

103. Torrance, Reality and Scientific Theology, 76.

104. In a discussion of Torrance's "ana-logic and critical realism," Spjuth clearly distinguishes Torrance's critical realism from a "representational position" (naïve realism); see Spjuth, *Creation, Contingency and Divine Presence*, 94–101. With a phrase borrowed from Nancey Murphy, Spjuth characterizes Torrance's critical realism as "chastened modern," ibid., 98. In this he is surely right. See Habets, "Theological Interpretation of Scripture in Sermonic Mode."

105. See P. M. Achtemeier, "The Truth of Tradition: Critical Realism in the Thought of Alasdair MacIntyre and T. F. Torrance," *SJT* 47 (1996): 355–74; J. D. Morrison, "Heidegger, Correspondence Truth and the Realist Theology of Thomas Forsyth Torrance," *EvQ* 69 (1997): 139–55; and Morrison, *Knowledge of the Self-Revealing God in the Thought of Thomas Forsyth Torrance*, Issues in Systematic Theology 2 (New York: Peter Lang, 1997).

products of our enquiry into 'reality', so that our assertions about 'reality' acknowledge their own provisionality. Knowledge, in other words, although in principle concerning reality is independent of the knower, is never itself independent of the knower.[106]

The critical realism advocated by Torrance connects the knower and the known together in personal union, thus putting the knower (theologian) under a certain obligation to offer a rational account of that which exists independently of the knower (theology). By this means it is obvious that for Torrance and his scientific theology, as for Einstein and his natural science, epistemology follows ontology. With this critical realism in place in both science and theology, Torrance explores on many occasions the interrelated and mutual coherence of both disciplines on each other through a historical and a constructive approach. It will reward us to examine this briefly now.

In his work *The Ground and Grammar of Theology*, Torrance traces the development of Christian theology on the natural sciences and argues for a Christian science for today such as that developed by the early church.[107] Through the doctrine of *creatio ex nihilo*, the early church developed "three masterful ideas"[108] that powerfully affected all subsequent thought in natural as well as theological science.[109] The first idea was the rational unity of the universe, given the fact that God is the Creator of all. This provides the world with one pervading *taxis* or order. The second idea was the contingent rationality or intelligibility of the universe.[110] In Greek thought, the human

---

106. N. T. Wright, *The New Testament and the People of God* (London: SPCK, 1992), 35 (italics in original).

107. Similar themes and treatments can be found throughout his *Christian Theology and Scientific Culture* (New York: Oxford University Press, 1981) and Reality and Scientific Theology.

108. Torrance, *The Ground and Grammar of Theology* (Charlottesville: University of Virginia Press, 1980), 48.

109. For a good recent history of the doctrine of *creatio ex nihilo* within the same general context as we are investigating here see McGrath, *A Scientific Theology*, vol. 1: Nature, 159–66.

110. This theme was also forcefully made by Eric L. Mascall, *Christian Theology and Natural Science: Some Questions in Their Relations* (London: Longmans, Green, 1956), 94, when he asked and answered the question of what kind of world the Christian God might be expected to have created, on the basis of what could be known of that God. His answer: a contingent and orderly one, the investigation of which would proceed by means of *a posteriori* examination. See Torrance's approving remarks in *Theological Science*, 61. In more recent times Wolfhart Pannenberg has also dealt with the idea of contingency but uses it to establish the priority of the future. See his *Systematic Theology*, vol. 2, trans. G. W. Bromiley (Grand Rapids: Eerdmans, 1994), 69–72. For a critique of Pannenberg's model of contingency see R. J. Russell, "Contingency in Physics and Cosmology: A Critique of the Theology of Wolfhart Pannenberg,"

mind was eternal. It was, due to the influence of the Orphic ideal, the spark of the divine. This led to the Greek idea of the apotheosis of the creature.[111] Christian theology rejected this dualism and instead operated with the distinction between created and uncreated light and rationality that exists between God and humanity. Creation *ex nihilo* meant that even the mind of the human person was created by the Creator in time. The consequence is that God gives human intelligence its own (contingent) rationality. The third idea is the corollary of the first and second points, the freedom of the universe—a contingent freedom.

This freedom is also found in the very being of God. When medieval theology adopted Aristotelian philosophy, the Greek notion of God as impassible and immutable was also adopted. In this way, Aristotle's Unmoved Mover became associated with the God of the Scriptures.[112] However, in patristic theology immutability and impassibility, as applied to God, were not associated with these philosophical ideas but were actually a challenge to it. It is true that God is not moved by, and is not changed by, anything outside the divine being, and that God is not affected by anything or does not suffer from anything beyond the divine being. But this simply affirms the biblical fact that God is transcendent and the one who created *ex nihilo*. The Fathers did not mean that God does not move Godself or that God is incapable of imparting motion to what God has made.[113] It does not mean that God is devoid of passion, of love, mercy, and wrath, and that God is impassibly and immutably related to our world of space and time in such a way that it is thrown back upon itself as a closed continuum of cause and effect.[114] Torrance acknowledges that "patristic theology was tempted constantly by the thrust of Greek thought to change the concepts of impassibility and immutability in this direction, but

Zygon 23 (1988): 23–43; and C. Mostert, *God and the Future: Wolfhart Pannenberg's Eschatological Doctrine of God* (London: T&T Clark, 2002), 97–104, 167–69.

111. Torrance, The Ground and Grammar of Theology, 55.

112. I have addressed these issues further in Myk Habets, "Third Article Theology and the *Filioque*," in *Ecumenical Perspectives on the Filioque for the 21st Century*, ed. Myk Habets (London: T&T Clark, forthcoming).

113. See Torrance, *The Trinitarian Faith: The Evangelical Theology of the Ancient Catholic Church* (Edinburgh: T&T Clark, 1995), 235–56.

114. Torrance, *The Ground and Grammar of Theology*, 65. See a modern Thomistic support for this reading of the Fathers in Thomas G. Weinandy, *Does God Change? The Word's Becoming in the Incarnation* (Petersham. MA: St. Bede's, 1985); and followed up by *Does God Suffer?* (Edinburgh: T&T Clark, 2000). A further volume applying these insights to contemporary issues is *Divine Impassibility and the Mystery of Human Suffering*, ed. James F. Keating and Thomas J. White (Grand Rapids: Eerdmans, 2009).

it remained entrenched within the orbit of the Judeo-Christian doctrine of the living God who moves himself, who through his free love created the universe, imparting to its [sic] dynamic order, and who through the outgoing of his love moves outside of himself in the incarnation."[115]

This is the God who was not always Creator but became Creator. This implies the notion that even in the life of God there is change. Nor was God eternally incarnate, for in Jesus Christ God became what God was not without ceasing to be what God was. This teaching altered the whole concept of God, of God's being and act, in the early centuries of our era. Torrance sees this doctrine being clearly articulated first by Athanasius and then in our own day by Karl Barth[116] in his account of the being of God in God's act, and of the act of God in God's being, inseparably bound up with the transcendent freedom of God in God's love.[117] In fact, this principle that God is revealed in God's being and act and act and being is one of the principal tenets of both Barth and Torrance's theological work.

According to Torrance and the scientific tradition within which he stands, the order evident in the natural world is totally contingent and yet ordered, and so conforms to the Christian truth of the creative action of God. Drawing on the work of James Clerk Maxwell (1831–1879), Torrance seeks to drive out all dualisms in our understanding and method in favor of what Maxwell presented in terms of unitary modes of thought about nature.[118] Torrance repeatedly argued that Maxwell's strong Christian faith was the foundation of his scientific method, like John Philoponos well before him.[119] Torrance suggested that for

---

115. Torrance, *The Ground and Grammar of Theology*, 65–66.

116. For his indebtedness to Barth on this matter see Thomas F. Torrance, "Introduction to Karl Barth," in *Theology and Church, Shorter Writings 1920–1928* (London: SCM, 1962), 7–54. It should be noted that Torrance first received insight into this key doctrine from his Edinburgh mentor Hugh Ross Mackintosh. See Torrance, "Hugh Ross Mackintosh: Theologian of the Cross," *SBET* 5 (1987): 162–63.

117. "Dogmatic thinking arises from the fact that God has acted in human history in a final and saving way, and that what he has given us in His revelation is Himself, His own divine being: His Being in His Act; His Act in His Being," Torrance, *Theological Science*, 343; and *The Ground and Grammar of Theology*, 67.

118. On November 4, 1979, Torrance preached the sermon at the James Clerk Maxwell Memorial Service, held at Corsock Parish Church in Kirkcudbrightshire, marking the centenary of Maxwell's death. In 1982, Torrance would edit and write the preface and introduction to James Clerk Maxwell, *A Dynamical Theory of the Electromagnetic Field* (Edinburgh: Scottish Academic, 1982).

119. Thomas F. Torrance, "John Philoponos of Alexandria, Sixth Century Christian Physicist," *Texts and Studies*, vol. 2. (London: Thyateira House, 1983): 261–65. Torrance's collected essays on John Philoponos are published as *Theological and Natural Science* (Eugene, OR: Wipf and Stock, 2002). Also see *Philoponos and the Rejection of Aristotelian Science*, ed. R. K. Sorabji (Ithaca, NY: Cornell University Press,

Maxwell, the Christian doctrine of creation offered a lens through which the rationality and intelligibility of the created order could be understood and pursued.[120] Here again Torrance is arguing that proper theological reflection (science) has affected and driven natural scientific investigation, and not vice versa.

With an understanding of a unitary and ordered universe and scientific reflection on it that refuses to operate with inherent *a priori* foundations, together with a *kataphysic* approach to reality and truth, Torrance built up his form of critical realism. When he applies it to dogmatics, Torrance is clear that objective reality, which in this case is God in God's self-givenness, has ontological priority over all of our human referencing. Theological thinking, as with all scientific thinking, must be properly realist. It is out of this "theological realism" that Torrance sees the doctrine of the *homoousion* as a faithful expression and disclosure model of the oneness in being in the relation of the incarnate Son with the Father. Ultimately, Torrance's theological realism is grounded in God and calls the church back to a truly rational worship of God (*logike latreia*). This point was made clear in an essay on theological realism in which Torrance wrote: "It is as our communion with God the Father through Christ and in the Spirit is founded in and shares in the inner Trinitarian consubstantial or *homoousial* communion of the Father, Son and Holy Spirit, that the subjectively-given pole of conceptuality is constantly purified and refined under the searching light and quickening power of the objectively-given pole in divine revelation. Within that polarity Christian theology becomes what it essentially is and ought always to be, *logike latreia*, rational worship of God."[121]

IV. POLANYI AND A PHILOSOPHY OF SCIENCE

During our survey of Torrance's theological method, we have seen that he repeatedly draws on many philosophers of science, especially Michael Polanyi. Given the fact that Torrance is referred to as a philosopher of science in his

---

1987), 1–40; and E. M. Macierowski and R. F. Hassing, "John Philoponus on Aristotle's Definition of Nature: A Translation from the Greek with Introduction and Notes," *Ancient Philosophy* 8 (1988): 73–100.

120. Torrance, *Transformation and Convergence*, 216–20.

121. Thomas F. Torrance, "Theological Realism," in *The Philosophical Frontiers of Christian Theology: Essays Presented to D. M. MacKinnon*, ed. B. Hebblethwaite and S. Sutherland (Cambridge: Cambridge University Press, 1982), 193.

own right,[122] it is necessary to examine further Torrance's insights derived from Polanyi.

Throughout Torrance's writings the name of the Hungarian medical doctor, chemist, and philosopher of science Michael Polanyi (1891–1976) appears repeatedly. By Torrance's own admission, Polanyi had a pervasive impact on his philosophy of science and his philosophy of religion. Numerous theologians have used Polanyi's work, and an examination of his philosophy of science is of importance to an understanding of Torrance's own position.[123] In Weightman's study of the interaction between Torrance and Polanyi, he argues that "the part Polanyi plays in Torrance's attempt to relate his Barthian theology to the modern scientific world . . . is crucial to comprehending what Torrance is all about."[124]

It is clear from the evidence and Torrance's own comments that Torrance used the philosophy of Polanyi at key points in his theology to further clarify or illustrate basic axioms and commitments that Torrance had already formed. That Torrance did not read Polanyi into his theology like some *a priori* philosophy imposed upon the biblical evidence is obvious.[125] Torrance distinguished between what may be termed *foundational* and *illuminative* roles for philosophies such as Polanyi's. Clearly, Torrance's use of Polanyi's philosophy is in the sense of *illumination*, not *foundation*.

According to Torrance, his first association with Polanyi was in reading a work of his around the year 1958, well after Torrance's fundamental thoughts on the relation between science and theology, and his natural theology, had been formulated. Torrance's first published use of Polanyi can be dated to May 1963, as found in a paper on "The Problem of Theological Statement Today."[126] This was followed by his first extensive interaction with Polanyi's thought in

---

122. R. J. Palma, "Thomas F. Torrance's Reformed Theology," *RefR* 38 (1984): 26–29.

123. Polanyi's use by numerous theologians has been well documented. See for instance A. Dulles, "Faith, Church and God: Insights From Michael Polanyi," *TS* 45 (1984): 537–50 (especially 537). One commentator sees Polanyi as a modern Martin Luther(!); R. Gelwick, "Michael Polanyi—Modern Reformer," *Religion in Life* 34 (1965): 224–34.

124. Colin Weightman, *Theology in a Polanyian Universe: The Theology of Thomas Torrance* (New York: Peter Lang, 1994), 1.

125. Weightman's *Theology in a Polanyian Universe* has as its basic premise that Torrance adopted Polanyi's philosophy *in toto* and built his own theology upon it. This is not supported by the evidence and is a distortion or overemphasis of the facts. Torrance's Auburn Lectures from 1939 on science and theology illustrate this point well. See The Thomas F. Torrance Manuscript Collection, Special Collections, Princeton Theological Seminary Library, Box 22: "Science and Theology," with "Theology and Science." Also see Torrance, "Michael Polanyi and the Christian Faith—A Personal Report," *TAD* 27 (2000–2001): 26–32.

Theological Science (1969). Torrance maintained that while these lectures were originally given in the United States in 1959, the material relating to Polanyi was written during the revision of the work for publication during the 1960s.[127] From the 1960s on, Torrance consistently drew on insights from Polanyi to illustrate his own theological points.[128] In 1968–69, Torrance joined Polanyi as a member of the Académie Internationale de Philosophie des Sciences, and over the years 1970–74 Torrance and Polanyi became friends.[129] An examination of Torrance's use of Polanyi shows that he considers Polanyi's *Personal Knowledge* (1958)[130] to be among the most important of Polanyi's works.[131]

Torrance regards Polanyi as standing at the end, and so representing the capstone, of the Maxwellian–Einsteinian restructuring of the epistemological foundations of natural science, and he does so with "unrivalled delicacy and refinement."[132] The appeal of Polanyi for Torrance is the way he makes religious belief compatible with his philosophy of science.[133]

Of central importance to Torrance's theological program is the nature of the correspondence between knowing and being. For Torrance, as for Polanyi from whom he draws, knowing is correlated to being. We advance in knowledge as we "hook our thoughts onto the structures of reality. In doing so

---

126. Originally a lecture delivered at the University of Tübingen, May 1963, and found in Torrance, *Theology in Reconstruction* (Eugene, OR: Wipf and Stock, 1996), 46–61.

127. Alister E. McGrath, *T. F. Torrance: An Intellectual Biography* (Edinburgh: T&T Clark, 1999), 230.

128. Weightman's suggestion that Torrance first heard of Polanyi through Sir Bernard Lovell as early as 1946 is, while plausible, not probable, and Torrance himself dismisses such an early link. See Weightman, *Theology in a Polanyian Universe*, 230–31.

129. Torrance, "Michael Polanyi and the Christian Faith—A Personal Report," 26–32. On Polanyi's death in 1976 Torrance became his literary executor. Upon the death of Magda, Polanyi's wife, Torrance handed the role over to their son John Polanyi, a Nobel Laureate professor of chemistry in Toronto. In 1978, Torrance delivered a lecture on Polanyi's thought at the opening of the Michael Polanyi Seminar Room in the Philosophy Department of the University of Manchester. Torrance, "The Framework of Belief," in *Belief in Science and in Christian Life: The Relevance of Michael Polanyi's Thought for Christian Faith and Life*, ed. T. F. Torrance (Edinburgh: Handsel, 1980), 148.

130. Michael Polanyi, *Personal Knowledge: Towards a Post-Critical Philosophy* (Chicago: University of Chicago Press, 1958). Other Polanyi works of importance for our study include his *The Tacit Dimension* (New York: Doubleday, 1966), and *Meaning*, with Harry Prosch (Chicago: University of Chicago Press, 1975).

131. This is the main work Torrance interacts with specifically in his article "The Framework of Belief," 1–27.

132. Torrance, *Christian Theology and Scientific Culture* (New York: Oxford University Press, 1981), 61.

133. Torrance, "The Framework of Belief," 15. This point is also made by W. R. Thorson, "Scientific Objectivity and the Listening Attitude," in *Objective Knowledge: A Christian Perspective*, ed. P. Helm (Leicester: Inter-Varsity, 1987), 62.

'we presume that a correlation is possible between our human conceiving and the inner structure of reality itself, and we carry out all our operations in that belief.'[134]

Knowing, for Einstein, Polanyi, and Torrance, involves hierarchical structures.[135] Einstein outlined a hierarchical structure that could be applied to each particular science: the physical, the theoretical, and the meta-theoretical. Polanyi advanced beyond this and proposed a hierarchy of sciences. The various scientific disciplines themselves could be stratified from lower to higher levels, with the higher levels having an influence over the lower levels and not, as in Newtonian science, with a mechanistic reading of the lower levels up into the higher. Torrance called this the principle of coherent integration from above.[136] When Torrance adopted this stratified structure of the sciences, he, not surprisingly, placed theology as the highest level of knowing, as it is the science of theology that has to do with the knowledge of God; this is the highest possible form of knowing.[137] Here we have a modern interpretation of theology as the queen of the sciences.

One of the more important themes that Polanyi develops and that Torrance uses is that of the fiduciary component of human knowledge. Over and against the triumph of reason over belief, which had come to dominate modern scientific activity, Polanyi argues convincingly for a "post-critical philosophy" similar to that of Augustine in the fourth century.[138] According to Polanyi, Augustine taught that all knowledge was a gift of grace for which we

---

134. Weightman, *Theology in a Polanyian Universe*, 235, quoting Torrance, *Reality and Scientific Theology* (Edinburgh: Scottish Academic, 1985), 27.

135. Torrance, *Space, Time and Resurrection* (Edinburgh: Handsel, 1976), 188–92.

136. Torrance, *Christian Theology and Scientific Culture*, 36. In another work appearing in the same year, *Divine and Contingent Order*(reprint, Edinburgh: T&T Clark, 1998), 20, Torrance explains: "[there is] an ontological stratification in the universe comprising a sequence of rising levels, each higher one controlling the boundaries of the one below it and embodying thereby the joint meaning of the particulars on the lower level." For further insights into this methodology, with special reference to the methodological insights of Duns Scotus and Kurt Gödel, see Thomas F. Torrance, "Intuitive and Abstractive Knowledge: From Duns Scotus to Calvin," in *De Doctrina Ioannis Duns Scoti. Congressus Scotisticus Internationalis. Studia Scholastico-Scotistica* 5,ed. C. Balic (Rome: Societas Internationalis Scotistica, 1968), 291–305; and Torrance, *Space, Time and Incarnation*(Edinburgh: T&T Clark, 2005),86–90.

137. Torrance, *Space, Time and Resurrection*, 190.

138. Polanyi was a Jew whose religious life is ambiguous at best. He was influenced early on by Dostoevsky's and Tolstoy's visions of God and religion, later to become baptized into the Roman Catholic Church (1919). Through the 1940s he regularly attended an Anglican church and through the 1950s and '60s had regular contact with a number of Protestant theologians, among whom we could include Paul Tillich and later (early '70s), T. F. Torrance. Finally, Polanyi was influenced late in his life

must strive under the guidance of antecedent belief. He then cites Augustine: "Unless ye believe, ye shall not understand."[139] This fiduciary basis of knowledge ruled for a thousand years until Locke introduced an inherent dualism between knowledge and faith. "All belief," writes Polanyi, "was reduced to the status of subjectivity: to that of an imperfection by which knowledge fell short of universality."[140] To remedy this Polanyi offers the following corrective: "We must now recognize belief once more as the source of all knowledge. Tacit assent and intellectual passions, the sharing of an idiom and of a cultural heritage, affiliation to a like-minded community: such are the impulses which shape our vision of the nature of things on which we rely for our mastery of things. No intelligence, however critical or original, can operate outside such a fiduciary framework. While our acceptance of this framework is the condition for having any knowledge, this matrix can claim no self-evidence."[141]

This fiduciary element or post-critical philosophy of Polanyi's has had an enormous effect on theologians, including Torrance, as they can see that theological statements are developed in manners that are analogous to those associated with the natural sciences.[142] In both theology and the natural sciences, discovery begins with faith (belief), which leads to the truth, truth being a fundamental insight into the *real*, as it is independent of the knower. This does not mean that whatever one thinks is true or real. Rather, one works from one's own personal beliefs to explore, test, and refine them. Again using Augustine as his example, this time his *Confessions,* Polanyi writes, "His maxim *nisi credideritis non intelligitis* ["You will not understand unless you will have first believed"] expresses this logical requirement. It says, as I understand it, that the process of examining any topic is both an exploration of the topic, and an exegesis of our fundamental beliefs in the light of which we approach it; a dialectical combination of exploration and exegesis. Our fundamental beliefs are continuously reconsidered in the course of such a process, but only within the scope of their own basic premises."[143]

---

by the "cosmic theologian" Mircea Eliade. See the account of Polanyi's religious life in Weightman, *Theology in a Polanyian Universe,* 7–26.

139. Polanyi, *Personal Knowledge,* 266.

140. Ibid.

141. Ibid., 266–67.

142. Lesslie Newbigin in particular has developed many Polanyian themes in his works, especially *The Gospel in a Pluralist Society* (London: SPCK, 1989). See also the extensive use made of Polanyi in Colin Gunton, *Enlightenment and Alienation: An Essay Towards a Trinitarian Theology* (Basingstoke: Marshall, Morgan and Scott, 1985).

143. Polanyi, *Personal Knowledge,* 267.

Carl Henry, the preeminent theological foundationalist of contemporary theology, criticized aspects of Torrance's scientific theology over several publications, the most sustained being in volume three of his magnum opus *God, Revelation and Authority*.[144] Henry was particularly critical of what he saw as the illogical presuppositions of Torrance's intuitive theology. Torrance rejected the form of propositional revelation espoused by Henry in favor of a "personal knowing."[145] Reality is to be known in faith through an existential encounter with the ultimate Reality—Jesus Christ the incarnate Word (*Logos*).

Henry saw the critical mistake of Torrance's epistemology, derived in part from Kierkegaard but more from Polanyi, to lie in his seeming rejection of any objective revelational knowledge.[146] From Kierkegaard, Torrance was committed to the idea that the truth of God is communicated through personal relations, not, as Henry would have it, objectively. However, Torrance held that theology that accepts the absolute primacy of its proper object of inquiry could be considered both rational and scientific—hence objective. Torrance understood Kierkegaard's "truth as subjectivity" as in fact theological objectivity and realism, the subject's proper relation to the object.

Henry appears to misread Torrance (and Polanyi) at this point by interpreting the notion of personal knowledge, which acknowledges the necessity for "responsible commitment" (Polanyi's term for personal knowledge) in terms of subjectivism. This is especially so when "personal knowledge" applied to religious knowing is virtually equated with biblical "faith."[147] Using Polanyi's epistemology as he does, Torrance would no doubt respond to this criticism by saying that Henry and other critics are perhaps looking to an impersonal procedure that operates along detached and mechanical lines and ultimately appeals to the concept of autonomous reason. This autonomous reason is then directed at an external authority, in this case the Holy Scriptures, and a system of propositional truth is worked out in a purely impersonal but logical way. It is this program that Torrance is particularly concerned to eradicate.[148]

---

144. Carl F. H. Henry, *God, Revelation and Authority*, vol. 3 (Waco, TX: Word, 1980), especially 214–24. Also see Carl Henry, "Presuppositions and Theological Method," Part 1, Tape 172a; "Presuppositions and Theological Method," Part 2, Tape 172b (Edinburgh: Rutherford House, n.d.), http://tapesfromscotland.org/Rutherfordhouseaudio.htm.

145. For his definition of this term see Torrance, ed., *Belief in Science and in Christian Life*, 141.

146. Henry, *God, Revelation and Authority*, 3:221.

147. For the convergence between Polanyi's "personal knowledge" and biblical faith see W. R. Thorson, "The Biblical Insights of Michael Polanyi," *JASA* 33 (1981): 129–38.

148. A full examination of Torrance and Henry's differences can be found in Myk Habets, "Beyond Henry's Nominalism and Evangelical Foundationalism: Thomas Torrance's Theological Realism," in

This use of Polanyi further explains Torrance's form of realism, which we have already examined. It is this commitment to realism that constitutes one of Torrance's main reasons for drawing on the work of Polanyi. In Polanyi Torrance found a philosophical ally, and one who illustrated Torrance's own point in the natural sciences as Torrance sought to do in Christian theology.

Conclusion

From this reading of Torrance's account of a strictly *scientific* theology, we are given an introduction into an understanding of his theological *oeuvre*. Critics of Torrance's work have often misunderstood his basic scientific hermeneutics and epistemology, and on that basis dismissed his various insights as either unbridled theological speculation in a Barthian mold or the idiosyncratic ravings of a maverick theologian. It is obvious that neither is the case. From his scientific theology we are led to ask, however, about the nature of his understanding of natural theology and a theology of nature, and, in turn, his doctrine of Scripture. We turn our attention to each of these issues in the next two chapters.

Gospel, Truth and Interpretation: Evangelical Identity in Aotearoa New Zealand, Archer Studies in Pacific Christianity, ed. Tim Meadowcroft and Myk Habets (Auckland: Archer Press, 2011), 205–40.

3

Natural Theology
And a Theology of Nature

There exists within Torrance's dogmatics a consistent and deeply foundational interrelation between science and dogmatics on the epistemic or methodological level, and between theology and the natural sciences on the practical level.[1] It comes as no surprise then to turn our attention, as Torrance himself does, to the question of the definition and place of natural theology.[2] The way in which Torrance understands the relationship that exists between natural theology and revealed theology, it can be argued, reflects his growing appreciation of the importance of forging rigorous links between theology and the natural sciences.[3] The legitimacy and status of natural theology is highly contested in Reformed theology generally and amongst post-Barthian scholarship especially. This is no less true amongst Torrance scholarship. Thus

---

1. This thesis has been defined and defended in J. H-K. Yeung, *Being and Knowing: An Examination of T. F. Torrance's Christological Science*(Hong Kong: China Alliance, 1996), especially 65–72.

2. Natural theology has long been the topic of considered debate amongst theologians and has been supported by such figures as Anselm of Canterbury, Thomas Aquinas, René Descartes, G. W. Leibniz, and John Locke, each in their respective ways. Contemporary scientist-theologians leading the dialogue between these two disciplines apart from Torrance include the following: I. Barbour, J. Polkinghorne, S. Hauerwas, and especially the multi-volume series from Alister E. McGrath, *A Scientific Theology,vol. 1: Nature, vol. 2: Reality, vol. 3: Theory*(Grand Rapids: Eerdmans, 2003); and *The Science of God* (London: T&T Clark, 2004). For an overview of McGrath's three-volume series see his Templeton Lecture "Scientific Method and the Reconstruction of Theology: Introducing 'A Scientific Theology,'" Lecture for the John Templeton Oxford Seminars on Science and Christianity, Harris Manchester College, (July 24, 2003), http://www.metanexus.net/archives/message_fs.asp?ARCHIVEID=8363. McGrath has continued to refine his concept of natural theology in the successive works *The Open Secret: A New Vision for Natural Theology* (Oxford: Blackwell, 2008) and *A Fine-Tuned Universe: The Quest for God in Science and Theology*(Louisville: Westminster John Knox, 2009).

3. Roland Spjuth, *Creation, Contingency and Divine Presence: In the Theologies of Thomas F. Torrance and Eberhard Jüngel*(Lund: Lund University Press, 1995), 68–93.

Torrance's appeal to a "new" natural theology invites close consideration and comment.

Natural theology generally refers to the attempt to show that belief in God's existence can be defended with references to reason or the natural order that ought to be acceptable to anyone, not simply those who already believe in God's existence.[4] Torrance challenges this traditional practice and seeks in his theology a "transposition"[5] and "transformation"[6] of natural theology. This is often called Torrance's "new" natural theology.

Natural theology is to be distinguished from a theology of nature, a related yet different enterprise. A theology of nature may refer to a doctrine of creation, or more generally to a theological perspective on the world, including the natural sciences. It seems that in Torrance's new natural theology we find three concepts in play—natural revelation, natural theology, and a theology of nature—and yet these are not fully and finally distinguished in his dogmatics. This introduces a level of ambiguity into Torrance's work. No wonder Elmer Colyer once wrote that "Torrance's reconstruction of natural theology is one of the most difficult aspects of his theology."[7]

In terms of the natural sciences, Torrance admits that they discover, or better, come under the compulsion of God's revelation, but they do so by means of a *kataphysic* approach to discovering the order inherent in the world. Torrance thus accepts a limited role for what can be called natural theology based on natural revelation. However, natural revelation never gets one beyond the first level in the stratification of reality (as detailed in chapter two). This level is intuitive, experiential, and empirical. At its edges it occasionally bleeds into the second level and becomes a natural theology (and it is precisely here that Torrance's work becomes controversial, creating differences of opinion even amongst Torrance scholars). A theology of nature then becomes the focus of the second two levels, as the theologian operates at these levels from faith and not simply from reason. In these two higher levels the Trinitarian act of creation

---

4. For this textbook definition of natural theology and a critical appeal to reclaiming a dogmatic natural theology in the Reformed tradition see Michael Sudduth, *The Reformed Objection to Natural Theology* (Farnham: Ashgate, 2009), 1. It is noteworthy that Sudduth doesn't include a single reference to Torrance in his entire work. A helpful taxonomy of five types of natural theology can be found in David Fergusson, "Types of Natural Theology," in *The Evolution of Rationality: Interdisciplinary Essays in Honor of J. Wentzel van Huyssteen*, ed. F. LeRon Shults (Grand Rapids: Eerdmans, 2006), 380–93.

5. Torrance, *Space, Time and Resurrection* (Edinburgh: Handsel, 1976), ix.

6. Torrance, *The Ground and Grammar of Theology* (Charlottesville: University of Virginia Press, 1980), 92.

7. Elmer M. Colyer, *How To Read T. F. Torrance: Understanding His Trinitarian and Scientific Theology* (Downers Grove, IL: InterVarsity, 2001), 192.

and the christological purpose for creation (not simply the world)[8] is the focus of attention. Torrance's new natural theology is thus a combination of natural revelation, a limited role for natural theology, and a Trinitarian theology of nature. But this is to run ahead of the discussion.

Given the large amount of space in Torrance's work dedicated to the interrelation between science and theology, it is expected that Torrance would turn to the issue of a natural theology, and in light of his dependence in many areas upon his *doktorvater* Karl Barth, the issue is of some significance. Barth, as is well known, initially denied any role to what is termed natural theology in his debates with Emil Brunner.[9] However, in Barth's later works he did allow for a modified form of natural theology in his theological system.[10] Torrance moves beyond Barth over the understanding and place of natural theology and shows here, as elsewhere, that he is not a "Barthian epigone."[11] Rather, Torrance

---

8. Scientists can discover truths about the world but not necessarily have anything to say to a doctrine of creation which requires belief in a Creator, which, in the Christian tradition, already puts one within the orbit of the doctrine of the Trinity and God's being and act.

9. For the debate see K. Barth and E. Brunner, *Natural Theology: Comprising "Nature and Grace" by Professor Dr. Emil Brunner and the reply "No!" by Dr. Karl Barth*, trans. P. Fraenkel (London: Geoffrey Bles, The Centenary Press, 1946). By "natural theology" Barth meant a systematic discourse about God based on something other than revelation in Jesus Christ, something he could not find in Calvin. Brunner, on the other hand, argued that the Christian message can be heard by men and women only if some natural capacity for the word remained in them after the fall. Consequently, by "natural theology" Brunner meant God's objective revelation of God's self in nature, not the subjective appropriation received through Christ in Scripture. Clearly there is a measure of semantic ambiguity at play in this debate. Both authors went on to elaborate their views further, Barth in the monumental *Church Dogmatics* and Brunner in *The Divine-Human Encounter*, trans. A.W. Loos (1944) and *Revelation and Reason*, trans. O. Wyon (1941). Further commentary on the debate can be found in E. A. Dowey, *The Knowledge of God in Calvin's Theology* (New York: Columbia University Press, 1952); T. H. L. Parker, *Calvin's Doctrine of the Knowledge of God*, 2nd ed. (Grand Rapids: Eerdmans, 1959); G. Hunsinger, *How to Read Karl Barth: The Shape of His Theology* (Oxford: Oxford University Press, 1991), 76–102; and K. Tanner, "Creation and Providence," in *The Cambridge Companion to Karl Barth*, ed. J. Webster (Cambridge: Cambridge University Press, 2000), 111–26.

10. Karl Barth, *Church Dogmatics*, II/1, trans. W. B. Johnston et al., ed. G. W. Bromiley and T. F. Torrance (Edinburgh: T&T Clark, 1957), 85–98.

11. Contrary to the view of S. Rehnman, "Barthian Epigoni: Thomas F. Torrance's Barth-Reception," *WTJ* 60 (1998): 271–96. The biographical reflections of Alasdair Heron's time spent under Torrance provides further, firsthand evidence: "Edinburgh dogmatics under Torrance was not, however, characterized by any kind of uncritical Barthianism. In the theology I learned at New College in the 1960s (and taught there in the 1970s), Barth was an important source and a significant authority, but one with whom one had a perfect right to disagree and who was certainly not to be regarded as having said the last word on any subject. It may seem banal to say so, but we were not 'Barthians' in any narrow sense of the word at all . . . . I went on at Torrance's encouragement to do research in Patristics; and my

is prepared to build upon Barth's foundation in ways that Barth himself did not or would not do.[12] John Morrison expresses the relation well when he states:

> Torrance's relation to Barth and Barth's theological thought is complex and multileveled. On the whole, Torrance defends and develops Barth's theological thinking in and from Jesus Christ, while constructing an agenda that is simultaneously related and distinct. Where Torrance does differ with aspects of Barth's thinking, criticism is given in understated tones. Subsequent theological reformulation and construction are intended to advance Barthian thinking in ways which, in terms of the Christocentric-Trinitarian goal, Barth himself could and ought to have taken. The issue of "natural theology" is a good example of this connective-constructive development between Torrance and Barth.[13]

Natural Theology in Historical Context

The concept of natural theology holds a tentative place in the history of theological thought, with advocates arguing strongly for it and others who argue just as strongly against it.[14] Torrance contends that traditional natural

first published article ventured to attempt to correct Barth on the *filioque* question with the help of Anselm, Augustine, and Vladimir Lossky! That was characteristic of Torrance's influence." A. I. C. Heron, "Karl Barth: A Personal Engagement," in *The Cambridge Companion to Karl Barth*, ed. J. Webster (Cambridge: Cambridge University Press, 2000), 297–98.

12. Torrance clearly asserted this in "Reply to Donald Macleod," Tape 199, http://tapesfromscotland.org/Rutherfordhouseaudio.htm (Edinburgh: Rutherford House, 1999), at 0:34–1:05, when he said: "People take me for a Barthian . . . but I'm an Athanasian. I owe more to him than to anyone else, and where I differ from him I differ from him at Athanasius. And again I differ from him on Calvin." Later he says, "If you want to categorize me, I am an Athanasian, or a Calvinian; not a Calvinist." (41:49–41:54). A similar point is made by Colin Weightman, *Theology in a Polanyian Universe: The Theology of Thomas Torrance* (New York: Peter Lang, 1994), 139–47. While Weightman's thesis that "the universe to which Torrance will attempt to relate his own theology is a *Polanyian* universe" is less than obvious, his point that Torrance self-consciously moves through and beyond Barth is not.

13. John D. Morrison, "Thomas Torrance's Reformulation of Karl Barth's Christological Rejection of Natural Theology," *EvQ* 73 (2001): 66.

14. The entire history of the debate is not the focus of this small section. For an important background to this study see P. Barth, *Das Problem der natürlichen Theologie bei Calvin* (Munich: C. Kaiser, 1935); G. Gloede, *Theologia naturalis bei Calvin* (Stuttgart: Kohlhammer, 1935); P. Maury, "La Théologie naturelle d'après Calvin," in *The Bulletin de la Soc. de l'Hist. du Protest. Francais*, LXXXIV (1935): 267–79; and T. F. Torrance, *Calvin's Doctrine of Man* (London: Lutterworth, 1949), 128–30. For a history of the place of natural theology in the Reformed tradition more generally see Michael Sudduth, *The Reformed Objection to Natural Theology* (Farnham: Ashgate, 2009).

theology flourishes during periods in which dualist modes of thought prevail in science and philosophy, given the fact that knowledge is allegedly derived by way of abstraction from sense experience or deduction from observations.[15]

According to Torrance, the integrated theological understanding of God and the world became ambiguous in the thought of John of Damascus in the eighth century due to the Neoplatonic-Byzantine dualism between the unknowable, unnameable God and the conceptual categories that were in operation at the time.[16] John of Damascus introduced Aristotelian notions of space and motion and of the Unmoved Mover into his theology, thinking this would close the gap between God and the world. It did not. However, John of Damascus did not separate his natural theology from the activity of God in revelation and redemption. The Damascene placed his doctrine of the Trinity[17] alongside his Neoplatonic notion of God, resulting in a rigid apophaticism alongside a robust doctrine of *theosis* in which one can participate in the *energies* of God but not in God's *essence*.[18]

As for the West, Torrance saw Thomas Aquinas building on the foundations of natural theology laid by John of Damascus. But in his case, the division is between natural and supernatural knowledge, which is rooted in the Augustinian-Aristotelian dualism in his thought.[19] Given the stress on the transcendence of God over creation, this necessitated within the Augustinian tradition some intermediate realm of "grace" as constituting the practical or effective relation between God and nature or God and humanity. Alongside this there is a bifurcation between signs and things signified and between thought and being, or idea and event, necessitating an intermediary realm of representations, images or ideas "in the middle," as it were. Within this context, natural theology became the prime contender for closing the gap between God and the world by means of a "logical bridge," and that is what the famous "Five

---

15. Torrance, *The Ground and Grammar of Theology* (Charlottesville: University of Virginia Press, 1980), 76.

16. With Pseudo-Dionysius this gap widens, under Torrance's critique, as he advocates a supra-transcendental approach to God that relativizes and devaluates even the concept of God as Father. Ibid., 78.

17. Plagiarized from Pseudo-Cyril, according to ibid., 79.

18. For an argument against the essence-energies dualism in relation to a doctrine of *theosis* see Myk Habets, "'Reformed Theosis?' A Response to Gannon Murphy," *TT* 65 (2009): 489–98; and "Theosis, Yes; Deification, No," in *The Spirit of Truth: Reading Scripture and Constructing Theology with the Holy Spirit*, ed. Myk Habets (Eugene, OR: Pickwick, 2010), 124–49.

19. Especially in his work Summa contra Gentiles. See N. Kreitzmann, The Metaphysics of Theism: Aquinas's Natural Theology in Summa contra Gentiles I (Oxford: Clarendon, 1997); and Torrance, The Ground and Grammar of Theology, 79.

Ways," by which natural knowledge of God were claimed to be demonstrated, sought to do.[20] Torrance concluded that in more recent times philosophy in the West has followed this basic dualist way of thinking in espousing a positivist philosophy.

What Torrance rejects is the attempt to find a way of reaching God by logical reasoning. Rather, what Torrance allows and wants to foster is the reality that in creation we are confronted by the order pervading the universe and this order points to the uncreated and creative *Logos* of God, in whose image, by the grace of God, we ourselves are created, "so that as we contemplate the rational order in the creation, we are directed above and beyond ourselves to the one God, the Lord of creation."[21]

It is difficult to see how Torrance's justification for his new natural theology is different from the one he wants to reject. The only real difference seems to be the rationale for the order found in nature; for the philosopher it is *logos*, for the Christian it is the *Logos*. However, the real difference is discerned when Torrance is placed within his Reformed heritage. For the Reformers, like the early church, natural theology came to occupy a developed and important place as an apologetic tool. The distinctive element of a Reformed natural theology however, is its subordinated role to divine revelation. This is the key conception Torrance wishes to retain in his own natural theology. McGrath echoes this thought with his opinion that "Torrance may be regarded as having restored natural theology to its traditional place within Reformed theology, while at the same time taken seriously the objections which Barth raised against it."[22]

---

20. Torrance, *The Ground and Grammar of Theology*, 80. A similar application of this form of natural theology is found in many contemporary Christian scientists. For example, S. L. Jaki, *The Road to Science and the Ways to God* (Chicago: University of Chicago Press, 1978), argues that the big bang is convincing evidence to prove the existence of God as Creator. In his chapter "The Gravitational Paradox," in *Cosmos in Transition* (Tucson, AZ: Pachart, 1990), Jaki argued that "gravitational paradox" proves the existence of a creator God. Equally convinced are those scientists—Christian and atheist—who are convinced that natural theology does *not* necessarily lead one to a conviction about the existence of God. See P. Davies, *The Runaway Universe* (London: J. M. Dent, 1978), chapter 8, and Stephen W. Hawking, *A Brief History of Time* (Toronto: Bantam, 1988). Hawking is an outspoken advocate of atheism and finds no place for God in the universe. Similarly, one of the most influential critiques of natural theology has come from Richard Dawkins, *The Blind Watchmaker: Why the Evidence of Evolution Reveals a Universe without Design*(New York: W. W. Norton, 1986).

21. Torrance, The Ground and Grammar of Theology, 77.

22. Alister E. McGrath, *T. F. Torrance: An Intellectual Biography*(Edinburgh: T&T Clark, 1999), 147. In Molnar's opinion McGrath has misunderstood Torrance's intentions in utilizing a natural theology and when McGrath uses such a natural theology for apologetic purposes Molnar believes McGrath has

Like Calvin, Torrance places natural theology squarely within the self-revelation of God. Throughout Book 1 of the *Institutes* Calvin reiterates the notion that creation is a "mirror" of God, a favorite metaphor of his.[23] According to Calvin, real knowledge of God is obtained through this "mirror" or the natural order. He writes:

> Since the perfection of blessedness consists in the knowledge of God, he has been pleased, in order that none might be excluded from the means of obtaining felicity, not only to deposit in our minds that seed of religion of which we have already spoken, but so to manifest his perfections in the whole structure of the universe, and daily place himself in our view, that we cannot open our eyes without being compelled to behold him. His essence, indeed, is incomprehensible, utterly transcending all human thought; but on each of his works his glory is engraven in characters so bright, so distinct, and so illustrious, that none, however dull and illiterate, can plead ignorance as their excuse . . . . In attestation of his wondrous wisdom, both the heavens and the earth present us with innumerable proofs not only those more recondite proofs which astronomy, medicine, and all the natural sciences, are designed to illustrate, but proofs which force themselves on the notice of the most illiterate peasant, who cannot open his eyes without beholding them.[24]

However, while real knowledge of God is obtained from the natural order, for Calvin this is not a *saving* knowledge but simply enough knowledge to hold the knower accountable.[25] As Calvin wrote, "Therefore, though the effulgence which is presented to every eye, both in the heavens and on the earth, leaves the ingratitude of man without excuse, since God, in order to bring the whole human race under the same condemnation, holds forth to all, without exception, a mirror of his Deity in his works, another and better help must

---

betrayed Torrance's intent. Paul D. Molnar, "Natural Theology Revisited: A Comparison of T. F. Torrance and Karl Barth," *ZDTh* 21 (2005): 54, n. 9.

23. "The elegant structure of the world serving us as a kind of mirror, in which we may behold God, though otherwise invisible." John Calvin, *The Institutes of the Christian Religion*, trans. H. Beveridge (London: Clarke, 1953), 1.5.1; see also 1.5.11; 1.6.1; 1.15.4.

24. Calvin, *Institutes*, 1.5.1–2.

25. See the discussion of Calvin's "point of contact" and his "natural theology" in D. E. Tamburello, *Union With Christ: John Calvin and the Mysticism of St. Bernard* (Louisville: Westminster John Knox, 1994), 36–39, and in the older although still useful work of E. D. Willis, *Calvin's Catholic Christology: The Function of the So-Called Extra Calvinisticum in Calvin's Theology* (Leiden: Brill, 1966), 101–31.

be given to guide us properly to God as a Creator."[26] This "better help" is only found through the Word and Spirit of God. Calvin does not develop a natural theology in the sense that one can come to a full and saving knowledge of God *independent* of God's self-revelation in the Son and through the Holy Scriptures! However, Calvin does lay the foundation for a valid and indeed rich natural theology that is subservient to, and from that position complementary to, revealed theology. From this perspective, according to Calvin, creation takes on a deep sense of significance to those with "sanctified spectacles" (another of his favorite metaphors) by which to see God through and in God's creation. In Calvin's words, "For as the aged, or those whose sight is defective, when any books however fair, is set before them, though they perceive that there is something written are scarcely able to make out two consecutive words, but, when aided by glasses, begin to read distinctly, so Scripture, gathering together the impressions of Deity, which, till then, lay confused in our minds, dissipates the darkness, and shows us the true God clearly."[27]

The Reformed tradition developed this Calvinian insight, as witnessed by many of the official creeds and confessions of that tradition. The Reformed tradition came to refer to nature and Scripture as the two "books" of God.[28] Both books were written by the same author and so each was legitimate to study, but each in its own way and for its own ends. As McGrath correctly notes, this had considerable importance in holding together Christian theology and piety and the emerging interest and knowledge of the natural world in the seventeenth and eighteenth centuries, and "may be considered as an integral element of the Reformed tradition prior to Barth."[29] With Barth, however, natural theology was to be seen in an altogether different light.[30]

---

26. Calvin, *Institutes*, 1.6.1.

27. Calvin, *Institutes*, 1.6.1; 14.1.1.

28. The Gallic Confession of Faith (1559) contains a statement on natural theology, and The Belgic Confession (1561) contains the "two books" wording when it affirms the two ways of knowing God: "First, by the creation, preservation and government of the universe, which is before our eyes as a most beautiful book, in which all creatures, great and small, are like so many characters leading us to contemplate the invisible things of God, namely, his eternal power and Godhead, as the Apostle Paul declares (Romans 1.20). All of these things are sufficient to convince humanity, and leave them without excuse. Second, he makes himself known more clearly and fully to us by the aid of his holy and divine Word; that is to say, as far as is necessary for us to know in this life, to his glory and our salvation."

29. This was especially the case in England, as McGrath, *T. F. Torrance*, 178–79, clearly articulates. Indeed, Sudduth, *The Reformed Objection to Natural Theology*, provides ample evidence that a form of natural theology is innate to Reformed theology, receiving its most concentrated focus in the seventeenth century, waning after the impact of Barth, but receiving attention again in our own day through the likes of Alvin Plantinga, Nicholas Wolterstorff, William Alston and others.

Barth considered human reason corrupt due to the fall, and so it is unable to reach a proper knowledge of God. Instead of relying on natural reason, argued Barth, we must rely solely on God's self-revelation to humanity in the incarnate person of the Son. In his *Church Dogmatics* Barth stated:

> Jesus' message about God the Father must not be regarded as if Jesus had expressed the familiar truth, that the world must have and really has a creator, and then had ventured to designate this Creator by the familiar name of 'Father'—not as if on his part he intended what all serious philosophy has named as the highest cause, or as the highest good, as *esse a se* or as the *ens perfectissimum*, as universal, as the ground of meaning and the abyss of meaning, as the unconditioned, as the limit, the critical negation or the origin; intended it and dedicated it by the name of Father, not altogether unknown to religions language, gave it a Christian interpretation and, as it were baptism. To that we can but say that this entity, the supposed philosophical equivalent of the Creator God, has nothing to do with Jesus' message of God the Father, with or without the name of Father attached.[31]

Barth considered natural theology an attempt on the part of humanity to discover God *independent* of God's self-revelation to humanity. To Barth, this corrupted the very ground and grammar of theology.[32] The original sin was, according to Barth, autonomy, and this was what he saw lying behind all attempts at a natural theology.[33] Once natural theology of this kind is entertained, then theology is reduced to anthropology. Barth was clearly reacting against the Ritschlian School of his time, as well as the Kantian philosophy that he rightly saw as a threat to orthodox Christian faith. Barth repeatedly insisted—indeed it can be argued that it forms the heart of his theology—that there is no knowledge of God apart from God's revelation of God's own self.[34] Natural theology, according to Barth's reading of the

---

30. According to Tamburello, "Karl Barth's claim that God comes and creates his own point of contact with grace is not, as he seems to think, compatible with Calvin's thought." *Union With Christ*, 37.

31. Karl Barth, *Church Dogmatics*,I/1, trans. G. W. Bromiley, ed. G. W. Bromiley and T. F. Torrance, 2nd ed. (Edinburgh: T&T Clark, 1975), 391.

32. See the articulation of this point in Colin Weightman, *Theology in a Polanyian Universe: The Theology of Thomas Torrance* (New York: Peter Lang, 1994), 155–61.

33. R. Prenter, "Das Problem der natürlichen Theologie bei Karl Barth," *TLZ* 77 (1952): 607–11.

34. See for instance Karl Barth, *Church Dogmatics*,II/1, trans. W. B. Johnston et al., ed. G. W. Bromiley and T. F. Torrance (Edinburgh: T&T Clark, 1957), 3–4, 69, 206–7.

situation, thus stood for an attempt to know God independent of God's self-revelation. It was, in short, idolatrous.

When Barth read Reformed history he saw it contradicting Calvin's proposal on natural theology by making natural theology the necessary prolegomena to theology proper. When viewed against the background of his debate with Emil Brunner and the rise of the pro-Hitler "German Christians," it is easy to see how Barth made an immediate connection between an independent natural theology and the recreated German churches as state churches.[35] When an autonomous or independent natural theology is allowed to exist, one that finds a logical bridge from nature to God, it sets itself up in antithesis to revealed theology and becomes enslaved to the prevailing cultural and ideological concerns of the contemporary culture, in this case that of National Socialism. Barth thus sought to argue against any natural theology and maintain the exclusivity of God's self-revelation in Jesus Christ. With the end of World War II and the radically changed climate within European philosophy and theology, Barth softened in his opposition to natural theology.[36] More in keeping with what we see in Calvin's theology, he allowed natural theology to play a part in knowledge of God that is subordinate to that of revealed theology.[37]

How does Torrance understand Barth's rejection of natural theology? Barth does not object to natural theology because he maintains some kind of deistic dualism between God and the world in which there is no active relation, nor with some form of Marcionite dualism between redemption and creation, or with a skepticism coupled with a false fideism. On the contrary, Torrance

---

35. Barth, CDII/1, 127. According to J. Barr, *Biblical Faith and Natural Theology* (Oxford: Clarendon, 1993), 113, the connection Barth made between natural theology and National Socialism was dubious at best. In this work Barr presents a biblical argument for the legitimacy of natural theology.

36. According to McDowell the later Barth did not change direction on the issue of natural theology, as some have supposed, but rather *extended* the "witness" concept to include creation in *CDIV/3.1*. John C. McDowell, "A Response to Rodney Holder on Barth on Natural Theology," *Them*27 (2002): 43.

37. See Karl Barth, *The Christian Life* (Edinburgh: T&T Clark, 1981), 120–22, and *Church Dogmatics,*IV/3.1, trans. G. W. Bromiley, ed. G. W. Bromiley and T. F. Torrance (Edinburgh: T&T Clark, 1961), 139: "It is given, therefore, quite irrespective of whether the man whom it addresses in its self-witness knows or does not know, confesses or denies, that it owes this speech no less than its persistence to the faithfulness of the Creator . . . . However corrupt man may be, they illumine him, and even in the depths of his corruption he does not cease to see and understand them . . . they are not extinguished by this light, nor are their force and significance destroyed . . . . As the divine work of reconciliation does not negate the divine work of creation, nor deprive it of meaning, so it does not take from its lights and language, nor tear asunder the original connection between creaturely *esse* and creaturely *nosse*."

contends, Barth's position rests upon an immense stress on the concrete activity of God in space-time, in creation as in redemption, and upon his refusal to accept that God's power is limited by the weakness of human capacity or that the so-called natural reason can set any limits to God's self-revelation to humankind.[38] Torrance's reading of Barth's natural theology is that Barth had an interactionist understanding of the relation between God and the world in which God has *already* established an ontological and cognitive bridge between the world and God. Torrance writes, "Thus Barth's objections to traditional natural theology are on grounds precisely the opposite of those attributed to him!"[39]

Torrance contends that if nature is in some way deistically detached from God then nature can, in some measure, substitute for God by providing out of itself a bridge to the divine. This is the form of natural theology that Torrance rightly reads Barth as critiquing and rejecting.[40] The other side of the deistic coin is seen in an over-immanentism, as when an Aristotelian notion of divine *entelechy* is embedded in nature and then reinforced with a Neoplatonic notion of infused grace and enlightenment. The result is that all being is intrinsically analogical to the divine, and humanity endowed with grace is inherently capable of participating in God.[41] This is what Torrance typically describes as "divinization," an idea he rejects outright as being alien to the gospel and alien to the doctrine of *theosis* as advocated by the early church.[42]

Torrance interprets Barth's position on natural theology to be the first half of what Calvin maintained, that is, that natural theology is *subordinate* to revealed theology. However, Calvin made this point first and moved, if we can put it so crudely, from natural to revealed theology and then back again. Barth, however, operated in the opposite direction. For Barth natural theology merely grants one a mistaken idea or knowledge of God that is turned into an idol. According to a Barthian assessment of all natural theologies, they "begin their journey with their backs turned towards God and, with all brilliance and

---

38. Torrance, *The Ground and Grammar of Theology*, 87.

39. Ibid., 87.

40. Especially in Barth's attack on the Augustinian metaphysics advocated by Erich Pryzwara, and Emil Brunner's attempt to provide a basis for a Protestant natural theology on the double ground of nature and grace. See ibid., 88–89.

41. Ibid., 88.

42. Torrance rejects any and all formulations of a *natural* divinization as alien to the gospel. However, he does accept the legitimate *theosis* of human beings through the radical irruption of grace such that the gospel witnesses to in the incarnation of the Word in space-time, made possible by the hypostatic union. See Myk Habets, *Theosis in the Theology of Thomas Torrance*, Ashgate New Critical Thinking in Religion, Theology and Biblical Studies (Farnham: Ashgate, 2009).

ingenuity, end at a deity who cannot be the God of Christian grace whom they seek."[43] It is this autonomous and independent bias of traditional natural theology that Barth was reacting to, and only that, according to Torrance, "What Barth objects to in natural theology is not its rational structure as such, but its *independent* character, that is, the autonomous rational structure which it develops on the ground of 'nature alone' in abstraction from the active self-disclosure of the living God."[44]

The result is that Torrance believes Barth holds that natural theology has a warranted place within the locus of revealed theology. As Barth once famously declared, "God may speak to us through Russian communism, through a flute concerto, through a blossoming shrub or through a dead dog . . . . God may speak to us through a pagan or an atheist, and in that way give us to understand that the boundary between the Church and the profane world still and repeatedly takes a course quite different from that which we hitherto thought we saw."[45] Like Calvin before him, the natural order is a revelation of God, most especially to those who have already been enlightened by the Word of God. According to Torrance,

> Barth can say that *theologia naturalis* is included and brought to light within *theologia revelata*, for in the reality of divine grace there is included the truth of the divine creation. In this sense Barth can interpret, and claim as true, the dictum of St Thomas that grace does not destroy nature but perfects and fulfils it, and can go on to argue that the meaning of God's revelation becomes manifest to us as it brings into full light the buried and forgotten truth of the creation. In other words, while knowledge of God is grounded in his own intelligible revelation to us, it requires for its actualisation an appropriate rational structure in our cognising of it, but that rational structure does not arise unless we allow our minds to fall under the compulsion of God's being who he really is in the act of his self-revelation and grace, and as such cannot be derived from an analysis of our autonomous subjectivity.[46]

---

43. James J. Buckley and William McF. Wilson, "A Dialogue with Barth and Farrer on Theological Method," *HeyJ* 26 (1985): 286.

44. Thomas F. Torrance, "The Problem of Natural Theology in the Thought of Karl Barth," *RelS* 6 (1970): 125.

45. Barth, *CD* I/1, 60–61.

46. Torrance, "The Problem of Natural Theology in the Thought of Karl Barth," 128–29.

By such means Torrance seeks to remain faithful to Barth's insistence against traditional natural theology, if by natural theology one means an independent and autonomous inquiry into the knowledge of God by means of logical deduction. But if Barth is saying that *theologia naturalis* is to be entertained within or underneath a prior *theologia revelata*, then Torrance argues that Barth is simply restating the central concerns of Calvin at this point.[47]

Torrance on and beyond Barth

From his reading of Barth Torrance derives the following principles, both theological and scientific, regarding a natural theology: theologically, the God we come to know through Jesus Christ is the Father, the Son, and the Holy Spirit in God's own eternal and undivided being. Natural theology (of the traditional kind) can only bring to mind some being of God (or a god) in general; hence, natural theology abstracts the existence or being of God from God's act, so that if it does not begin with deism it ends up there. As Torrance stated in *Space, Time and Resurrection*:

> I do not deny that there is a proper place for rational argumentation in what is traditionally known as 'natural theology', for I find it contradictory to operate with a deistic disjunction between God and the universe, which presupposes belief in the existence of God but assumes at the same time that he is utterly detached and unknowable . . . . This demands, doubtless, a proper natural theology in which form and content, method and subject-matter, are not torn apart – that is, not a 'natural theology' as an *independent* conceptual system, *antecedent* to actual or empirical knowledge of God upon which it is then imposed, quite unscientifically, as a set of necessary epistemological presuppositions![48]

However, if to know God through God's saving act in our world is to know God as triune, then the doctrine of the Trinity belongs to the very ground and grammar of our knowledge of God (hence the title of one of his works).[49]

---

47. An insightful articulation of Barth's views on natural theology is given by McDowell, "A Response to Rodney Holder on Barth on Natural Theology," 32–44. The article is a correction of the views presented by Rodney D. Holder, "Karl Barth and the Legitimacy of Natural Theology," *Them*26 (2001): 22–37.

48. T. F. Torrance, *Space, Time and Resurrection* (Edinburgh: Handsel, 1976), 1.

49. T. F. Torrance, *The Ground and Grammar of Theology* (Charlottesville: University of Virginia Press, 1980), 89.

Natural theology then has a legitimate place in Christian theology, albeit a specific and localized one: it is posterior to that of revealed theology and not, as many sectors had made it, a necessary *praeambula fidei*.[50] For this reason, Torrance maintains that natural theology is the "rational intrastructure" of revealed theology.[51] Another way of putting it is to say that even natural theology is in service to the christocentric theology evident in Calvin, Barth, and Torrance (indeed also in Luther!). Natural knowledge of God is not in competition with revealed knowledge through the Word and the Spirit within Calvin's, Barth's, or Torrance's theology. Nature, illuminated by Scripture, reveals the work of the one God, the Spirit no less than the Father and the Son.[52] When natural theology is once again brought within the orbit of a robust revealed theology then it can, as Barth suggested and Calvin maintained, be a useful and meaningful tool for Christian theology.[53] It is in this very specific sense that Torrance accepts and works with a natural theology.

It will be instructive to see at this point how Torrance is actually drawing on the theology of Calvin here more so than Barth apparently did. Calvin allowed natural theology (*cognitio dei Creatoris*) to play a part in his theology and he too gave it a distinctive place, before that of the knowledge of God as Redeemer (*cognitio dei Redemptoris*).[54] In the early chapters of Book 1 of the

50. For Torrance's definition and treatment of a Roman Catholic natural theology functioning as a *praeambula fidei* see: Torrance, "Preface," in *Space, Time and Resurrection*, ix; *Reality and Evangelical Theology* (Philadelphia: Westminster, 1982), 33; *The Ground and Grammar of Theology*, 147; and *God and Rationality*(London: Oxford University Press, 1971), 133. Torrance concludes that a traditional Roman Catholic doctrine of natural theology functioning as a *praeambula fidei* resulted in Roman Catholic theology being subordinated to philosophical ontology; Torrance, *Theology in Reconstruction*(Eugene, OR: Wipf and Stock, 1996), 178.

51. T. F. Torrance, *Reality and Scientific Theology*(Edinburgh: Scottish Academic, 1985), 61–62. Torrance borrowed the term "rational intrastructure" from H. Bouillard, *The Knowledge of God*, trans. S. D. Femiano (New York: Herder and Herder, 1968), 62. Torrance considers Bouillard's work on Barth's natural theology to be of "outstanding importance"; see Thomas F. Torrance, "The Problem of Natural Theology in the Thought of Karl Barth," *RelS* 6 (1970): 134.

52. Torrance, *The Ground and Grammar of Theology*, 90; and "The Problem of Natural Theology in the Thought of Karl Barth," 128. Perhaps the clearest and most concise articulation of Torrance's position here is found in the "Preface" to his work *Space, Time and Resurrection*, ix–x. See also Torrance, *Space, Time and Incarnation*, 69–70.

53. See Torrance, *Reality and Scientific Theology*, 39, The Ground and Grammar of Theology, 90–91, Transformation and Convergence in the Frame of Knowledge: Explorations in the Interrelations of Scientific and Theological Enterprise (Grand Rapids: Eerdmans, 1984), 293–95, and Theological Science (reprint, Edinburgh: T&T Clark, 1996), 9–10. For Barth's suggestion that natural theology is made clear through revealed theology see K. Barth, "Church and Culture," Theology and Church: Shorter Writings 1920–1928, trans. L. Pettibone Smith (London: SCM, 1962), 342. See Calvin, *Institutes*, 2.6.1.

Institutes Calvin develops a basis for a natural theology through a knowledge of ourselves as beings created in the *imago Dei*. This is clearly seen in the famous opening paragraphs of his magisterial work the 1559 *Institutes*, 1.1.1–2:

> Our wisdom, in so far as it ought to be deemed true and solid Wisdom, consists almost entirely of two parts: the knowledge of God and of ourselves. But as these are connected together by many ties, it is not easy to determine which of the two precedes and gives birth to the other. For, in the first place, no man can survey himself without forthwith turning his thoughts towards the God in whom he lives and moves; because it is perfectly obvious, that the endowments which we possess cannot possibly be from ourselves; nay, that our very being is nothing else than subsistence in God alone . . . . On the other hand, it is evident that man never attains to a true self-knowledge until he have previously contemplated the face of God, and come down after such contemplation to look into himself.[55]

Because of the created image all people are able to discern a supreme being. They may not call that being "God," but nonetheless the knowledge of God is there. Because of the fall this "natural" knowledge must be supplemented with further revelation. However, Calvin does not see the knowledge of God in creation obliterated by the fall; it simply needs supplementing. In *Institutes* 1.3.1 we are told by Calvin, "That there exists in the human minds and indeed by natural instinct, some sense of Deity, we hold to be beyond dispute, since God himself, to prevent any man from pretending ignorance, has endued all men with some idea of his Godhead, the memory of which he constantly renews and occasionally enlarges, that all to a man being aware that there is a God, and that he is their Maker, may be condemned by their own conscience when they neither worship him nor consecrate their lives to his service."[56]

We would naturally expect this to be knowledge of the Redeemer, but before Calvin enters into that he first mentions "the need of Scripture, as a guide and teacher, in coming to God as Creator."[57] This takes Calvin's discussion to

---

54. See how Torrance works his way appreciatively through Calvin's doctrine of the *imago Dei* and into the discussion on natural theology in Torrance, *Calvin's Doctrine of Man*, 154–83.

55. See further in Edward A. Dowey, "The Structure of Calvin's Thought as Influenced by the Two-Fold Knowledge of God," in *Calvinus Ecclesiae Genevensis Custos*, ed. W. Neuser (Frankfurt: Peter Lang, 1984), 135–48.

56. Calvin, *Institutes*, 1.3.1.

the end of Book 1. With Book 2 he takes up the theme of the fall (2.1–5) and then centers on knowledge of God as Redeemer:

> The whole human race having been undone in the person of Adam, the excellence and dignity of our origin, as already described, is so far from availing us, that it rather turns to our greater disgrace, until God, who does not acknowledge man when defiled and corrupted by sin as his own work, appear as a Redeemer in the person of his only begotten Son. Since our fall from life unto death, all that knowledge of God the Creator, of which we have discoursed, would be useless, were it not followed up by faith, holding forth God to us as a Father in Christ.[58]

Natural theology is not redundant; it is useful to knowledge of God. However, while distinct, it is not a *separate* category from knowledge of God as Redeemer. Alasdair Heron has correctly described this process within Calvin thus: "In the same way, however, that faith does not abolish or do away with the *cognitio dei Creatoris*, nor does it subsume it under the *cognitio dei redemptoris*. Instead, it establishes it in the fullest sense by setting humans once more in a proper relation to their Maker."[59] Herein lay the limits of natural theology for Calvin and, strikingly, for Torrance too.

Alongside Torrance's close reading of Calvin in reformulating a natural theology we must also see the importance that the natural sciences played in Torrance's thinking. Torrance went beyond Barth in exploring more deeply the connection between the basic concepts of theological science and natural science than Barth allowed for himself.[60] The result of this exploration is that natural theology should be natural both to theological science and to natural science. A natural science of this sort will necessitate dialogue between the theological and natural sciences within their common sharing of the rational

---

57. Calvin, *Institutes*, 1.6; 1.10. In 1.6.1–2 Calvin uses the famous analogy of likening the Scripture to a pair of spectacles.

58. Calvin, *Institutes*, 2.6.1.

59. A. I. C. Heron, "*Homo Peccator* and the *Imago Dei* According to John Calvin," in *Incarnational Ministry: Essays in Honor of Ray S. Anderson*, ed. C.D. Kettler and T.H. Speidell (Colorado Springs: Helmers and Howard, 1990), 42. Heron is self-consciously basing much of his discussion on a reading of Torrance, *Calvin's Doctrine of Man* (London: Lutterworth, 1949).

60. Torrance, *The Ground and Grammar of Theology*, 94, although Barth did envisage others to go where he did not when he wrote that he would leave the problem of investigating the relationship between theology and natural science to "future workers in the field of Christian doctrines of creation," Barth, *CD* III/1, x.

structures of space-time conferred on the universe by God in God's creating of it, and within their common sharing in the basic conceptions of the unitary rationality of the universe, its contingent intelligibility, and contingent freedom.[61] A consequence of Torrance's natural theology is the idea, a favorite of his, that men and women, especially those involved in scientific endeavor, are the priests of creation (a theme explored in more detail in chapter 6).[62]

> So far as theological science is concerned it is imperative that we operate with a *triadic relation* between God, man, and world, or God, world, and man: for it is this world unfolding its mysteries to our scientific questioning which is the medium of God's revelation and of man's responsible knowledge of him. This implies, however, once more, that there is a necessary and inescapable connection between theological concepts and physical concepts, spiritual and natural concepts, positive and natural science, for it is in that connection that the changed status of natural theology has its place.[63]

Like Calvin and Barth, Torrance is clear that natural theology (it would be better to say natural revelation at this point) plays an important role in Christian dogmatics—not as some kind of necessary prolegomena, but rather as an illustration or further illumination of God after God's self-revelation through the incarnation.[64] This conclusion stems from Torrance rigorously thinking through the implications of what a contingent universe means. Contingency implies rationality and freedom. It also reveals the fact that the immanent rationality of the universe is unable to give any *final* account of itself. The universe itself is determinate and knowable, but over against the creation God remains free in God's eternal self-existence and cannot therefore be known in the determinate way in which created things are known.

In a 1969 work, Torrance stated categorically that "it is no longer possible to operate scientifically with a separation between natural theology and revealed

---

61. He is also drawing on the insights of the "new science," which seeks to explain lower levels of order in terms of higher levels. See Torrance, *The Ground and Grammar of Theology*, 142 and *The Christian Frame of Mind*, 60.

62. Torrance, *The Ground and Grammar of Theology*, "Man the Priest of Creation," 1–14, and "Theological Science," 111–145. See also Torrance, *Reality and Scientific Theology*, 68–69.

63. Torrance, *Reality and Scientific Theology*, 69. For an appreciation of this aspect of Torrance's work see Palma, "Thomas F. Torrance's Reformed Theology," 29–31. This triadic relation is explained in more detail in Chapter Six below.

64. These themes are developed in detail in Thomas F. Torrance, "Incarnation in Space and Time," in *Space, Time and Incarnation*(Edinburgh: T&T Clark, 2005), 52–90.

theology any more than between geometry and physics."⁶⁵ In the preface to his 1976 work *Space, Time and Resurrection* Torrance relates his last discussion with Karl Barth, late in the summer of 1968, shortly before Barth's death:

> I put a number of questions to him, mostly bearing on the interrelation between theological and natural science .... I was anxious to get Karl Barth's reaction to the way in which I explained to a Thomist or a physicist his attitude to natural theology by referring to Einstein's account of the relation of geometry to experience, or to physics .... Karl Barth expressed full agreement with my interpretation of his thought, and said, rather characteristically, of the relation of geometry to physics, "I must have been a blind hen not to have seen that analogy before."⁶⁶

In order to further explain the connection between natural and revealed theology Torrance draws the following conclusions, which I quote here in full:

> In theology, this means that natural theology cannot be undertaken apart from actual knowledge of the living God as a prior conceptual system of its own, or be developed as an independent philosophical examination of rational forms phenomenologically abstracted from their material content, all antecedent to positive theology. Rather must it be undertaken in an integrated unity with positive theology in which it plays an indispensable part in our inquiry and understanding of God. In this fusion 'natural' theology will suffer a dimensional change and will be made *natural* to the proper subject-matter of theology. No longer extrinsic but intrinsic to actual knowledge of God, it will function as a sort of 'theological geometry' within it, in which we are concerned to articulate the inner material logic of knowledge of God as it is mediated within the organized field of space-time.⁶⁷

Torrance maintains that theology is scientific because of its objectivity, and he "moves natural theology from its previous position of prolegomena into positive theology proper."⁶⁸ It is a valid question, however, to ask whether Torrance's

---

65. Torrance, *Space, Time and Incarnation*, 69.
66. Torrance, *Space, Time and Resurrection*, ix–x.
67. Torrance, *Space, Time and Incarnation*, 70.
68. Ted Peters, "Theology and Science: Where Are We?" *Zygon* 31 (1996): 335. Of some importance to Torrance's understanding of natural theology but not of particular importance to our immediate study

"natural theology" is in fact what the tradition has termed *natural theology* at all.[69] In an interaction with Torrance's conception of natural theology, Colin Gunton prefers to maintain a distinction between natural theology and "a theology of nature" rather than constructing, as Torrance does, a transformed natural theology.[70] This position has merit in that traditionally natural theology refers to knowledge of God from nature, whereas Torrance wishes our knowledge of God to be derived only from God's self, with nature then becoming a second order display of God's being and act.

However, given Torrance's adoption of certain Calvinian insights into the place and function of natural theology, his position is not as straightforward as Gunton suggests. Torrance wants to develop a consistent and appropriate way of coordinating but not confusing natural revelation, natural theology, and a theology of nature so that natural science can be used by theologians, and also, theology can be instructive to natural scientists, thus overcoming the ingrained dualism between the two disciplines throughout modernity. It is this aspect of his work that I believe he intended as a further development of the tradition. And it is this aspect of his work that has occasioned much confusion and controversy.

The Coordinated and Contested Nature of New Natural Theology

In Torrance studies one finds three major views represented: first, that Torrance's theology sponsors a natural theology that functions in an apologetic way (Alister McGrath); second, that Torrance's theology is consistently Barthian and allows no place for a traditional natural theology at all, even though Torrance was at times inconsistent with these intentions (Paul

---

is the idea of the "social coefficient of knowledge." Torrance treats this in one place only, *Reality and Scientific Theology*, 98–130. For an interaction with Torrance on this point see Colin Weightman, *Theology in a Polanyian Universe: The Theology of Thomas Torrance* (New York: Peter Lang, 1994), 170–73, Elmer M. Colyer, *How To Read T. F. Torrance: Understanding His Trinitarian and Scientific Theology* (Downers Grove, IL: InterVarsity, 2001), 353–55, 370, and *The Nature of Doctrine in T. F. Torrance's Theology* (Eugene, OR: Wipf and Stock, 2001), 95–127.

69. See a brief history of the term and definition in McGrath, *A Scientific Theology, vol. 1: Nature* (Grand Rapids: Eerdmans, 2003), 241–305, pages 279–86 being an evaluation of Torrance's natural theology.

70. See Colin Gunton, *A Brief Theology of Revelation* (Edinburgh: T&T Clark, 1995), 63. I think this is the position of Molnar, "Natural Theology Revisited," as well. Molnar, it seems to me, uses Barth as a reading guide for Torrance at this point such that Torrance's new natural theology is strictly speaking a theology of nature.

Molnar);⁷¹ and third, that Torrance consistently speaks of natural theology in the way we would normally speak of a theology of nature, and there is no inconsistency within his thought on this issue (Elmer M. Colyer, and W. Travis McMaken).⁷² It is my contention that there is a fourth way to read his theology, one that seeks to bring the natural and theological sciences into dialogue, which allows a soft apologetic role to natural theology, and yet, one that does not allow any strictly logical bridge to God from unaided human reason on the basis of natural revelation. I also contend that Torrance was less than clear or consistent in his use of and development of his transposed form of natural theology.

The advance that Torrance's so-called new natural theology provides is a rationale for why and how natural science can conduct its own examination of reality seemingly independently of theology, and yet still reveal truth (natural revelation), and how theologians can draw upon such research and use it in an illustrative and even mildly apologetic manner (natural theology). "Some of us are also deeply indebted to scientists who under God have helped to clarify for us an understanding of the space-time world in which the Creator Word became incarnate, and within which we are *committed to preach the Gospel* of his saving love to all people until Christ Jesus comes again, and makes all things new. Then we shall no longer know the truth in dim or partial ways, but shall see Christ face to face, and know him as we are known by him."⁷³

---

71. Paul D. Molnar, "Natural Theology Revisited: A Comparison of T. F. Torrance and Karl Barth," *ZDTh* 21 (2005).

72. W. Travis McMaken, "The Impossibility of Natural Knowledge of God in T. F. Torrance's Reformulated Natural Theology," *IJST* 12 (2010): 319–40; and Elmer M. Colyer, "A Response to Paul Molnar's Essay, 'A Natural Theology Revisited'" (unpublished paper delivered at the Thomas F. Torrance Theological Fellowship Annual Meeting, 2009), 1–22. Colyer notes that "Tom was kind enough to read the manuscript of my book, *How to Read T. F. Torrance*, before I sent it off for publication. Next to the footnote where I assert that 'There is reason to believe that Torrance may regret calling this reformulated version "natural theology,"' Tom put three very large exclamation points" (3). Colyer takes these exclamation points as affirmations of his interpretation. Colyer and McMaken are in agreement that Torrance is developing Barth's aversion to all forms of traditional natural theology. McMaken appeals to the term *Aufhebung* in his argument that Torrance and Barth affirm, negate, then reconstitute nature in their theologies (McMaken, "The Impossibility of Natural Knowledge," 11–12). Colyer for his part sees Torrance co-opting natural theology by radically transforming it into something compatible with the core of Barth's criticism of traditional natural theology (Colyer, "A Response," 3–4, Appendix 1:12–13).

73. T. F. Torrance, "Thomas Torrance Responds," in *The Promise of Trinitarian Theology: Theologians in Dialogue with T. F. Torrance*, ed. E. M. Colyer (Lanham, MD: Rowman & Littlefield, 2001), 303 (italics mine). Torrance always maintained he was an evangelist, both to modern culture and to contemporary theologians! Thus "the preaching of the Gospel" mentioned here has an apologetic tone to it. The clearest statement we have of that is his statement: "I am primarily interested in the Gospel; and preaching. I am a missionary. And all my thinking is missionary and evangelistic. My theology is evangelistic and

Yet another fascinating example of how Torrance uses a form of new natural theology is given, without additional comment, in a memoir of his boyhood in China, 1913–1927,[74] in which he gives a fascinating account of the religious beliefs of the Chinese Xiang people among whom his parents worked as missionaries. We are told that the Xiang priest worshiped the one God whom they called *Abba Chee*, the Father Spirit, believed in the need for a Mediator or *Abba Malach*, and Sin-bearer, and sacrifice to take away sin. There was a family sacrifice of a goat or lamb at the altar on the roof of each house marked by a White Stone or *O-pee*, and the yearly atonement ritual involving the priest, a *Nehushtan*, a sacred rod with a serpent entwined around it, and a sacred scroll to represent the Word of God. The scroll was empty other than bearing a death's head at the top to indicate the "Word of God" and the "Redeemer," the Divine Savior, the Lamb of God, who was to come into the world. The annual ceremony involved purification rites and a ceremony "rather like the 'scape goat' described in the Old Testament." What significance did Torrance draw from this? "When my father heard what the *Oir Be-Bo* related to him, he was astonished, and opening his Bible he read to him the Leviticus account in the Old Testament of the rites for the Day of Atonement," to which the priest "in his excitement nearly leapt off the bench he was sitting on (I can still see him in my mind), and explained, 'those are our lost Scriptures.'"[75] His father then went on to read from John's Gospel and explain how Jesus Christ is *the*Lamb of God who takes away the sin of the world. The result was that "The Oir priest believed the good news of the Gospel my father proclaimed to him, and he and his sons were baptised." In a final comment Torrance states, "That is an experience I shall never forget."[76]

It is clear that for Torrance natural revelation is never considered the logical or necessary bridge to faith such that Christ would be sidelined or where nature rivals the incarnation. The rationality that natural science investigates (or in fact certain tribal religious reflect!) is a contingent rationality that is not to be confused with ultimate rationality, the *Logos*of God. Faith, by contrast, comes by hearing the word of God, but God can and may use secondary media

---

missionary. I am concerned in that kind of way with the Gospel," T. F. Torrance, "Reply to Donald Macleod," Tape 199, http://tapesfromscotland.org/Rutherfordhouseaudio.htm (Edinburgh: Rutherford House, 1999), 14:34–14:55.

74. The Thomas F. Torrance Manuscript Collection, Special Collections, Princeton Theological Seminary Library, Box 10, "My Boyhood in China, 1913–1927," 39–40. This is not dated but correspondence on a possible publication of the work dates it to around the year 2000.

75. Ibid., 40.

76. Ibid.

(communism, a flute, a dead dog, and natural theology) in bringing one to faith. In addition to this, theology, working as it does on scientific principles, has something to contribute to the natural sciences (a theology of nature). In this regard, Torrance wrote of the dialogue between theology and science, stating that such dialogue "can also help natural science, in view of its recurring temptation to resolve contingence away, to remain faithful to the nature of contingent reality . . . and therefore to remain open to the realization that the universe is what it is as a whole because of its implication in a transcendent rational order, in God."[77] I call this a soft apologetic approach.

According to this perspective, natural theology can reveal truth and reality. It can also reveal a deep-seated awareness of the existence of God, but it can only rise to the level of revealing a god but not the Trinity, an inherent order in the world but not the *Logos*, and it *may* lead one on to further questions that would more properly be directed to theology. But it may not! Einstein was not a Christian, nor are many contemporary scientific figures, not to mention those from history.

All of which is not to say that Torrance has presented his position very clearly. In my opinion, his work contains within it mixed signals, ambiguous tendencies, and contradictory trajectories. All the elements of a coherent revision of the coordination between natural revelation, natural theology, and a theology of nature are there, but he did not use such lucid language or present his views with the rigorous comprehension exhibited elsewhere in his dogmatics. This has led his interpreters to differ over an evaluation of his position on natural theology.

Alister McGrath has provided the most extensive treatment of this aspect of Torrance's work and gone beyond it in presenting his own "new vision for natural theology." Over a number of works McGrath has constructed an account of natural theology that includes the formative views of Torrance before offering his own account.[78] According to McGrath, Torrance only allowed natural theology to act as an *ancilla theologiae* ("handmaid to theology"), and so in his own account natural theology can only ever be done from within dogmatic theology.[79] As such McGrath argues that revealed theology precedes natural theology as it assumes creation and a Creator.[80] But he also

---

77. T. F. Torrance, *Divine and Contingent Order* (reprint, Edinburgh: T&T Clark, 1998), 84.

78. Alister E. McGrath, *A Scientific Theology*, vol. 1: *Nature*; vol. 2: *Reality*; vol. 3: *Theory* (Grand Rapids: Eerdmans, 2003); *The Science of God* (London: T&T Clark, 2004); *The Open Secret: A New Vision for Natural Theology* (Oxford: Blackwell, 2008); and *A Fine-Tuned Universe: The Quest for God in Science and Theology* (Louisville: Westminster John Knox, 2009).

79. McGrath, *A Scientific Theology*, vol. 1: *Nature*, 283–86.

allows the study of nature to disclose truth to the observer, by appeal to Torrance's stratification of truth and reality. Here McGrath and Torrance are very close and, as Holder has pointed out, in this case in reference to McGrath, "bewilderingly circular and confusing, if not confused."[81] The specific causes for Holder's bewilderment are McGrath's twin convictions that, on the one hand, a Christian natural theology allows the believer to see in all of creation the truth, beauty, and goodness of the triune God already known;[82] and yet on the other hand that this allows nature to function as a pathway toward this same God for secular culture as a whole.[83]

Molnar offers the same critique of Torrance's theology:

> Still, there is an ambiguity in Torrance's thought about the intelligibility of the universe. On the one hand he claims that the universe in its contingency and by its nature points beyond itself to God when in fact it does not necessarily do so, except to one who already believes. On the other hand he correctly insists that the universe pointing to God represents our interpretation in faith and that the Holy Spirit is necessary to know this in a proper way.[84]

Torrance is ambiguous about this because on the one hand he insists that even his 'new' natural theology can only make sense in light of revelation while on the other hand he wants to say that natural theology, bracketed from revelation, can still help us somehow in our quest for God.[85]

On the one hand Torrance insists that a proper natural theology cannot be bracketed at all, but must function within the ambit of revelation. But on the other hand his thinking suggests that creation itself cries for an explanation grounded in the Christian God and he believes that this "silent" cry is a touchstone for discussion between theology and science.[86]

---

80. McGrath, *A Scientific Theology, vol. 1: Nature,* 295.

81. Rodney D. Holder, *The Heavens Declare: Natural Theology and the Legacy of Karl Barth* (West Conshohocken, PA: Templeton, 2012), 192.

82. McGrath, *The Open Secret*, 147.

83. Ibid., 147–48.

84. Molnar, "Natural Theology Revisited," 55, n. 11.

85. Ibid., 74

86. Ibid., 78–79. Molnar is referring to Torrance, *Reality and Scientific Theology* (Edinburgh: Scottish Academic, 1985), 42–43, 58, where Torrance contends that creation "does more than raise a question for it seems to *cry silently* for a transcendent agency in its explanation and understanding" (58).

One can't have it both ways, according to Holder and Molnar, and they are right. And yet Holder points out that natural and theological science exhibit complementarity in a way similar to quantum systems in that "they offer two mutually exclusive ways of probing reality."[87] Holder then notes how similar Torrance's view here is to Stephen Jay Gould's notion of "non-overlapping magisteria" before stating that "the natural sciences and theology should not tread on each other's toes and are indeed complementary. Nevertheless, there are areas of overlap when it comes to broader questions such as the metaphysical underpinnings of science and the use of commonly shared rational modes of inquiry—especially perhaps when the latter are applied to the data of faith." He then notes, perceptively, "Torrance may agree in part with this, though he would very strongly circumscribe the latter point."[88]

This accords well with the way in which David Fergusson discerns differing functions for natural theology. According to Fergusson, deployment of a natural theology may be in one of the five following ways: foundationally, as seen in modern epistemological projects; deistically, to demonstrate religious truth; soft apologetics, as proofs of general revelation; hard apologetics, to be used as defeating arguments against objections to the Christian faith; and dialogically, where the claims of revelation can coexist with scientific knowledge.[89] On such a schema I would equate Torrance's position with the dialogical approach, and at times it even gives hints of the soft apologetics position.

Natural theology traditionally conceived is thus rejected by Torrance as leading one away from the exclusive self-revelation of God in Jesus Christ. It leads to deism, and from there to atheism or idolatry. However, in his transposed version of natural theology what Holder notes above is, I think, correct. And it is for this reason that Torrance took such an active interest in the natural sciences and sought a constructive dialogue between it and theology. But there are limits to what natural science can reveal of truth and reality, and thus theology always has the upper hand and the final word.

---

87. Holder, *The Heavens Declare*, 148. The comments are made in reference to Torrance, *Theological Science* (reprint, Edinburgh: T&T Clark, 1996), 102.

88. Ibid. According to Molnar this thinking is simply a contradiction within Torrance's dogmatics. Molnar, "Natural Theology Revisited."

89. David Fergusson, "Types of Natural Theology," in *The Evolution of Rationality: Interdisciplinary Essays in Honor of J. Wentzel van Huyssteen*, ed. F. LeRon Shults (Grand Rapids: Eerdmans, 2006), 380–93. The specific terms are mine, not Fergusson's. Fergusson sees the first three options as incompatible with the theology of Barth, however the last two he holds out as valid and even necessary.

One of the most perspicuous instances of this transposed place for natural theology in Torrance's dogmatics is given in his highly suggestive volume *Space, Time and Incarnation*:

> In theology, this means that [traditional] natural theology cannot be undertaken apart from actual knowledge of the living God as a prior conceptual system on its own . . . rather must it be undertaken in an integrated unity with positive theology in which it plays an indispensable part in our inquiry and understanding of God. In this fusion 'natural' theology will suffer a dimensional change and will be made *natural* to the proper subject-matter of theology. No longer extrinsic but intrinsic to actual knowledge of God, it will function as a sort of 'theological geometry' within it, in which we are concerned to articulate the inner material logic of knowledge of God as it is mediated within the field of space-time.[90]

Molnar simply finds all such claims on the part of Torrance to be ambiguous and inconsistent features of his otherwise Barthian-themed approach to natural theology. To this effect he writes:

> But he has also acquiesced, at least to a certain degree and perhaps in his desire for agreement with Henri Bouillard, to the temptation to find a natural theology (in the sense that he himself rejects) that would unite scientific theology and natural science. And that is why he can say that while there is no logical way to understand the onto-relations which concern us in Christian theology, still 'we do have access to the set of conditions within which the distinctive kind of order they embody spontaneously manifests itself, and by indwelling that order we can come up with the anticipatory conceptions or basic clues we need in developing our cognition of it.'[91]

What this highlights, I believe, is that much of what Torrance calls a new natural theology is actually a theology of nature (creation). This is the main burden of his thought in this area. He maintains that natural theology is located within revealed theology, and thus *theology of nature* is the best epithet for this

---

90. T. F. Torrance, *Space, Time and Incarnation* (Edinburgh: T&T Clark, 2005), 69–70.

91. Molnar, "Natural Theology Revisited," 80, citing T. F. Torrance, *Reality and Evangelical Theology* (Philadelphia: Westminster, 1982),164. Molnar believes that one of the main reasons for Torrance's inconsistency here is his failure to take the concept of sin seriously enough.

enterprise. But what is often overlooked or misunderstood is that he does have something *new* to say in this area: he does hold to a limited version of natural theology, but allows this to be chastened by his Trinitarian commitments. Hence the need to distinguish in his work between what may be called natural revelation (which creates the conditions for scientific inquiry but cannot act as a *preambula fidei*), natural theology (which can be used evangelistically by Christians), and a Trinitarian theology of nature. The natural sciences do disclose reality and truth, although in and of themselves they cannot account for this in any satisfactory way. The natural sciences share a common commitment to order and reality, and in that common commitment there is much to learn for each discipline, hence the need for dialogue. Natural theology is thus legitimate, but only if it remains at the lowest level of the stratification of truth.[92] Revealed theology is required if one is to penetrate the higher levels of reality, given the fact that levels of reality are open upward but not reducible downward.[93] Torrance's new natural theology holds out the promise that for some, such a natural theology can be used by the Spirit to remove grounds for doubt. As far as this is recognized I am in agreement with Holder's assessment: "Torrance's own observations about science open up possibilities for a more traditional natural theology, despite his intentions."[94]

However, for Torrance, traditional natural theology can never play the part of providing a logical bridge to God or servicing a program of supposed proofs for the existence of God. Torrance's vision for a transposed natural theology is best summarized in the foreword to his work *Reality and Scientific Theology*: "What is ultimately envisaged is a reconstruction of the very foundations of modern thought and culture, similar to that which took place in

---

92. George Hunsinger, "Light from Light: From Irenaeus and Torrance to Aquinas and Barth," in *Light from Light: Scientists and Theologians in Dialogue*, ed. G. O'Collins and M. A. Myers (Grand Rapids: Eerdmans, 2012), 218, points to just this move in Torrance: "Torrance's idea of 'ontological stratification' sometimes seems to move in the latter direction [a bottom-up approach]." In Hunsinger's view this is incompatible with what Torrance asserts elsewhere. Also useful is the chart Hunsinger provides on page 235, according to which I am arguing that Torrance's theology of reason and revelation accords with his type 3 "correlationist" position, as long as the imagery is of two independent circles, one (revelation) bigger than the other (reason).

93. This point is made clearly in Torrance, *Divine and Contingent Order*, 20, when he cites Polanyi to the effect that "all meaning lies in the higher levels of reality that are not reducible to the laws by which the ultimate particulars of the universe are controlled." On this principle more generally see the helpful account of emergence in dialogue with the theology of Karl Barth (and by implication Torrance) provided by Ross H. McKenzie, "Emergence, Reductionism and the Stratification of Reality in Science and Theology," *SJT* 64 (2011): 211–35.

94. Holder, *The Heavens Declare*, 167.

the early centuries of the Christian era, when the unitary outlook of Judaeo-Christian thought transformed that of the ancient world."[95]

Divergent interpretations of what Torrance was doing in invoking the concept of natural theology in his dogmatics will continue to occupy the attention of his interpreters. What is clear, however, is the way in which natural theology, or a theology of nature, is in service to dogmatics, as revealed in the Son by the Spirit and witnessed to in Holy Scripture. An early account of this is given in a sermon Torrance preached on Gen. 1:1 in 1941, when he proclaimed, "It is only *in Christ* that we can understand God and nature. In Christ we can return to the long ago yesterday of the Bible when mountains were petrified poetry, when the rocks were unhewn altars, when the hills were libraries, and the winds mighty organs that could thunder and tremble and wail and cry and sing at the touch of the finger of God."[96]

One need not linger in the thicket of nature too long, but must come in from the cold to the fold of God and God's Word. As such we move in the next chapter from nature to revelation, from creation to Christ, and ask about the relation of the Word incarnate to the word written.

---

95. Torrance, *Reality and Scientific Theology*, x.

96. The Thomas F. Torrance Manuscript Collection, Special Collections, Princeton Theological Seminary Library, Box 42, "Sermon on Gen 1.1: Alyth, Sept 28, 1941," 11 (slightly altered).

4

Realist Theology
And Theological Realism

Torrance's academic publications are often noted as being dense and convoluted works that are hard for the expert, let alone the novice, to navigate. While in my opinion such claims are exaggerated, Torrance's subject matter is profound and technical, and reliable guides to his work are useful. Often, however, his work is misunderstood by those who either have not read his entire corpus and seek to interpret the parts from the whole, or others who jump to hasty and unwarranted conclusions about this or that aspect of his work, and on such a basis accuse him of holding ideas that they say necessarily flow from such concepts. One outspoken critic of Torrance's dogmatics was the influential evangelical scholar Carl Henry. The nature of his objections to Torrance's theological science, and Torrance's reply, are the subject of this chapter, in which I argue that we must look beyond Henry's nominalism and evangelical foundationalism to Thomas Torrance's theological realism.

CARL HENRY VS. THOMAS TORRANCE

The careers of Carl Henry and Thomas Torrance share many similarities in their general outlines, and yet they could not have charted more different courses in theology had they tried. Both men were born in 1913 and lived into their 90s. Both were professors of theology: Henry at Fuller Theological Seminary, which he helped to establish; Torrance at the University of Edinburgh. Both were prolific authors: Henry's magnum opus being the six-volume *God, Revelation and Authority*;[1] many consider Torrance's magnum opus to be *The Christian Doctrine of God* (and *The Trinitarian Faith*).[2] Both were also editors of significant theological journals: Henry of the popular *Christianity*

---

1. Carl F. H. Henry, *God, Revelation and Authority*, 6 vols. (Waco: Word, 1976–83).

Today,[3] and Torrance of the *Scottish Journal of Theology*. Both were international speakers and first-order systematic theologians. Finally, both were guardians of what they considered orthodoxy: Henry of the evangelical heritage that developed out of fundamentalism,[4] and Torrance of an orthodoxy developed in line with the Great Tradition.

While clearly of the same mind regarding a range of theological beliefs, Henry and Torrance did not share the same epistemic commitments. Thus their theological methods were drastically different, and this resulted in what can only be considered radically differing theologies. They disagreed considerably when they met on several occasions, and this spilled over into their respective *oeuvres*. What follows is a focused reflection on what may be considered the heart of their theological disagreement: the nominalism of Henry versus the realism of Torrance.

In *God, Revelation and Authority*, Henry sought to establish the foundations of an apologetic theology. This was an evangelical response to modernity on modernity's terms, with the aim of establishing the intellectual coherence and academic credibility of a Christian "world-life view," as Henry termed it. In volume one, *God Who Speaks and Shows*, he sets forth the nature of theology, and in volumes two, three, and four he comments at length upon fifteen foundational theses on divine revelation. Volumes five and six, *God Who Stands and Stays*, develop a classically orthodox approach to the doctrine of God. The ordering of the work is important; Henry treats method before theology proper, for Scripture is epistemologically prior to God in his theology. To be clear, it was Henry's express conviction that the foundation for correct theology can only be found in the divine revelation of God as deposited in the Holy Scriptures.

Henry defined revelation as "that activity of the supernatural God whereby he communicates information essential for man's present and future destiny. In revelation God, whose thoughts are not our thoughts, shares his mind; he communicates not only the truth about himself and his intentions, but also that concerning man's present plight and future prospects."[5] Revelation is thus

---

2. T. F. Torrance, *The Christian Doctrine of God: One Being Three Persons*(Edinburgh: T&T Clark, 1996); *The Trinitarian Faith: The Evangelical Theology of the Ancient Catholic Church* (Edinburgh: T&T Clark, 1995).

3. While *Christianity Today* has become a popular, lay-driven magazine, it started out as a theological magazine-journal in opposition to *The Christian Century*.

4. Even though, in Grenz's estimation—correct, in my opinion—Henry remained a fundamentalist in many respects. Stanley J. Grenz, *Renewing the Center: Evangelical Theology in a Post-Theological Era*(Grand Rapids: Baker, 2000), 87.

objective and available to unaided human reason. So insistent was Henry on this point that he rejected all attempts by the so-called neo-orthodox of his day (read here Barth, Bultmann, and Brunner especially) to establish a relational and participatory theology whereby only those united to Christ and enlivened by the Spirit could know God. Henry wrote, "If a person must first be a Christian believer in order to grasp the truth of revelation, then meaning is subjective and incommunicable"; and further, "the new birth is not prerequisite to a knowledge of the truth of God."[6]

According to Henry, the Bible is almost entirely propositional in content. Thus God communicates in order to convey truths in the form of propositional sentences.[7] The purpose of theology is to take such sentences and form doctrines or propositions from them. In this regard, we might note the affinities of Wayne Grudem's approach to systematic theology with that of Henry, when Grudem defines theology as "any study that answers the question: 'What does the whole Bible teach us today?' about any given topic."[8] John Franke calls this the "concordance conception of theology," which has characterized evangelical theology in general to the extent that it has assumed the methodology of post-Reformation Protestant scholasticism.[9] In a programmatic passage, Henry sets forth his "basic epistemological axiom" as follows: "Divine revelation is the source of all truth, the truth of Christianity included; reason is the instrument for recognizing it; Scripture is its verifying principle; logical consistency is a negative test for truth and coherence a subordinate test. The task of Christian theology is to exhibit the content of biblical revelation as an orderly whole."[10]

One may inquire about the relationship between Scripture and general revelation, given the epistemological axiom above. Henry states, "The scriptural revelation takes epistemological priority over general revelation, not because general revelation is obscure or because man as sinner cannot know it, but because Scripture as an inspired literary document republishes the content of general revelation objectively, over against man's sinful reductive dilutions and misconstructions of it."[11]

---

5. Henry, *God, Revelation and Authority*, 3:457.

6. Ibid., 1:229.

7. Ibid., 1:181–409.

8. Wayne Grudem, *Systematic Theology: An Introduction to Biblical Doctrine* (Grand Rapids: Zondervan, 1994), 21. Grudem's definition is insufficient and deficient in that it ignores the interplay in all knowing between tradition, reason, and experience.

9. See John R. Franke, *The Character of Theology: An Introduction to its Nature, Task, and Purpose* (Grand Rapids: Baker, 2005), especially 88–89.

10. Henry, *God, Revelation and Authority*, 1:215 (italics in original). This is not to deny that the Triune God is Christianity's basic ontological axiom. Ibid., 1:219.

It was Henry's conviction that general revelation was sufficient for the independent use of reason for knowledge of God. He thus believed that special revelation was an objective given. In a 1964 work, *Frontiers in Modern Theology*, Henry, in Grenz's words, "charted an agenda that proved to be an apt summary of his entire theological program:"[12] "If Christianity is to win intellectual respectability in the modern world, the reality of the transcendent God must indeed be proclaimed by the theologians—and proclaimed on the basis of man's rational competence to know the transempirical realm."[13]

This is not to say that Henry was an advocate of natural theology; he wasn't. Henry was a Biblicist who rigorously upheld the inerrancy and infallibility of Scripture.[14] Thus, right thinking about God can only be found through Scripture, for here alone one finds the authoritative word of God in objective form. While Henry does allow that revelation is personal, simply because God and humans are personal, his theology amounts to a rejection of personal revelation in favor of an absolute propositional revelation. This is asserted in his Thesis Ten: "God's revelation is rational communication conveyed in intelligible ideas and meaningful words, that is, in conceptual-verbal form."[15] Henry clarifies that he is opposed to all definitions of revelation that "restrict God's disclosure to *self*-revelation, or to *cosmic*revelation, or to *historical*revelation, in express contrast to a divine disclosure of truths and information."[16] Henry cites Karl Barth and Thomas Torrance as two such champions of the sort of dialectical and existential (read, non-evangelical) theology he opposes.

Focusing specifically upon Torrance's doctrine of the knowledge of God drawn largely from the 1969 work *Theological Science,* Henry devotes an entire chapter of *God, Revelation and Authority*to rebutting Torrance's position.[17] In Henry's estimation, Torrance's formulation of what he terms "theologic" is evangelically inadequate and an example of the "unstable neo-Protestant

---

11. Ibid., 1:223.

12. Grenz, *Renewing the Center,*92.

13. Carl F. H. Henry, *Frontiers in Modern Theology A Critique of Current Theological Trends*(Chicago: Moody, 1964), 154–55, cited in Grenz, *Renewing the Center*, 92.

14. For his defense of inerrancy, infallibility, and inspiration, see Henry, *God, Revelation and Authority*, 4:103–219. Henry did not, as many other fundamentalist-evangelicals have done, including the Evangelical Theological Society, make inerrancy a badge of evangelical orthodoxy. See Carl F. H. Henry, "Reaction and Realignment," *Christianity Today*20 (July 2, 1976): 30.

15. Henry, *God, Revelation and Authority*, 3:248.

16. Ibid., 3:248.

17. Chapter 14: "The Logos and Human Logic," in ibid., 3:216–29.

formulation of man's knowledge of God."[18] What, exactly, Henry takes exception to is Torrance's attempt to relate human logic to the logic of God in a non-formal way.

Acknowledging that Torrance rises above the neo-orthodox (a pejorative and inaccurate term in itself) antithesis of propositional and personal revelation by locating revelation in Jesus Christ, himself the Truth and the one who manifests the truth, Henry then accuses Torrance of "unjustifiably converting the fact that God objectifies God's own self for us and meets us in Jesus Christ into an eclipse of general revelation, a devaluation of the prophetic revelation, and a cognitive deflation of all Logos-revelation."[19] What Henry takes umbrage to is the idea that outside of Jesus there is no knowledge of God.[20] Henry appeals to the Old Testament in the first instance (then to nature, history, and the conscience) as evidence that God has spoken in propositional form through prophets, kings, priests, and directly in divine manifestations. Henry considers these to be defeating arguments against Torrance's insistence that outside of Christ there is no knowledge of God. But this is to misunderstand Torrance's position that Jesus Christ is epistemologically determinative and thus there is no knowledge of God outside of Jesus Christ, given that Christian theology as a science is posterior to an actual encounter with an actual event. We have already seen this in our discussion in the last chapter of Torrance's new natural theology.

Henry agrees with Torrance that humanity after the fall is estranged from God and thus cannot think rightly—about God, truth, or reality. However, argues Henry, that does not mean that we must attribute this to an "epistemic deficiency" in humanity whereby only through regeneration and repentance one may actually know God.[21] Henry then levels his charge against Torrance:

> Torrance here overstates the deformity of human reason in relation to divine revelation; he disregards the general revelation that penetrates man's reason and conscience with the knowledge of God which confronts him consciously with light and truth and knowledge and in relation to which he is culpable. The change in logical structure which a revelation is held to require, it develops, is

---

18. Ibid., 3:216.
19. Ibid., 3:217.
20. This is the fourth of Torrance's five points as to what characterizes theological science. Torrance, *Theological Science* (reprint, Edinburgh: T&T Clark, 1996), 137; and Torrance, *The Christian Doctrine of God*, 1.
21. Henry, *God, Revelation and Authority*, 3:218. See Torrance, *Theological Science*, 147.

nothing less than a rejection of the law of contradiction and if that be the case—so we shall argue, against Torrance—nonsense can be regarded as divine truth.[22]

Henry was not one to lack rhetorical flourish or force a point!

Interpreting Torrance accurately, I think, Henry shows that according to Torrance only Jesus, who is the Logos, can know the Truth through human concepts and statements because Christ is the God-man. For all other people our statements point away from ourselves to some objective truth, but for Christ he is the Truth incarnate. Thus his statements don't point away from himself but to himself. Torrance can thus say: "Theological knowledge and theological statements participate sacramentally in the mystery of Christ as the Truth."[23] As such revelation is, for Torrance, *uniquely* personal and *uniquely* propositional to Christ, and mediated to others to the extent that they participate in Christ.[24] It is thus faith (revelation) in Christ, and not philosophy, which forms the conceptual bridge between God and humanity.

What Henry pushes back against is Torrance's dialogical/dialectical theological method. According to Henry, truth and statements of the truth correspond such that the truth is objectively known despite the condition—fallen or otherwise, Christian or not—of the subject. Henry's correspondence theory of truth (similar to Wittgenstein's "picture language")[25] comes up squarely against Torrance's realistic theory of truth. In Henry's estimation, all such dialogical/dialectical reasoning only has the options of "either saying nothing or of stating gibberish."[26]

Henry appears to misunderstand Torrance's claim that only those united to Christ genuinely know Christ. Torrance, it seems to me, does not insist that there is no general revelation, simply that general revelation does not provide enough information for the unredeemed person to come to a *saving* knowledge of God. This is the new natural theology discussed in the previous chapter.[27] Henry also appears to adopt something of a Thomistic theology of conversion whereby reason acts as a genuine and natural *praeambula fidei*, the means by

---

22. Henry, *God, Revelation and Authority*, 3:218.

23. Torrance, *Theological Science*, 150, cited by Henry, *God, Revelation and Authority*, 3:219.

24. Torrance, *Theological Science*, 42, 148, cited by Henry, *God, Revelation and Authority*, 3:219

25. See David Munchin, *Is Theology a Science? The Nature of the Scientific Enterprise in the Scientific Theology of Thomas Forsyth Torrance and the Anarchic Epistemology of Paul Feyerabend* (Leiden: Brill, 2011), 205–9, for a description of various correspondence theories of truth, including that of Torrance.

26. Henry, *God, Revelation and Authority*, 3:221.

27. See Paul D. Molnar, *Thomas F. Torrance: Theologian of the Trinity* (Surrey: Ashgate, 2009), 93–99.

which one is led to faith. Any other view, Henry avers, amounts to fideism—the blind leap of faith, the theology of which Kierkegaard is mistakenly the poster child. In short, what Henry would seem to take exception to in this part of his argument is Torrance's Reformed doctrine of election whereby faith itself is a gift imparted to the believer. In relation to the work and role of human reason, Henry is a semi-Pelagian, as opposed to Torrance's commitments to the Reformation solas: *sola gratia, sola fidei,* and *solus Christus*. In Henry's best estimation, "the insistence on a logical gulf between human conceptions and God as the object of religious knowledge is erosive of knowledge and cannot escape a reduction to skepticism."[28] And finally, "We are therefore back to the emphasis that the laws of logic belong to the *imago Dei*, and have ontological import."[29]

Henry is particularly critical of what he sees as the illogical presuppositions of Torrance's intuitive theology. Torrance rejects the form of propositional revelation espoused by Henry in favor of a "personal knowing." Reality is to be known in faith through an existential encounter with the ultimate Reality—Jesus Christ the incarnate Word (Logos). Henry believes this amounts to mysticism, something he is not favorably disposed to. We will deal with the mystical nature of Torrance's theology in the next chapter.

Henry sees the critical mistake of Torrance's epistemology, derived in part from Kierkegaard but more from Polanyi, to lie in his seeming rejection of any objective revelational knowledge. From Kierkegaard, Torrance is committed to the idea that the truth of God is communicated through personal relations, not, as Henry would have it, "objectively" and even dispassionately.[30] However, Torrance holds that theology that accepts the absolute primacy of its proper object of inquiry can be considered rational and scientific—hence objective. Torrance understands Kierkegaard's "truth as subjectivity" as in fact theological objectivity and realism, the subject's proper relation to the object.

Henry misreads Torrance (and Polanyi, if he read him at all) at this point and interprets the notion of "personal knowledge," which acknowledges the necessity for "responsible commitment"—Polanyi's term for personal knowledge—in terms of subjectiv*ism*. This is especially so when "personal knowledge" is applied to religious knowing and is virtually equated with biblical "faith."

---

28. Henry, *God, Revelation and Authority*, 3:229.
29. Ibid., 3:229.
30. Recall Torrance's account of his job interview for Princeton University in J. I. Hesselink, "A Pilgrimage in the School of Christ: An Interview with T. F. Torrance," *RefR* 38 (1984): 57–58.

Using as he does Polanyi's epistemology, Torrance would no doubt react to this criticism that Henry, and other critics, are perhaps looking to an impersonal procedure that operates along detached and mechanical lines, ultimately appealing to the concept of autonomous reason. Autonomous reason is then directed at an external authority, in this case the Holy Scriptures, and a system of propositional truth is worked out in a purely impersonal but logical way. It is this program that Torrance is particularly concerned to eradicate.

This use of Polanyi further explains Torrance's form of realism in his theological method discussed earlier. As we have already noted, it is the commitment to *critical* realism that constitutes one of Torrance's main reasons for drawing on the work of Polanyi. In Polanyi, Torrance found a philosophical ally and one who illustrated in the natural sciences what Torrance sought to do in Christian dogmatics.

Not only does Torrance appeal to Polanyi, but also the theological method of Athanasius, Anselm of Canterbury, John Calvin, and not least, Karl Barth. Throughout his reading of the tradition Torrance develops what we have seen him call a *kata physic* form of theological methodology that is as applicable to the sciences as it is to the humanities, and here specifically to Christian dogmatics. An overview of Torrance's theology illustrates his methodology, and an examination of his use of Scripture in particular highlights the fundamental differences between the fundamentalist orientation of Henry's—and popular evangelicalism's—theological methodology and biblical hermeneutics.

As can be gleaned from this brief survey of Henry's critique of Torrance's theological method, Henry's theology must be characterized as rationalist, foundationalist, and nominalist. As Grenz observed, Gordon H. Clark, Henry's professor of philosophy when he was a young student at Wheaton College, was perhaps the single most important intellectual influence on Henry's thought, giving it its rationalist-oriented worldview.[31] Not all would agree with this assessment. "Put simply, if the term 'foundationalist' is to be applied to Henry's theological outlook, his sounds more like that of a soft than a hard foundationalist,"[32] writes Mavis Leung. Chad Brand agrees when he writes, "Is Henry a foundationalist? If one means by "foundationalist," the search for Cartesian certainty through the discovery of indubitable and noninferential truth claims arrived at through reason or reflection, then the answer is a resounding, "no." . . . It might be correct, on the other hand, to call Henry

---

31. Grenz, *Renewing the Center*, 90.

32. Mavis M. Leung, "With What is Evangelicalism to Penetrate the World? A Study of Cary Henry's Envisioned Evangelicalism," *TJ* 27 (2006): 240.

a scriptural foundationalist."[33] And further, "In regards to Scripture, Henry is certainly a firm, biblical foundationalist; in regards to the outworking of the theological implications of biblical asseverations, it appears that Henry is a soft foundationalist, one who is willing to admit that all our claims to understanding are subject to the eternal bar of God's judgment."[34]

Torrance "*Contra Evangelical Mundum*"

Henry is not alone in his critique of Torrance and others who adopt a similar theological method. The example of an appreciative critic of Torrance's, Colin Gunton, will be useful. Gunton first met Torrance at a student conference in 1963, when Gunton was a student and Torrance was a keynote speaker. Since then the two men were known to each other and respected each other's work, despite disagreeing on many points. Gunton later organized a day conference in Torrance's honor at the King's College's Research Institute in Systematic Theology, and he contributed to a volume of essays interacting with Torrance's theology edited by Elmer Colyer in 2001. In this essay, Gunton appreciatively critiqued Torrance's doctrine of God,[35] and elicited a short response by Torrance.[36]

Gunton's critique of Torrance's method is best explored through his published lectures *Revelation and Reason*, where Torrance's idea of "theological science" is critiqued in chapter 2, §2.[37] Gunton focuses his lectures on the relationship between revelation and reason. In the wake of Enlightenment philosophy, revelation was consigned to the periphery of human knowledge, if not rejected outright, and in its place reason assumed the center. Whereas patristic thinkers simply assumed divine revelation, post-Enlightenment theology felt it had to establish a basis from which revelation could be accepted and then utilized by human reason. Thus it was that foundationalism found

---

33. Chad O. Brand, "Is Carl Henry a Modernist? Rationalism and Foundationalism in Post-War Evangelical Theology," *TJ* 20 (1999): 18.

34. Ibid., 19.

35. Colin Gunton, "Being and Person: T. F. Torrance's Doctrine of God," in *The Promise of Trinitarian Theology*, 115–37. Paul Molnar has provided a thorough critique of Gunton's essay in *Divine Freedom and the Doctrine of the Immanent Trinity: In Dialogue with Karl Barth and Contemporary Theology* (London: T&T Clark, 2002), 317–30.

36. Torrance, "Thomas Torrance Responds," in *The Promise of Trinitarian Theology: Theologians in Dialogue with T. F. Torrance*, ed. E. M. Colyer (Lanham, MD: Rowman & Littlefield, 2001), 314–18.

37. Colin Gunton, *Revelation and Reason: Prolegomena to Systematic Theology*, ed. Paul H. Brazier (London: T&T Clark, 2008), 49–51; also see 33–36. The work is based on tape recordings of a seminar program for MA students given by Gunton at King's College, London, 1999–2000.

its way into theology. Gunton refers to this as "faith seeking foundations," a phrase coined by Ronald Thiemann, and an obvious play on Anselm's "faith seeking understanding." Gunton uses a definition of foundationalism as the proposition that every coherent belief system rests upon certain convictions. These convictions are assumed to be true, or even self-evident, and thus provide stability for the framework of belief. The coherence of many other beliefs depends upon the acceptance of these beliefs as true.[38] In his use of Thiemann, Gunton believes Torrance is a foundationalist of a sort, in that his appeal to ground revelation in something else, namely in the ability to causally explain revelation as coming from God; thus belief in God is the foundation. According to Gunton, "By intuition Torrance does mean, well, integrity, a kind of integration of data rather than leaping into another world [revelation]. There is a very rationalistic side to Tom Torrance; he would use a foundationalist argument if he could."[39] It is unclear in the context what Gunton means exactly by the phrase, "if he could." He goes on to say that Locke and Schleiermacher are certainly foundationalists, thus we may aver that Torrance is a qualified foundationalist of some sort.

When Gunton turns his attention to Torrance directly, he examines his use of "science" to describe his theological method. Science in this context is the activity in which we observe objects and reduce the description of their workings into a coherent explanation. Thus Torrance allows God the Object to impose God's self on us rather than appealing to philosophical foundations or some such. By means of a Polanyian integration, the scientist then integrates all the evidence into a logical coherence. Thus Torrance reads from the Object (God) to the subject (the inquiring mind).

Later in the work, under a discussion of Vatican II, Gunton provides a chart that depicts Torrance's view of revelation as act and event. In it, Gunton explains that when revelation means Jesus Christ it is different from revelation as a series of propositions.[40] And so, when we come to ask if revelation is personal or propositional, as Henry does, unless Torrance's twofold view of revelation is

---

38. Gunton is using the definition provided by Ronald Thiemann, *Revelation and Theology: The Gospel as Narrated Promise*(Notre Dame: University of Notre Dame Press, 1985), 13–15. Thiemann's work is critical of Torrance's "epistemological foundationalism" and in its place a coherentist account of epistemology is offered. For a critical interaction see Tom McCall, "Ronald Thiemann, Thomas Torrance and Epistemological Doctrines of Revelation," *IJST* 6 (2004): 148–68.

39. Gunton, *Revelation and Reason*, 35.

40. Ibid., 98. This distinction approximates Torrance's distinction between "Coherence-statements" and "existence-statements" in Torrance, *Theological Science*(reprint, Edinburgh: T&T Clark, 1996), 164–72.

acknowledged, there is going to be confusion. It will appear that Torrance does not believe in propositional revelation, leaving many evangelicals to assume that Torrance is merely a sophisticated mystic for whom doctrine is either Gnosticism, known only to the initiated (something we have seen Henry accuse Torrance of in other words), or one is a liberal or postmodern theologian for whom there is no truth but only personal experience. Torrance is neither.[41]

Gunton contrasts Torrance's view with that of Roman Catholicism, even post-Vatican II. According to this view, God's personal act presupposes all our traditions and writings such that Church tradition must be considered as authoritative as Scripture, given that both affirm the same content of propositional truth. If we were to apply this to Henry and some other evangelicals, then we would have to conclude that a commitment to a strong propositional revelation that is not nuanced in the twofold way that Torrance does necessarily ends up in a form of narrow foundationalism, so that classic Roman Catholicism and fundamentalist-evangelicalism are actually operating out of the same theological methodology and epistemology.

So much for the evaluation and critique of Torrance by Henry and others. It will reward us to consider the essence of Torrance's reply to Henry before forming some critical conclusions.

THOMAS TORRANCE VS. CARL HENRY

In 1981 Torrance presented the Payton Lectures at Fuller Theological Seminary (subsequently published as *Reality and Evangelical Theology*), wherein he was "concerned to establish a realist basis in evangelical theology in contrast with the nominalism that prevails so widely among so-called 'evangelicals'"![42] Torrance singled out Carl Henry as one such exemplar.[43] In answer to a student's question on the extent of the atonement Torrance replied, and I reproduce it here in full:

---

41. Interestingly, in Torrance's opinion the fundamentalist and the liberal are not that far removed from each other when it comes to their epistemic commitments. They share "a fatal deistic disjunction between God and the World" in that they both cut short the ontological reference of biblical and theological statements to God. See Torrance, *Space, Time and Resurrection* (Edinburgh: Handsel, 1976), 2–3.

42. J. I. Hesselink, "A Pilgrimage in the School of Christ: An Interview with T. F. Torrance," *RefR* 38 (1984): 60.

43. Carl Trueman writes in "Admiring the Sistine Chapel: Reflections on Carl F. H. Henry's *God, Revelation and* Authority," *Them* 25 (2000): 48, "If the twentieth century 'evangelical renaissance' in North America has produced a Michelangelo, that exemplar is surely Carl Henry," citing Gabriel Fackre.

You see there is nowhere in the Christian faith, there is no such thing as partial representation, as partial substitution. It's a total act and therefore the total being comes under the death and resurrection of Christ and therefore under the judgment of the cross. So that you, whether you are good or evil—Christ died for you. Now for you with your good as well as your evil comes under the judgment of the cross. Now that applies to the whole of creation. That applies to this creation that God made to be good but which has become estranged from him. So there you have to take seriously, dead seriously, the fact that the Creator became creature, made atonement for the whole creation, consecrated the whole creation for God, not part of it. Now this is very important, you see.

Carl Henry, for example, in a discussion with me on this very issue, would not agree that Christ died for all of him. There is still an integrity in his reason that doesn't come under the judgment of the cross, you see. So I said to him, Carl Henry, do you believe in a partial substitution, and therefore there is something in your reason, Carl Henry, that hasn't really come under the judgment of the cross of Christ? And that's why you are a rationalist.

So you see that is the point; and this is where the gospel comes at its hardest. It's a good man, a righteous man, a man who is rich in goodness, it's as impossible for him to be saved as it is a camel to go through the eye of a needle. And yet that's possible for God, you see. And so the more we cling to our rationality, the more we cling to our goodness, the more difficult it is for us to have salvation.[44]

Torrance, of course, is accurate in his assessment of Henry. According to Henry, the fall affects the will and not the mind: "Man wills," writes Henry, "not to know God in truth, and makes religious reflection serviceable to moral revolt. But he is still capable of intellectually analyzing rational evidence for the truth-value of assertions about God."[45]

Echoing the same critique, Donald Bloesch rightly observed that Henry and other fundamentalist-evangelicals provided a "transcendence in ontology but not in epistemology, for they are confident that human reason can lay

---

44. Thomas F. Torrance, "The Ground and Grammar of Theology," lectures given at Fuller Theological Seminary, 1981: Lecture 6, Q&A, 20:54–22:42, http://www.gci.org/audio/torrance.

45. Carl F. H. Henry, *God, Revelation and Authority*, 6 vols. (Waco: Word, 1976–83), 1:226–27. Henry locates the *imago Dei* in the cognitive capacity of humanity, and does not see this as inoperative after the fall. See ibid., 1:394, 405; 2:136.

hold of the truth of divine revelation apart from special grace."[46] He then outlines a four-stage taxonomy of ways in which contemporary Christianity has sought to respond to the challenges of modernity. Henry is allocated to stage one, a theology of restoration, which Bloesch characterizes as a return to the rationalistic idealism of the early Enlightenment: "In this approach we arrive at truth by beginning with universal principles and then proceeding to deduce particular conclusions."[47]

Like Torrance and Bloesch, John Webster makes a trenchant and enlightened case for the need for reason itself to be sanctified and converted if it is to be of use in thinking theologically: "Christian theology is an aspect of reason's sanctification . . . good Christian theology can only happen if it is rooted in the reconciliation of reason by the sanctifying presence of God."[48] This is a central point that Henry misses, even rejects. According to Henry, reason is a natural faculty seemingly unaffected by the fall. As such, reason is not involved in the drama of God's saving work. As Webster notes of this approach, "Consequently, 'natural' reason has been regarded as 'transcendent' reason."[49] Conversely, "Holy reason is eschatological reason,"[50] argues Webster. Torrance accepts the basic orientation of Webster's claims with his dialogical/dialectical method in dogmatics.[51]

---

46. Donald G. Bloesch, *A Theology of Word and Spirit: Authority and Method in Theology* (Downers Grove, IL: InterVarsity, 1992), 252.

47. Bloesch, *A Theology of Word and Spirit,* 253. Bloesch identifies the influence of Gordon Clark on Henry, along with the influence of Descartes and Leibniz.

48. John Webster, *Holiness* (Grand Rapids: Eerdmans, 2003), 10.

49. Ibid., 10.

50. Ibid., 12.

51. With Bobby Grow I have outlined what this form of dialogical method is in thesis nine of "Theses on a Theme," in *Evangelical Calvinism: Essays Resourcing the Continuing Reformation of the Church*, ed. Myk Habets and Robert Grow (Eugene, OR: Pickwick, 2012), 439–41. One example from Torrance where he directly comments on his rejection of strictly logical forms of reasoning and theology occurs in a recorded dialogue with Donald Macleod in which he is speaking of the logicalizing nature of theology within post-Reformation Calvinism. Torrance writes that this emphasis upon logical relations is what he cannot understand about such Calvinism. He asks, "What is the relation between you and your salvation? Is it a logical relation? What's the relation of the death of Christ to your salvation? Is it a logical relation? Or a causal relation? Or a temporal relation? It's none of these things. It's a relation of the Holy Ghost. It's God's act! Same act you have in the virgin birth. Same act you have in the resurrection of the dead, and it's that mighty act of God which you cannot construe in human logic or causal connections. Now that is what we are concerned with, it's what Calvin was concerned with. That's why he could say a person is damned, it happens *acidentaliter, per accidens*," used over 300 times in Calvin's writings! "This is the opposite of logical relation." Thomas Torrance, "Reply to Donald Macleod," Tape 199 (Edinburgh: Rutherford House, 1999, http://tapesfromscotland.org/Rutherfordhouseaudio.htm), 16:16–17:05, 17:26.

Gunton too, follows this basic epistemological stance in discussing Christian claims to knowledge. Gunton glosses 1 Cor. 1:22, "For Jews demand signs and Greeks desire wisdom, but we proclaim Christ crucified, a stumblingblock to Jews and foolishness to Gentiles, but to those who are the called, both Jews and Greeks, Christ the power of God and the wisdom of God," as: "Modernists seek certainty; postmodernists deny it? What do we claim and proclaim?"[52] We proclaim Christ, of course. But knowledge that comes by faith is of a different sort, or at least requires a different epistemic orientation—that which comes by faith.

Torrance directly accuses Henry of being a nominalist in his insistence that revelation is propositional and not at the same time personal. Then follows an example: "This paper is white" is not the truth, according to Torrance, but is a statement about the truth; however, according to Henry, "This paper is white" is the truth itself. Torrance is thus a metaphysical realist against Henry's nominalism, presumably in the sense that Torrance thinks Henry rejects universals. Torrance then draws a comparison with law when he says, "I thought lawyers would have seen through this much clearly and more early." Juridical law is based upon actual law and is utterly consistent. A clue is thus found in juridical law—law testifies to actual Law, which imposes itself upon us. Thus it may be that Torrance's little book on juridical law may say more about his hermeneutics and method than has previously been thought.[53]

In Tom McCall's estimation, Torrance is a modest foundationalist.[54] While this, in McCall's opinion, is better than Thiemann's coherentism, it is not without its problems. He writes, "Torrance's epistemological foundationalism will likely continue to draw criticism from his detractors . . . but the general position seems to be a stable one. If there is a problem with his theology of revelation it will appear when he relates his doctrine of revelation to scripture."[55] McCall was on the money, and Henry was one such detractor to make this point. It is thus to Torrance's doctrines of knowledge, revelation, and Scripture that we must briefly turn.

---

52. Colin Gunton, *Revelation and Reason: Prolegomena to Systematic Theology,* ed. Paul. H. Brazier (London: T&T Clark, 2008), 17.

53. Thomas F. Torrance, *Juridical Law and Physical Law: Toward a Realist Foundation for Human Law* (Eugene, OR: Wipf and Stock, 1997). In this work it is legal positivism Torrance is reacting to with his realist epistemology.

54. Tom McCall, "Ronald Thiemann, Thomas Torrance and Epistemological Doctrines of Revelation," *IJST* 6 (2004): 164–65.

55. Ibid., 165.

THEOLOGICAL REALISM

According to Torrance, the truth can be known and apprehended by the human person and this knowledge represents a genuine disclosure of that which is real. Christian theology and natural science operate with an understanding of knowledge that has its "ontological foundations in objective reality." We have already seen this in our examination of Torrance's scientific theology and in his defense of a critical realism.[56] Both science and theology recognize

> the impossibility of separating out the way in which knowledge arises from the actual knowledge that it attains. Thus in theology the canons of inquiry that are discerned in the process of knowing are not separable from the body of actual knowledge out of which they arise. In the nature of the case a true and adequate account of theological epistemology cannot be gained apart from substantial exposition of the content of the knowledge of God, and of the knowledge of man and the world as creatures of God . . . this means that all through theological inquiry we must operate with an *open* epistemology in which we allow the way of our knowing to be clarified and modified *pari passu* with advance in deeper and fuller knowledge of the object, and that we will be unable to set forth an account of that way of knowing in advance but only by looking back from what has been established as knowledge.[57]

Torrance is a critical realist, not a positivist. Torrance also rejects a "naïve realism" in which there is a direct correspondence between knowledge and reality. Unless Torrance is misunderstood, we must understand that realism involves at least three elements, identified by Andrew Moore as: ontological (realism vs. idealism); epistemological (realism vs. empiricism), and semantic (realism vs. linguistic idealism).[58] While obviously interconnected, these three elements are distinct, and confusion often results from insufficiently distinguishing between them in a person's work. As David Munchin has

---

56. Alister McGrath characterizes Torrance's method as "scientific realism" in *A Scientific Theology, Volume 2: Reality* (Grand Rapids: Eerdmans, 2002), 130. The alternative to scientific realism would be constructive empiricism, whereby theories are empirically adequate but may not necessarily correspond to reality.

57. Torrance, *Theological Science* (reprint, Edinburgh: T&T Clark, 1996), 10.

58. Andrew Moore, *Realism and Christian Faith: God, Grammar and Meaning* (Cambridge: Cambridge University Press, 2003), 1.

observed, "The debate concerning realism becomes therefore a matter of epistemic degrees."[59] Torrance can then assert:

> Belief is not something that is freely chosen or arbitrary, that is, without evidential grounds, for that would be highly subjective, a mere fancy. Nor is it something hypothetical or conditional, for then it would not be genuine, since we would entertain it, as it were, with our fingers crossed. Rather does belief arise in us, as we have seen, because it is thrust upon us by the nature of the reality with which we are in experiential contact. It arises as we allow our minds to fall under the compelling power of an intelligible structure or order inherent in the nature of things which we cannot rationally or in good conscience resist. That is to say, belief has to be understood strictly within the context of rational submission to the claims of reality upon us and of obligation towards the truth laid upon us by truth itself.[60]

This leads us to ask about the relationship between Scripture and theology within Torrance's scientific theology.

SCRIPTURE AND DOGMATICS

There is an inseparable relation between Scripture and dogmatics for Torrance, which may be explained around three interrelated movements. First, dogmatics explains Scripture and Scripture explains Christ. Second, Christ explains Scripture. Third, dogmatics is only rightly conducted when Christ is rightly known.[61] As a consequence, Scripture stands in a middle relation between Christ and dogmatics, as a witness to Christ, but it needs illumination from both ends, from Christ and from dogmatics. The result is that Christ the Word is known both through and in the word written, which means the written word has a unique and normative authority in our knowledge of Christ in the present.

There is a *theological* reason for Torrance's method. For Torrance, revelation is always divine self-disclosure in which God communicates *God's own self* to God's creatures. This self-revelation was made decisively through

---

59. David Munchin, *Is Theology a Science? The Nature of the Scientific Enterprise in the Scientific Theology of Thomas Forsyth Torrance and the Anarchic Epistemology of Paul Feyerabend*(Leiden: Brill, 2011), 190.

60. Torrance, "The Framework of Belief," in *Belief in Science and in Christian Life: The Relevance of Michael Polanyi's Thought for Christian Faith and Life*, ed. T. F. Torrance (Edinburgh: Handsel, 1980), 13.

61. These relations are articulated in Robert T. Walker, "Editor's Foreword," in *The Incarnation: The Person and Life of Christ* (Downers Grove, IL: IVP Academic, 2008), xxvi.

the incarnation. Scripture thus plays a secondary (but indispensable) role to the self-revelation of God through Christ. In Torrance's theology, revelation determines both Scripture and the *depositum fide*. The *depositum fide* is a gracious work of God in which knowledge of God through Christ is made possible in a personal and participatory way in the knower.

While Scripture is an imperfect and inadequate text, when it is appropriated by God's full, final and Holy Word—Jesus Christ—it is made to serve the reconciling revelation and infallible communication of God's truth. Thus explicating the relationship between the Word incarnate and the word written becomes one of Torrance's central tasks. In a sermon on Matt. 18:1-22, "Christ in the Midst of His Church," Torrance narrates the relationship between Christ and Scripture by means of a meditation on the fact of "Christ in us." Christ lodges permanently within us by means of the words of Scripture, but they are more than merely human words. They are "creative words," "personal words," "life-giving words," which create personal communion and presence. They "germinate in the human heart and create room for Christ there."[62] Christ and Holy Scripture are in such an intimate union that Torrance can say, "It is as we allow the Word of the Gospel to saturate our minds and imaginations, to penetrate into our memories, and to master all our thinking, that Christ is born within us, that all that He is and has done becomes, as it were, imprinted upon us within, and becomes so truly and permanently the very centre of our being that we are transformed into His image and likeness, and even partake of His nature."[63] Here the goal of Scripture is clearly stated,[64] related as it is to the Word incarnate. We also begin to see how Torrance clarifies how the christological analogy and the Chalcedonian formula are integral to his understanding of the relation between the word written and the Living Word.[65]

Torrance's use of Scripture avoids both fundamentalist and Roman Catholic forms of foundationalism on the one hand, and liberal and neo-Protestant idealism on the other hand; both approaches Torrance considers to be mistaken.[66] In relation to fundamentalist-evangelicalism, Christian dogmas or doctrines are not to be read directly off the pages of Scripture in a

---

62. Thomas F. Torrance, "Christ in the Midst of His Church," in *When Christ Comes and Comes Again*(London: Hodder and Stoughton, 1957), 110.

63. Ibid.

64. For more on the ultimate goal of salvation, see Myk Habets, *Theosis in the Theology of Thomas Torrance*, Ashgate New Critical Thinking in Religion, Theology and Biblical Studies (Farnham: Ashgate, 2009).

65. For his articulation of this point see Torrance, *The Atonement: The Person and Work of Christ*,ed.Robert T. Walker (Downers Grove, IL: IVP Academic), 333–40.

propositionalist kind of way: "The assumption that the Scriptures are impregnated with universal, changeless divine truths which can be read off the sentential sequences of the inspired text, provided that it is properly or authoritatively interpreted, is admittedly the view that was long held, and often still is held, by Roman Catholic and Protestant fundamentalism alike."[67] Fundamentalisms of this sort result in a position in which faith is placed *in* Scripture directly rather than in that to which Scripture bears witness—God's being and act. To mistake the text of Scripture for the truths it seeks to reveal is to adopt some form of nominalism or extreme realism.[68] According to Torrance, "In a scientific theology, on the contrary, we are concerned not with thinking thoughts, far less with thinking statements themselves, but with thinking realities through thoughts and statements, and with developing an understanding of God from his self-revelation mediated to us by the Holy Scriptures in the Church, in which the connections we think are objectively and ontologically controlled by the intrinsic connections of God's *self-communication* as Father, Son and Holy Spirit."[69]

The second position Torrance distances himself from is that of liberalism or neo-Protestantism, in which Christian dogmas or doctrines are reached by simple empirical observations of uninterpreted facts—that is, simply existentially.[70] This form of neo-Protestantism is considered the by-product

66. Torrance deals with both fundamentalism and liberalism on many occasions. See for instance, *God and Rationality* (London: Oxford University Press, 1971), 36; *Space, Time and Resurrection* (Edinburgh: Handsel, 1976), 1–26; and *Reality and Evangelical Theology* (Philadelphia: Westminster, 1982), 52–83. Barth avoided both positions as well, but in Hunsinger's words he labeled the two extremes "literalism" and "expressivism." See George Hunsinger, "Beyond Literalism and Expressivism: Karl Barth's Hermeneutical Realism," in *Disruptive Grace: Studies in the Theology of Karl Barth* (Grand Rapids: Eerdmans, 2000), 210–25. In his own work John Webster labels both poles as "objectification" and "spiritualisation" respectively, and argues that both are pneumatologically deficient. See Webster, *Holy Scripture: A Dogmatic Sketch* (Cambridge: Cambridge University Press, 2003),33–36.

67. Torrance, *Space, Time and Resurrection,* 7–8. Similar ideas are expressed in Torrance, *Reality and Evangelical Theology*, see especially 17.

68. As background to Torrance's discussion on truthfulness and the truth see Thomas F. Torrance, "Truth and Authority: Theses on Truth," *ITQ* 39 (1972): 215–42, especially thesis 5. Torrance's commitment to critical realism is also at play here.

69. Torrance, *Space, Time and Resurrection,* 8.

70. Torrance believes contemporary existentialists have distorted the referring function of language so that people are thrown back upon themselves to supply meaning, something already seen in late medieval times. Torrance concludes that modern exegesis has much in common with the allegorical exegesis of the Augustinian tradition and that "as we look back upon allegorical exegesis with a little pathetic ridicule, so they in the days ahead will look back upon modern existentialist exegesis with the same sort of pathetic ridicule because it was oblique and rejected the *intentio recta*." Torrance, "Truth and Authority," 221, cf.

of the scientific world of Newton. This was a radically dualist conception of science that carried over into theology, exemplified, as Torrance notes, by Hermann's distinction between *Geschichte* and *Historie*.[71]

DEPTH EXEGESIS

In distancing himself from these two positions Torrance argues that what the theologian is really seeking to do is penetrate the depths of meaning to which Scripture bears witness. Thus a genuinely *theological* reading of Scripture is attempted. The theologian "operates with the whole apostolic tradition in its stratified depth in order to allow himself to be directed from all sides to the objective realities under the creative impact of which all the apostolic tradition incorporated in the New Testament took its rise and shape in the primitive church."[72] Throughout this process the theologian is under the influence of the self-revelation of God in Jesus Christ and the Holy Spirit, through Scripture and beyond. This process involves a form of spiraling upward from one level to another as successive layers of meaning and order are uncovered. This is the essence of Torrance's depth exegesis, realist hermeneutics, and theological interpretation of Scripture.[73]

Torrance is highly indebted to Barth's doctrine of Scripture, especially his 1930 work on Anselm, *Fides Quaerens Intellectum,* which Torrance considers to be the turning point in Barth's theological method.[74] Scripture contains a word of God in rational form. This word is not an end in itself but is accompanied by the living Word of God in the *event* of revelation.[75] In a sermon, Torrance

---

219. The turn to theological interpretation of Scripture may yet challenge Torrance's assumptions here, as many within this field are attempting to reinstate something of the allegorical approach.

71. Torrance, *Space, Time and Resurrection*,8–9, and *Preaching Christ Today* (Grand Rapids: Eerdmans, 1994), 42–43.

72. T. F. Torrance, *Space, Time and Resurrection*(Edinburgh: Handsel, 1976), 10.

73. See Kurt Richardson, "Revelation, Scripture, and Mystical Apprehension of Divine Knowledge," in *The Promise of Trinitarian Theology*, ed. Elmer M. Colyer (Lanham, MD: Rowman & Littlefield, 2001), 185–203; and Colyer, *The Nature of Doctrine in T. F. Torrance's Theology* (Eugene, OR: Wipf and Stock, 2001). I am aware that the metaphors suggest an incompatible spiraling "upward" and a burrowing "downward," but these are simply analogies and thus spatial imagery is just that: imagery.

74. Torrance, *Karl Barth: An Introduction to His Early Theology, 1910–1931*(Edinburgh: T&T Clark, 2000), 183.

75. See the articulation of this in Barth, *Church Dogmatics,*I/1, trans. G. W. Bromiley, ed. G. W. Bromiley and T. F. Torrance, 2nd ed. (Edinburgh: T&T Clark, 1975), 113. According to a Barthian exposition of revelation as event, which Torrance subscribes to, "the term revelation refers *not to the objective self-manifestation alone, but equally to the act of faith in which it is heard and received and obeyed.*" Trevor Hart, *Regarding Karl Barth: Toward a Reading of his Theology*(Downers Grove, IL: InterVarsity,

explains this event when he says, "That is how God always speaks to us, not directly out of the blue, as it were, nor simply through the witness of others. It is when both these come together, the vertical Word of God from above, and the horizontal witness of others, that we know God and hear His Word personally and directly for ourselves."[76] Because of this event, true knowledge of the Object of our study is also true knowledge of the Subject—God. This involves penetrating into its inner rationality: the practice of depth exegesis.[77] Elsewhere Torrance refers to depth exegesis as a "cross-level movement of thought" in which we understand the text and the *realities* to which it bears witness.[78] It is also a "bi-polarity" (dialectic) between the words and the Word, the worldly form of revelation and its divine content that renders Scripture a *witness* to the self-revelation of God.[79] Torrance traces his method of depth exegesis back to the Athanasian difference between *lalia* and *Logos,* according to which the *lalia* or human words are to be interpreted in terms of the *Logos.*[80] On other occasions, Torrance refers to this method as a "stereoscopic" reading of Scripture, in which the *scope* of the Bible means its sacramental frame of reference, so that we must look not only at the text of Scripture but through it to the reality it signifies. When theologically interpreted, Jesus Christ becomes the *skopos* (scope, focus, and goal) of the Bible.[81] Torrance is explicit at this point: "Strictly speaking Christ himself is the scope of the Scriptures, so that it is only through focusing constantly upon him, dwelling in his Word and assimilating his Mind, that the interpreter can discern the real meaning of the Scriptures. What is required then is a theological interpretation of the Scriptures

---

1999),30 (italics in original). See Christina Baxter, "The Nature and Place of Scripture in the *Church Dogmatics*," in *Theology Beyond Christendom: Essays on the Centenary of the Birth of Karl Barth,*ed. John Thompson (Allison Park, PA: Pickwick, 1986), 35.

76. Torrance, "The Lamb of God," in *When Christ Comes and Comes Again*(London: Hodder and Stoughton, 1957), 56.

77. The term "depth exegesis" is taken from William Manson. See Torrance, *God and Rationality*(London: Oxford University Press, 1971),110; and Thomas F. Torrance, "Introduction," in William Manson,*Jesus and the Christian*(London: James Clarke, 1967), 9–14. The idea, however, Torrance attributes directly to the Greek Fathers. See Torrance, "Introduction: Biblical Hermeneutics and General Hermeneutics," in *Divine Meaning: Studies in Patristic Hermeneutics*(Edinburgh: T&T Clark, 1995), 5.

78. Torrance, *Reality and Evangelical Theology*(Philadelphia: Westminster, 1982), 99

79. Torrance, *Karl Barth: Biblical and Evangelical Theologian*(Edinburgh: T&T Clark, 1990), 111–12

80. See Torrance, *Space, Time and Resurrection,*5, 167.

81. This is articulated in Torrance, *Reality and Evangelical Theology*, 100–107; *Space, Time and Resurrection,*166–69; and *Theology in Reconstruction*(Eugene, OR: Wipf and Stock, 1996), 88–89.

under the direction of their ostensive reference to God's self-revelation in Jesus Christ and within the general perspective of faith."[82]

Accordingly, the function of theological understanding or *intelligere* is the act of reading (*legere*) the text embedded within (*intus*) the object. Torrance remarks: "God reveals himself to us by his Word in the Holy Scriptures, but our task in reading the outward text is to get at its inner meaning and basis, to read it at the deeper level of the solid truth on which the text rests. By a special act of the understanding that goes beyond mere reading, we penetrate into the objective *ratio* of the Word which enlightens and informs us."[83] *Ratio* carries within it a threefold sense: first, it refers to the means we employ (noetic *ratio*); second, to the end of our quest (ontic *ratio*); but ultimately, third, to the transcendent rationality of God behind all this (*ratio veritatis* or *ratio* of God). "*Ratio* is used then in a dimension of depth," writes Torrance, "of the ultimate Truth, the *ratio* of God himself; of the words and acts of God in Revelation, the *ratio* proper to the object of faith; and of man's knowledge of the object, the knowing *ratio* which corresponds to the *ratio* of the object."[84]

This final *ratio veritatis* is identical with God's being; it is the Divine Word consubstantial with the Father. Theological activity is derived from and is determined by the activity of God in the Word, for it is that Word (Christ) communicated through Holy Scripture that is the real object of our knowledge. When our statements are simply and formally identical with statements of the text of Scripture in which Christ speaks his Word to us, they are directly authoritative. Any other theological statements have a derived and thus lesser authority status and are constantly open to revision in light of the Word of God. Recall Vanhoozer's distinction between the magisterial authority of Holy Scripture and the ministerial authority of churchly interpretations.[85] But theology is not content merely to recite or repeat biblical texts; rather, it seeks to make statements about the truth revealed in the inner text, and so must seek a conformity to the truth at a deeper level beyond formal conformity to the external text. "Hence, scientific theological activity begins where straightforward biblical quotations end, precisely because it is the task of theology to penetrate to the solid truth upon which biblical statements rest."[86]

---

82. Torrance, *Reality and Evangelical Theology*, 107.
83. Torrance, *Karl Barth: An Introduction to His Early Theology*, 186.
84. Torrance, *Karl Barth: An Introduction to His Early Theology*, 187.
85. Kevin Vanhoozer, "Interpreting Scripture Between the Rock of Biblical Studies and the Hard Place of Systematic Theology: The State of the Evangelical (Dis)union," lecture delivered at Renewing the Evangelical Mission Conference held at Gordon-Conwell Theological Seminary (October 13–15, 2009).
86. Torrance, *Karl Barth: An Introduction to His Early Theology*, 188.

Torrance's method of depth exegesis or realist hermeneutics thus involves taking the biblical text and seeking to discern the inner, deeper structures of reality or truth inherent in it. It never leaves behind the text for another, for this is *Holy* Scripture,[87] but it never rests content on the mere *ipssisma vox*.

Torrance is insistent on the fact that the "voice" of God must be heard through Scripture alone—*sola scriptura*, but not *nuda scriptura*. In a sermon on Christ the Redeemer, Torrance asserts, "We cannot see Jesus just by piecing together picturesque historical detail about Him,"[88] clearly a rejection of the historical-critical method as an end in itself in biblical exegesis. Rather, "Jesus must be transfigured before our very eyes."[89] This is accomplished through his cross and resurrection, by means of which he now stands at the door of the church and knocks, and whose voice is heard inside the church "speaking to us out of the pages of the Bible."[90] Torrance speaks of this as a miracle: "We cannot see Jesus, for He has withdrawn Himself from our sight; and we will not see Him face to face until He comes again—but we *can hear* His *voice* speaking to us in the midst of the Church on earth. That is the perpetual miracle of the Bible, for it is the inspired instrument through which the voice of Christ is still to be heard . . . . The Church is, in fact, the Community of the Voice of God."[91]

Theology is an inherently rational discipline for the precise reason that faith itself is inherently rational. In revelation, God's very self is being communicated so that in the Word we are confronted with an Object that is Subject, that is, with one who is both person and message. "Hence, Christian Theology cannot tolerate the idea that faith is not rational in its own right and that it is the task of theology to give it rational interpretation through employing conceptual forms drawn from elsewhere."[92] From this premise Torrance concludes that the real issue is one of *ratio*, in both senses of the word, *rationality* and *method,* and this is what defines a scientific theology

---

87. For a recent account of what it means to call Scripture "holy" see Webster, *Holy Scripture: A Dogmatic Sketch* (Cambridge: Cambridge University Press, 2003). He also offers an account of Torrance's doctrine of Scripture in "T. F. Torrance on Scripture," *SJT* 65 (2012): 34–63, where he says on page 35, "His writings on these matters constitute one of the most promising bodies of material on the Christian theology of the Bible and its interpretation from a Protestant divine of the last five or six decades," before going on to note his relative absence in recent treatments of Scripture and theological interpretations of Scripture.

88. Torrance, "When Christ Comes to the Church," in *When Christ Comes and Comes Again* (London: Hodder and Stoughton, 1957), 26.

89. Ibid.

90. Ibid., 27.

91. Ibid.

92. Torrance, *Karl Barth: An Introduction to His Early Theology,* 182.

or dogmatics. Scientific theology or dogmatics is thus different from biblical theology, which remains content with the linguistic and phenomenological exegesis of the Scriptures. Theology must press on to inquire into the relation between biblical thought and speech and their source in the truth and being of God. It is the specific task of theology to inquire into what we ourselves have to say on the basis of the biblical revelation, and to articulate its relation to the object in such a way that our knowledge may be established as true. Torrance goes even further in suggesting that unless this happens "we have not engaged upon genuine exegesis, for then we are setting aside the all-important relation between the external text and the inner meaning and objective basis upon which it rests."[93] We may conclude from this that Torrance would only consider *theological* interpretation of Scripture as ultimately worthy of the epithet "Christian exegesis."

Torrance is trying to clarify how an exegesis of Scripture by a believer is different from that of an unbeliever. One could rephrase this somewhat to show that Torrance was pointing out the necessary ecclesial commitments and contexts for a correct reading of Scripture. According to Torrance, "The decisive point in interpretation is not reached until there is inquiry into the reality signified. True interpretation arises where perception of the meaning of the letter of Holy Scripture and understanding of the reality it indicates are one."[94] We see yet again Torrance's working out of his commitment in theological science to the *kata physic* nature of scientific inquiry, in which the method of inquiry is dictated by the object under study. "It belongs to the rationality of theology that the reason should operate only with objects of faith, for faith is the specific mode of rationality which is demanded of the reason when it is directed to the knowledge of God."[95]

A depth exegesis of Scripture can be illustrated by employing an analogy that Polanyi used in communicating what he meant by "tacit knowledge" and "indwelling": that of a blind man's walking stick. Gunton provides the following summary:

> When a blind man uses a stick . . . he learns about the world by their instrumentality, *from* them *to* the object of the knowledge. Employing these tools tacitly, we *indwell* them, "this indwelling

---

93. Ibid., 189. This is followed by a clarification: "No exegesis that is content only with noetic rationality can be regarded as properly scientific, for scientific activity must penetrate through noetic rationality into the ontic rationality of its basis and so lay bare its inner necessity."
94. Ibid., 189.
95. Ibid., 192.

being logically similar to the way we live in our body . . . . (Indwelling) applies here in a logical sense as affirming that the parts of the external world, when interiorised, function in the same way as our body functions when we attend from it to things outside." It is the fact that there is a real relation, in which there is a rational linkage between mind and matter, that makes the generalisation from body to tool to sophisticated theory a possibility . . . . The way in which our bodies and by extension our tools, both physical and theoretical, make a real indwelling in the world possible is fundamental to Polanyi's case. Without it, there would be no knowledge of the world at all. Thus the theory of indwelling is the obverse of the theory of tacit knowing.[96]

When applied directly to a realist hermeneutics, Scripture is the walking cane, the medium through which reality can be conceived, and yet it is not the reality itself but points to it.[97] According to Polanyi, things are only understood by indwelling them, not merely by observing them.[98] Hence when Torrance applies this philosophy of science, or epistemology, to theological method, he concludes that we only know the truth through indwelling the Word, both written and incarnate.[99] In this light, evangelical exegesis should not be the mere study of a text but a way of life in which God, through Christ, and by the Holy Spirit, leads us into a deeper communion with God's self through the word written.[100] The ends of exegesis are thus kept squarely at the forefront of Torrance's theological interpretation of Scripture.

---

96. Colin E. Gunton, "The Truth of Christology," in *Belief in Science and in Christian Life: The Relevance of Michael Polanyi's Thought for Christian Faith and Life*, ed. T. F. Torrance (Edinburgh: Handsel, 1980), 98.

97. It is Webster's contention that "the referential or signifying function of Scripture is . . . a primary element in Torrance's understanding of biblical interpretation." John Webster, "T. F. Torrance on Scripture," Keynote address at the annual meeting of the T. F. Torrance Theological Fellowship, Montreal (November 6, 2009), 12.

98. Michael Polanyi, "Science and Man's Place in the Universe," in *Science as a Cultural Force*.ed. H. Woolf (Baltimore: Johns Hopkins Press, 1964), 54–76; and Polanyi, *The Tacit Dimension*(New York: Doubleday, 1966), 21.

99. Webster, *Holy Scripture*, 68–106, presents a similar view.

100. Though not identical, see the sort of participatory exegesis recommend by Matthew Levering, *Participatory Biblical Exegesis: A Theology of Biblical Interpretation*(Notre Dame: University of Notre Dame Press, 2008).

INSPIRATION AND REVELATION

Torrance's revised Barthian doctrine of Scripture regards revelation as dynamic because it is initiated by Christ and enabled by the Holy Spirit. This means Scripture is not, strictly speaking, revelation but a vehicle for revelation or a medium through which God's revelation in Christ and by the Spirit can be given. Donald Bloesch is one of a number of contemporary evangelicals who follow this line of reasoning carefully. Bloesch maintains, "The Bible in and of itself is not the Word of God—divine revelation—but it is translucent to this revelation by virtue of the Spirit of God working within it and within the mind of the reader and hearer."[101] Scripture is a human medium of the divine Word and as such cannot be, according to Torrance, simply mistaken for God's living eternal Word, who is Jesus Christ. All human speech must have a reservation about it until all is revealed by God. Torrance brings out this eschatological character of revelation in his early work *Theological Science*:

> While God has made His Word audible and apprehensible with our human speech and thought, refusing to be limited by their inadequacy in making Himself known to us, He nevertheless refuses to be understood merely from within the conceptual framework of our natural thought and language but demands of that framework a logical reconstruction in accordance with His Word. Hence a theology faithful to what God has revealed and done in Jesus Christ must involve a powerful element of apocalyptic, that is epistemologically speaking, an eschatological suspension of logical form in order to keep our thought ever open to what is radically new.[102]

The relation between God's self-revelation and Scripture is fundamentally asymmetrical.[103] Indeed, Torrance is even willing to describe the Bible as a

---

101. Donald G. Bloesch, *Holy Scripture: Revelation, Inspiration, and Interpretation* (Downers Grove, IL: InterVarsity, 1994), 27. Bloesch's use of "translucent" is reminiscent of Torrance's language of Scripture as a "transparent medium" through which "the divine Light shines from the face of Jesus Christ into our hearts." Torrance, *Space, Time and Resurrection*(Edinburgh: Handsel, 1976), 12, and *Theology in Reconstruction*(Eugene, OR: Wipf and Stock, 1996), 257. In addition to Bloesch, see other contemporary evangelical theologians who share the same basic convictions, especially: Grenz, *Renewing the Center: Evangelical Theology in a Post-Theological Era*(Grand Rapids: Baker, 2000); and Alister E. McGrath, *A Passion for Truth: The Intellectual Coherence of Evangelicalism* (Leicester: Apollos, 1996), 53–118; and throughout *The Genesis of Doctrine: A Study in the Foundation of Doctrinal Criticism* (Grand Rapids: Eerdmans, 1990).

102. Torrance, *Theological Science*(reprint, Edinburgh: T&T Clark, 1996), 279–80.

product of human authorship and thus "faulty and errant."[104] However, due to the dual authorship of Scripture, Torrance regards its human imperfections as the very means through which God lays hold of our sinful, fallen human condition and redeems it. This is yet another reason he sees for not regarding the text of Scripture as the truth or as the word of God in any absolute or final sense. Scripture points to, and is the divinely chosen medium for, the revelation of God's eternal Word. I at least would want to affirm that it would thus be closer to the truth to say Holy Scripture *is* revelation, but must not be misunderstood as the *end* of revelation or as authoritative as Christ the Word.

Torrance develops this realist hermeneutic more fully in a discussion on the referring relation of language. If statements are absolutely adequate to the object, asks Torrance, then how can we distinguish the object from statements about it? If language and statements are to perform their denotative function adequately, directing us to reality/truth beyond themselves in such a way that there takes place a disclosure of reality/truth, then, Torrance concludes, they must have a measure of inadequacy in order to be differentiated from that to which they refer.[105] "The Scriptures of the Old and New Testaments rightly evoke from us profound respect and veneration not because of what they are in themselves but because of the divine revelation mediated in and through them. This is why we speak of them as 'Holy' Scriptures."[106] Barth's formulation of the dynamic between God's revelation in Christ and in Scripture was to propose his famous threefold distinction of the Word: the living Word, the written Word, and the proclaimed Word. Barth understands that only when the written or proclaimed Word is united with the revealed Word does it become revelation proper. Torrance, in line with Barth, considers the Word written to point to God's revelation. Yet for Torrance, revelation cannot be detached from the Bible, for in space-time this is how God has "uniquely and sovereignly coordinated the biblical word with his eternal Word, and adapted the written form and contents of the Bible to his Word, in such a way that the living Voice of God is made to resound through the Bible to all who have ears to hear."[107]

---

103. Torrance, *Reality and Evangelical Theology*(Philadelphia: Westminster, 1982),96.

104. Torrance, *Divine Meaning: Studies in Patristic Hermeneutics*(Edinburgh: T&T Clark, 1995), 10.

105. See the discussion in Torrance, "Truth and Authority: Theses on Truth," *ITQ*39 (1972): 229–31, especially 231.

106. Torrance, *Reality and Evangelical Theology*,95. In a footnote Torrance then directs the reader to Barth's *Church Dogmatics* I/2, trans. G. T. Thomson and Harold Knight, ed. G. W. Bromiley and T. F. Torrance (Edinburgh: T&T Clark, 1956), Ch. III on "Holy Scripture," 457–537.

107. Torrance, *Karl Barth: Biblical and Evangelical Theologian*(Edinburgh: T&T Clark, 1990),88.

Henry, Torrance, and Evangelicalism

Carl Henry's theological method falls foul of what Kevin Vanhoozer has dramatically termed "epic classicism," which conforms to Lindbeck's "cognitive-propositional" approach.[108] However, before Henry is dismissed as a fundamentalist fossil, I do think there are aspects of his critique and his perspective that are important to note and that most evangelicals will appreciate.

It can appear that Torrance sees Scripture as less than revelation and that it only *becomes* revelation through personal communion with Christ by the Spirit. Indeed, if that is the case then evangelicals would want to push back, with Henry, and say that our response to revelation does not make it revelation but rather makes it *revelatory* and personally affective. We must say, then, that Scripture *is* divine revelation, regardless of whether one is in union with Christ. In the words of Tom McCall, "Perhaps what Torrance needs is a strong dose of his own epistemological medicine. The trajectory of his thought might well result in belief in scripture as the written revelation standing in a direct but subordinate relation to the self-revelation of God in Jesus Christ."[109]

If this were the case then Torrance would be able to affirm, with Henry, that Scripture *is* revelation, without this being a denial that ultimate or final revelation is located in Jesus Christ alone. Scripture is revelation as far as it is a divinely given witness to the God revealed in Jesus Christ by the Spirit.

I conclude part one of this work with the words Marguerite Shuster penned to finish her short article on Torrance's theological method: "What is truth? The True Man said, 'I am the truth.' True men, responding in the faith of God's grace, can start nowhere else than to proclaim, 'Indeed, *he* is the truth.'"[110]

---

108. Kevin J. Vanhoozer, *The Drama of Doctrine: A Canonical Linguistic Approach to Christian Theology* (Louisville: Westminster John Knox, 2005), 83.

109. Tom McCall, "Ronald Thiemann, Thomas Torrance and Epistemological Doctrines of Revelation," *IJST* 6 (2004): 167.

110. Marguerite Shuster, "'What is Truth?' An Exploration of Thomas F. Torrance's Epistemology," *StudBT* 3 (1973): 56.

PART II

Select Themes within Torrance's Theological Oeuvre: Essays on Content

5

Mystical Theology
Reading Torrance as a Mystical Theologian Sui Generis

Moving from methodological concerns, the second part of our study addresses a number of theological themes found within the Torrance's dogmatics. On the surface, these themes may appear arbitrary; however, the deeper rationale that holds these three chapters together is that Torrance's work evidences mystical, integrated, and systematic elements, all of which are on display through the themes dealt with here.

THE MAKING OF MYSTICAL THEOLOGY

Torrance's work is most commonly associated with highly rational, even scientifically constructed theological discourse of the highest intellectual order (as seen in the last chapter). Indeed, he has often been criticized for his dense grammar and complex argumentation. While these critiques fail to account for the specific context within which Torrance chose to work and write, they do represent a central feature of his scientific approach to theology. It would be untrue and unfair, however, to suggest that Torrance was merely an academic commentator on theology. He was so much more than this. Torrance wrote as a Christian, as one who was utterly persuaded by the truth of the gospel and sought to persuade others of that same truth.

One of the central axioms by which Torrance conducted his theology was the conviction that to know God we must know his being in his act and his act in his being (he of course learnt this from Karl Barth). In order to do this, argued Torrance, we must not stand aloof from God like some detached observer, but instead indwell God through union and communion with Christ by the Spirit. In order to develop this approach he drew on the work of a now familiar group: scientists such as Albert Einstein, philosophers of science such as Michael Polanyi, church fathers such as Athanasius, and of course Karl Barth, in addition to a host of other voices from across the Great Tradition: from Anselm and Calvin in the West to John Philoponos and Orthodox figures in the East.

By means of such an appreciation of the Great Tradition Torrance's theology was expansive in a way that invited both meditation and critical response. He pushed boundaries, challenged long-held assumptions, and while committed to his Reformed heritage, understood that all traditions are living and thus require critical reflection and constructive contributions from successive generations. Perhaps this is the greatest invitation Torrance has left those of us working within the Reformed tradition, to reflect upon his work (along with the rest of the tradition) and add our own critical insights in service of the church.

Through Torrance's intimate involvement with thinkers from the East (both the living and the dead), his theology exhibits features not normally associated with Western, Reformed theology. One of these features is the place he affords Christian experience in his theology. As examined earlier, one of his key theological axioms is that one must do constructive theology as an *a posteriori* exercise, in light of the incarnation and our union with Christ, rather than in an *a priori* way in which scholastic theological metaphysics are imposed upon the Scriptures in such a way that God must conform to philosophical requirements quite independent of the triune God's self-revelation in Christ, through the Spirit, and in the word written. While the distinction should not be pressed, this is the difference for Torrance between dogmatics and systematic theology. This approach meant that Torrance made space for themes rather unfamiliar, albeit not unknown, in Western theology. Here I am specifically thinking of the way he so rigorously adapted a doctrine of *theosis* into his architectonic theology,[1] the way he was able to work out the implications of the Trinitarian ground and grammar of theology in his epistemology, and the way he was able to incorporate mystical themes into his scientific dogmatics. Torrance knew such themes would be foreign to and even unwelcome in much Western theology, and employed the phrase "the danger of vertigo" to express this in relation to *theosis*, for instance.[2] And yet Torrance felt constrained to

---

1. I have attempted to work out Torrance's commitment to *theosis* in a number of works, namely, "Reforming Theosis," in *Theosis: Deification in Christian Theology*, ed S. Finlan and V. Kharlamov, Princeton Theological Monograph Series 52 (Eugene, OR: Pickwick, 2006), 146–67; and comprehensively in *Theosis in the Theology of Thomas Torrance*, Ashgate New Critical Thinking in Religion, Theology and Biblical Studies (Farnham: Ashgate, 2009).

2. See for example in Torrance, *Space, Time and Resurrection* (Edinburgh: Handsel, 1976), 136–39. Cf. Habets, *Theosis in the Theology of Thomas Torrance*, 193–98.

speak in such terms, given the flow of the biblical narrative and the reality communicated through such concepts.

This is not to suggest that Torrance merely adopted existing concepts into his scientific dogmatics. Instead, what we find in Torrance's works are highly nuanced understandings of such notions as *theosis*, the *visio Dei*, and mysticism. I suggest that precisely because of the presence of many of these themes in his theology, Torrance may be regarded as a theological mystic—but one *sui generis*.[3] I also suggest that he was not always comfortable with the direction or implications of certain features of his own theology. This accounts for his dis-ease in his later works over the concept of natural theology, to take one example, and for his reticence to be identified as a mystic in any sense whatsoever, as another example.[4]

THE VISIO DEI

Within the Great Tradition the theme of *light* occupies an exalted place. This has notable roots in the New Testament's Johannine literature, which defines God as Light that is foreign to all darkness (1 John 1:5) and presents Christ as the Light of the world who sends out his disciples to be as lights to the world (John 8:12; cf. Matt. 5:14-16). The New Testament is also unanimous in its teaching that the saints and angels see God's face directly (Matt. 18:10; 1 Cor. 13:12; 1 John 3:2). If God is revealed to humanity as Light, and is able to be apprehended by such, can God also be inaccessible and transcendent, as Scripture affirms? This was the question put to the Hesychasts by Barlaam the Calabrian in the form of a bitter accusation.[5] The Hesychast monk Gregory

---

3. In Richardson's opinion, the presence of the following features unmistakably means Torrance made space for a form of mysticism in his dogmatics: "The mystical dimension of theological knowing are here: the doxological, the suprarational, the transcendent, the experiential, the surplus of knowing, mutual indwelling, and divine participation, all in the encounter with the Scripture." Kurt Richardson, "Revelation, Scripture, and Mystical Apprehension of Divine Knowledge," in *The Promise of Trinitarian Theology: Theologians in Dialogue with T. F. Torrance*, ed. E. M. Colyer (Lanham, MD: Rowman & Littlefield, 2001), 194–95.

4. I have no doubt that if Torrance were reading the title of this chapter today he would be not only horrified but annoyed at my suggestion that he is a theological mystic. However, I trust that upon a close reading of the argument his fears would be somewhat relieved and he would even appreciate the evaluation of his work and the place of mystery within it that I have argued for.

5. The question was initiated much earlier than the Hesychast controversy, of course. One thinks for instance of the "bittersweet" experiences of Symeon the New Theologian (949–1022) and the outrage he caused when he dared to speak of his own deification in personal terms. See Hilarion Alfeyev, *St. Symeon the New Theologian and Orthodox Tradition* (Oxford: Oxford University Press, 2000), who seeks to show the continuity and orthodoxy of Symeon's spirituality-theology. The present chapter has a similar intent

Palamas (1296–1359) undertook to answer Barlaam in his *Apodictic Treatises* (1336), followed by a series of letters in which he refuted Barlaam's theses, his famous *Triads in Defense of the Holy Hesychasts*(1338–1341), and finally in his *Hagioretic Tome* (1340). An essential piece of Palamas's reply was to develop the distinction between the *essence* of God and God's uncreated *energies*.[6]

Torrance rejected the Orthodox distinction between the essence and energies of God for a more personalistic account, though he never ventured a full-scale critique of the distinction, perhaps not wanting to cause undue offense on account of his close relations with the Eastern Orthodox Churches. That is not to say he did not specifically address the issue and gently make his objections known.[7] The essence-energies distinction and the theology that undergirds it are simply not acceptable to Torrance or to Western theology more generally, given the logically necessary impersonal implications of the doctrine. Torrance is far more inclined to accept, with critical corrections, something like the Rahnerian *Grundaxiom* that the economic Trinity is the immanent Trinity (the "vice versa" addition being critically rejected).[8]

Ever since the Nicene Creed represented the Son as "Light proceeding out of Light" this theme has played an important part in the Christian tradition,[9] especially within Byzantine Christianity, and has been intimately linked with doctrines of *theosis*.[10] This is evident even within Reformed theology. Thus Jonathan Edwards spoke analogously of *theosis* as the shining forth of light.[11] As

---

to that of Alfeyev's work, to show the continuity of Torrance's thought with the spirituality-theology of his own tradition.

6. See G. I. Mantzaridis, *The Deification of Man: St. Gregory Palamas and the Orthodox Tradition*,trans. L. Sherrard (Crestwood, NY: St. Vladimir's Seminary Press, 1984), 104–10.

7. See Torrance, *The Christian Doctrine of God: One Being Three Persons*(Edinburgh: T&T Clark, 1996), 187–88. I have dealt with Torrance's objections to the essence-energies distinction elsewhere; see "'Reformed Theosis?' A Response to Gannon Murphy," *TT* 65 (2009): 489–98; *Theosis in the Theology of Thomas Torrance*,154–59; and beyond Torrance in "Theosis, Yes; Deification, No," in *The Spirit of Truth: Reading Scripture and Constructing Theology with the Holy Spirit*,ed. Myk Habets (Eugene, OR: Pickwick, 2010), 124–49.

8. For a full-scale exploration of this Trinitarian theme with a limited focus on Torrance, see Paul D. Molnar, *Divine Freedom and the Doctrine of the Immanent Trinity*(London: T&T Clark, 2002), 167–96; 317–30.

9. For a survey of theological uses of the analogy of light see Kathryn E. Tanner, "The Use of Perceived Properties of Light as a Theological Analogy," in *Light from Light: Scientists and Theologians in Dialogue*,ed. G. O'Collins and M. A. Myers (Grand Rapids: Eerdmans, 2012), 122–30. According to Tanner, the analogy of light provides analogies for three main topics in theology: 1) the relationships between the persons of the Trinity; 2) God's creation of the world; and 3) God's presence within the world (122).

an example of such language, Ramsey cites Edwards's statement that believers are "little suns, partaking of the nature of the fountain of their light."[12]

Light was a favorite analogy for Torrance.[13] According to Torrance, for Christ to be Light necessitates his being Word also, the two being hypostatically related. "The very Light of God could not be consistently Light," Torrance writes, "and certainly could not be known as such, if Jesus Christ were not also Word of Word as well as Light of Light, and thus immutably, eternally God of God as both Light and Word."[14] This conclusion is drawn from the deduction that if Jesus Christ is of one and the same being with God (*homoousios*) as incarnate Son, this must apply to him also as incarnate Word of God.[15] This is consistent with the entire tenor of Torrance's method and theology examined in the earlier chapters: what God is toward us in God's self-revelation in Jesus Christ as the Word made flesh, he is in his own divine being.

Torrance forcefully reasons that "God is himself the supreme Light, unapproachable and invisible," and yet, "he is illuminatingly present in the world of thought."[16] How? God is visible through the things God has made

---

10. See V. Lossky, *The Vision of God*, trans. A. Moorhouse (Crestwood, NY: St. Vladimir's Seminary Press, 1973), 25–44; and *The Mystical Theology of the Eastern Church* (Crestwood, NY: St. Vladimir's Seminary Press, 1998), 217–35.

11. For a careful reading of Edwards's use of *theosis* see Kyle Strobel, "Jonathan Edwards and the Polemics of *Theosis*," *HTR* 105 (2012): 259–79.

12. Paul Ramsey, in J. Edwards, *Ethical Writings: The Works of Jonathan Edwards*, vol. 8, ed. P. Ramsey (New Haven: Yale University Press, 1989), 343, 347; cited in M. J. McClymont, "Salvation as Divinization: Jonathan Edwards, Gregory Palamas and the Theological Uses of Neoplatonism," in *Jonathan Edwards: Philosophical Theologian*, ed. P. Helm and O. D. Crisp (Aldershot: Ashgate, 2003), 139. Cf. J. Edwards, "A Divine and Supernatural Light. Immediately Imparted to the Soul by the Spirit of God, Shown to Be Both a Scriptural and Rational Doctrine," in *A Jonathan Edwards Reader*, ed. J. E. Smith, H. S. Stout, and K. P. Minkema (New Haven: Yale University Press, 1995).

13. The number of sermons and addresses Torrance devoted to the analogy of light is indicative of the importance of the analogy for Torrance. See The Thomas F. Torrance Manuscript Collection, Special Collections, Princeton Theological Seminary Library, Box 38, "Sermon on John 8.12: Whitekirk August 31, 1980"; "Sermon on 1 John 1.5, 1973"; and "Sermon on John 1.9: University Sermon, Leeds, Emmanuel Church, November 15, 1981," Box 39, "A Faith for Hard Times: the Living Light" (sermon, November 20, 1977); "Light: Its Theology and Physics" (sermon, Lawnswood School, Leeds: November 16, 1981); and "Light" (Kings College Chapel, Aberdeen: February 13, 1977); Box 40, Handwritten notes, "Light and Way"; and "The Light of the World: A Sermon," *The Reformed Journal* (December 1988).

14. Torrance, *Christian Theology and Scientific Culture* (New York: Oxford University Press, 1981), 107.

15. Torrance cites John Reuchlin (1455–1522), the German humanist and great uncle of Philipp Melanchthon, as first articulating this connection. Torrance, *Christian Theology and Scientific Culture*, 106.

16. Ibid., 87.

but is only knowable through the incarnate Word of God, Jesus Christ. True knowledge of God, even of God's uncreated and invisible Light, is "seen" and "known" only in Christ. In his own words, "Through the mystery of the invisibility of light God guards and reflects the mystery of his own invisible Light before which our creaturely finite minds falter and fail, but nevertheless he allows us, as St Paul expressed it, to 'see' him darkly or indirectly as in a mirror."[17]

Drawing heavily upon the insights of John Philoponos of Alexandria and John of the Cross, Torrance develops a theology of light—both scientifically and theologically.[18] God is unapproachable in the radiance of God's pure light. As one cannot look at the sun and see, one cannot see God and live. According to John of the Cross, this is so for two reasons. First, God is unapproachable because of the sheer invisibility of God's uncreated Light. God is infinite and transcendent, and our finite capacities have no means by which we may see or comprehend this Light. Second, "God is unapproachable for us because of the inability of our impure minds to bear the sheer purity of his divine Light."[19] The utter holiness of God, which consumes all evil and impurity, overwhelms the sight of the sinner.

Torrance draws from this the following significant conclusions concerning knowledge of God. First, God must establish a degree of reciprocity between Godself and humankind in which God's uncreated Light adapts itself to the lowly understanding of fallen minds so that men and women may be elevated to communion with God in such a way that they may have access to God beyond their creaturely capacities.[20] This is a clear affirmation of *theosis* defined as the "elevation" of the person to communion with God.[21] Second, the reconciliation accomplished between God and humanity must ensure that guilt is expiated, sin is forgiven, and defilement is removed so that our minds may be equipped to "see" the divine Light. This is accomplished through the "two-fold relationship

---

17. Ibid., 91.

18. Hunsinger, "Light from Light: From Irenaeus and Torrance to Aquinas and Barth," in *Light From Light: Scientists and Theologians in Dialogue*, ed. G. O'Collins and M. A. Myers (Grand Rapids: Eerdmans, 2012) 208–35, has critically interacted with Torrance's use of the light analogy and brought him into dialogue with others in the tradition. Central to Hunsinger's interpretation of the analogy is that it is just that, analogical, thus Irenaeus's statement "[God] is most aptly called 'light,' but he is nothing like the light we know" (*Adversus haereses*, 2.13.4) becomes a central heuristic device for him. Ibid., 208, and further at 212 where it is referred to as a "formula."

19. Torrance, *Christian Theology and Scientific Culture*, 93.

20. Ibid.

21. Torrance expressly connects a theology of light to the concept of *theosis* in *The Trinitarian Faith: The Evangelical Theology of the Ancient Catholic Church* (Edinburgh: T&T Clark, 1995), 139, n. 102.

between God and humanity mediated through the incarnation and passion of God's beloved Son in Jesus Christ."[22] Drawing on and updating Irenaeus's commentary on the prologue of St. John's Gospel, Torrance writes: "We may express this today by saying that in Jesus Christ God's own transcendent Light in personal and concentrated form has moved directly into the physical world of luminous phenomena created by him and become uniquely man within the contingent structures and objectivities and patters of existence shaped and governed by the primacy of created light in the universe."[23]

George Hunsinger takes Torrance's account of the analogy of light to be less than satisfactory when compared to Irenaeus's description, on account of the fact that "more than Irenaeus, however, he wished to coordinate the uncreated Light of God with the created light, or contingent intelligibility, of the world . . . . In his desire to establish a positive connection between created and uncreated light, however, Torrance sometimes introduced a certain ambiguity into his discourse. He seemed to accord greater weight to the principle of eminence than to the principle of negation in use of analogical theological discourse. Eminence at the expense of negation runs the risk of obscuring God's difference from the world."[24] This is the same problem encountered earlier in chapter three, where critics of Torrance's use of a new natural theology failed to distinguish his use of natural theology from natural revelation and then from a theology of nature. What Hunsinger and others fear is that in places Torrance's theology does not emphasize clearly enough the radical difference between God and the world.[25] When doctrines of *theosis* and mystical theology are added into the mix, this (illegitimate) fear increases.

In Christ the invisible Light of God is made visible, and the "indissoluble oneness" with the eternal Word and Love of God is made accessible to humankind. Jesus Christ is the "Light of the world," and it is only in and through him that we are enlightened and may see and come to know the invisible God. Jesus Christ is thus "Light of Light" and "God of God," the two terms being synonymous, "thus he constitutes in the reality of his divine-human person both the invisible radiation and the creaturely reflection of the eternal Light which God is."[26] By becoming one with us in our human nature and

---

22. Torrance, *Christian Theology and Scientific Culture*, 94.
23. Ibid., 95. Cf. *The Ground and Grammar of Theology* (Charlottesville: University of Virginia Press, 1980), 129–30. Torrance drew heavily from his reading of Irenaeus at this point; see "Kerygmatic Proclamation of the Gospel: *The Demonstration of Apostolic Preaching* of Irenaios of Lyons," GOTR 37 (1992): 105–21.
24. Hunsinger, "Light from Light," 220.
25. Ibid., 215.

condition, the incarnate Son is both the eternal Word of God and a human word, both the uncreated Light of God and created light, in the indivisible unity of his life and person.[27]

The incarnation shows us what true humanity is. It reveals what true "seeing" or "knowing" God consists of,[28] for it is an accurate reflection (Calvin's "mirror") of the uncreated Light in a created human subject. In sermonic tone, Torrance writes:

> Jesus was completely and absolutely transparent with the Light of God. There was no darkness in him, nothing unreal, no deceit, no insincerity. He was utterly true and genuine, translucent with the sheer Truth of God himself, the one point in human existence where the divine Light shines through to the world purely and truly, unimpeded and unclouded by any distortion or refraction. Far from being less human because of that, he was more human than any other, indeed perfectly human, for with him the divine Light which is the source of all human life and light had its perfect way. He was so perfectly the man that he ought to have been that there was no gap in his nature resulting from a lapse from true humanity, as a result of which he was obliged to be what he was not but ought to be. The union between his human life and the humanising Light of the Creator was unbroken, so that it is through him that the eternal uncreated Light of God shines through to us.[29]

---

26. Torrance, *Christian Theology and Scientific Culture*, 95.
27. Ibid., 101–2.
28. Jesus Christ is both "luminous Word" and "audible Light." Ibid., 101.
29. Ibid., 96. In case he is misunderstood Torrance adds, "Jesus was not just the most perfect man, the most human being that ever lived, shot through and through with divine Light, but God himself in his divine Light living among us as man" (97).

"Transparency" in this discussion functions as an analogy for *theosis*.[30] To experience *theosis* is to become in a sense transparent. The goal of *theosis* is to reflect God's uncreated Light fully and completely, without spot or blemish; to mirror God absolutely. This is not possible for the darkened sinful vessels that we are. Consequently, only in the incarnate Light of the Son is *theosis* realized. "It is the living Light of God himself actively lived out among us as a human life, which continues to bear directly, personally, intimately upon the ontological depths of our human existence, searching, judging, cleansing, healing and renewing, and remains for ever the one light-bearing and life-giving Life for all mankind."[31] The incarnate Son of God is the Light of God and the Light of the world. It is only as one is united to this Light that one can apprehend it, reflect it, and be light oneself.[32] "Since it is in this enlightening and saving Life of the crucified and risen Jesus that the eternal Light and Life of God himself are mediated to us in a form in which we can share in death as well as life, it is through union and communion with Jesus that we are enabled to see the invisible God and live."[33]

What Torrance achieves in his theology of light is a remarkable description of mystical union that cuts through much of the confusion and debate between Eastern and Western views of mystical knowing, bringing to the fore as he does the christological aspects of *theosis*. Christ alone is the true human. He alone is able to participate fully in the divine life, for he remains divine (and human) in the hypostatic union. Through participating in the humanity of Jesus Christ the believer is drawn into the light and life of God— "divinized"—without losing

---

30. There is an interesting parallel in the doctrine of *theosis* articulated by Jonathan Edwards in response to a clergyman's objection that he taught that believers could participate in the divine *essence*, not simply in the divine *nature*: "A diamond or a crystal that is held forth in the sun's beams may properly be said to have some of the sun's brightness communicated to it; for though it hasn't the same individual brightness with that which is inherent in the sun, and be immensely less in degree, yet it is something of the same nature." Edwards, *Ethical Writings*, 8:640 (see 636–40). This is not to suggest that the language of participating in the divine *essence* is to be recommended, given as it is to such misunderstanding. However, Calvin, surely knowing the perils of such language, often speaks of an essential union in his *Institutes*. For a helpful clarification of Edwards's language here, see Strobel, "Jonathan Edwards and the Polemics of *Theosis*," 259–79.

31. Torrance, *Christian Theology and Scientific Culture*, 97.

32. See C. S. Lewis, "The Weight of Glory," in *Screwtape Proposes a Toast and Other Pieces* (London: Fontana, 1965), 106–7, for the same thought in his discussion of the glory that is to be experienced at the resurrection. Also note the pervasive use of theotic doctrine and imagery throughout Lewis's work; see Myk Habets, "Walking In *mirabilibus supra me*: How C. S. Lewis Transposes Theosis," *EvQ* 82 (2010): 15–27.

33. Torrance, *Christian Theology and Scientific Culture*, 99.

his or her created humanity in the process. To see God is to know God, and to know God is to know the incarnate Son who has made known the Father by the Spirit. "But we all, with unveiled face, beholding as in a mirror the glory of the Lord, are being transformed into the same image from glory to glory, just as from the Lord, the Spirit" (2 Cor. 3:18).

MYSTERY AND MYSTICISM

When the themes of light, knowledge, the *visio Dei*, and *theosis* are found in close proximity it is to be expected that some appeal could be made to the concept of mysticism in order to account for the ultimate experience of God.[34] While Torrance uses each of these concepts, he repeatedly rejects all allegations that his is a *mystical* theology.[35] Torrance rejects what he understands to be mysticism in favor of a highly developed notion of participatory knowing and personal indwelling in which the categories of light, vision, sight, and knowing come to the fore. In place of the term *mysticism* Torrance readily adopts the category of *mystery* and uses a doctrine of *theosis* in order to explain the spiritual aspect of personal participation in God (spiritual union).[36]

Because doctrines of *theosis* deal with the communing of the creature with the Creator, some form of mystery, or what is often termed mysticism, is assuredly involved. This mysticism must, however, be carefully defined. It is wrong to conclude that Torrance is a "mystic" or that his doctrine of *theosis* parallels that of Eastern or Western mysticism directly. Certainly mystical influences and themes are found within his theology, with certain aspects of *theosis* contributing in part to this. Torrance's attitude to the mystical tradition thus includes positive and negative elements. Like Calvin, Torrance sees union

---

34. This is made explicit in Kallistos Ware, "Light and Darkness in the Mystical Theology of the Greek Fathers," in *Light from Light: Scientists and Theologians in Dialogue*, ed. G. O'Collins and M. A. Myers (Grand Rapids: Eerdmans, 2012), 131–59.

35. For a concise account of mystical elements in Torrance's theology see Titus Chung, *Thomas Torrance's Mediations and Revelation* (Farnham: Ashgate, 2011), 127–33, whereupon he enters into a broader discussion of his intuitive theology.

36. Numerous references to mystery are found throughout Torrance's work. Among the unpunished material found in The Thomas F. Torrance Manuscript Collection, Special Collections, Princeton Theological Seminary Library, I note the following: "The Paschal Mystery of Christ and the Eucharist: General Theses," (New College Lecture), in Box 24, Main Lectures at New College and Box 29, lectures on ecclesiology (subsequently published as "Le mystere pascal du Christ et l'Eucharistie," *ISTINA* 4 [1975]: 404–34, and "The Pascal Mystery and the Eucharist: General Theses," *Liturgical Review* 6 [1976]: 6–12); "The Mystery of Christ," (draft), Box 25, lectures on Christology; "The Mystery of Christ," Box 26, Main Lectures at New College; and "The Mystery of the Kingdom," Box 54, Typescript and handwritten notes.

with Christ as an implied "mystical union" (*unio mystica*); however, such is his reticence over the word *mystical* that he prefers to speak of the "mystery of union" with Christ, a formula that he believes avoids unacceptable aspects of the notion of mysticism.[37]

In order to identify what Torrance rejects in the concept of mysticism, we may note his comments on Eastern apophaticism and on the Western mystical tradition. Torrance traces the Eastern Orthodox doctrine of apophaticism back to Neoplatonic and Pseudo-Dionysian philosophies, in which "the human spirit 'takes-off,' as it were, in a wordless and conceptless mystical vision of God."[38] For example, according to Hesychast teaching, unceasing prayer performed with the right bodily posture and breathing technique will eventually achieve "the union of the mind and heart." As McClymont reminds us: "In time, such prayer led on to a visionary experience by which it became possible for select individuals, in this present life and with their bodily eyes, to see the divine light, which was taken to be identical with that light that surrounded Jesus at the moment of his Transfiguration. In the teaching of St Gregory Palamas, the light seen by Hesychasts was a manifestation of the 'energies' of God, which he took to be distinct from the divine 'essence,' and yet uncreated and eternal just like the 'essence.'"[39]

For Orthodoxy, this vision of light forms the final goal of *theosis*. An examination of Torrance's theology of light and cognitive union with Christ makes it clear that he rejects such an Eastern apophatic theology. This is not to say that Torrance eschews all apophatic reticence in our knowledge of God,[40] but rather that he rejects the *doctrine* of apophaticism or negative theology as developed by such Eastern Orthodox writers as Lossky and Ware.[41] Richardson

---

37. While Torrance never uses the term "mystical union" in his work, he does affirm what Calvin meant by the term. See Calvin, *The Institutes of the Christian Religion*, trans. H. Beveridge (London: James Clarke, 1953), 3.11.10 (and 2.12.7 within the context of a discussion on divorce based on Matt. 19:4–6 "the two shall become one flesh").

38. Torrance, *Christian Theology and Scientific Culture* (New York: Oxford University Press, 1981), 104.

39. M. J. McClymont, "Salvation as Divinization: Jonathan Edwards, Gregory Palamas and the Theological Uses of Neoplatonism," in *Jonathan Edwards: Philosophical Theologian*, ed. P. Helm and O. D. Crisp (Aldershot: Ashgate, 2003),144–45.

40. Torrance, *Reality and Scientific Theology* (Edinburgh: Scottish Academic, 1985).

41. See V. Lossky, *In the Image and Likeness of God* (Crestwood, NY: St. Vladimir's Seminary Press, 1985), 13–29; and K. Ware, *The Orthodox Way* (London: Mowbrays, 1979), 12–32. For a good overview of Eastern versus Western approaches to the topic of apophaticism and mystery, see D. B. Clendenin, "The Mystery of God: Apophatic Vision," in *Eastern Orthodox Christianity: A Western Perspective* (Grand Rapids: Baker, 1994), 47–70. For a discussion of Platonism and the East see Lossky, *The Vision of God*,trans. A. Moorhouse (Crestwood, NY: St. Vladimir's Seminary Press, 1973), 64–65.

argues that, rather than drawing upon the Dionysian or Eckhartian traditions, Torrance developed his concept of mystical apprehension of God through the apophatic and kataphatic traditions of Athanasius and the Cappadocian Fathers.[42]

In its own way, the Augustinian-Thomistic tradition of theology endorses some form of conceptless mysticism in its formulation of the Beatific Vision. The Beatific Vision, a mute or wordless vision of God, functions as the goal of salvation in many Western, especially Latin, theologies. Aquinas rejected the necessity of a connection in the divine understanding (*intelligere*) and speaking (*locutio*). In response to the question posed by Peter Lombard as to how God and the blessed converse with one another, Aquinas answered that they converse "wordlessly" through intellectual vision alone.[43] Having examined Torrance's theology of the incarnate Son as both Word and Light of God, it is clear that Torrance rejects Latin forms of mysticism as well as Eastern forms.

Within both Eastern and Western theologies Torrance locates the same problem, arrived at by different routes, of a wordless or mute Deity behind the God of the economy. To counter these constructions, Torrance turns to Athanasius, Hilary, and Anselm, who affirmed with pro-Nicene theology that God's being is intrinsically eloquent and not mute, for God's Word dwells essentially within God.[44] Here we have the first steps in holding together the twin themes of sight and sound, Light and Word. This means, in Torrance's view, that the Light of God is not simply a mystical and mute experience but is intensely cognitive (cf. John 3:36; 6:30, 40; 12:39–40). In an unexpected move, Torrance identifies the ascetics of the patristic period as one model of how this cognitive participation may be attained: by way of *askesis*, or spiritual discipline![45] But then Torrance goes on to explain that we see in this example an attempt to know God in a way that is worthy of God: "To know God and to be holy, to know God and worship, to know God and to be cleansed in mind and soul from anything that may come between people and God, to know God

---

42. Kurt Richardson, "Revelation, Scripture, and Mystical Apprehension of Divine Knowledge," in *The Promise of Trinitarian Theology: Theologians in Dialogue with T. F. Torrance*, ed. E. M. Colyer (Lanham, MD: Rowman & Littlefield, 2001), 187.

43. Torrance, *Christian Theology and Scientific Culture*, 105.

44. This is another way in which the economic Trinity is to be read back into the immanent Trinity in basic conformity to Rahner's Trinitarian principle that "the economic Trinity is the immanent Trinity and immanent Trinity is the economic Trinity." See K. Rahner, *The Trinity*, trans. J. Donceel (New York: Seabury, 1974), 22. This is not to imply that Torrance endorses Rahner's axiom *simpliciter*.

45. See Lossky, *The Vision of God*, 103–20; and G. I. Mantzaridis, *The Deification of Man: St. Gregory Palamas and the Orthodox Tradition*, trans. L. Sherrard (Crestwood, NY: St. Vladimir's Seminary Press, 1984), 75–85, 87–115.

and be committed to him in consecration, love and obedience, go inseparably together."[46] This is both an important insight into Torrance's thinking and in some senses a surprising one. Given Torrance's self-styled aversion to mysti*cism* he is clearly not advocating the early ascetics' flights of mystical experience, but rather the rigorously practical way in which they applied themselves wholly to a vision or knowledge of God. It also highlights Torrance's familiarity with the Eastern tradition of knowledge/vision of God and so, by extension, it supports my contention that Torrance advocates a form of Christian mysticism.

To make my point succinctly, we may say that Torrance's theology asserts that the only way to know God is to become like God.[47] The way to become like God is to be united to the incarnate Son by the Spirit, and in Christ's humanity participate in the divine life in a creaturely way. In Richardson's assessment:

> Where Torrance discerns the mystical is in the communion of the redeemed with the Redeemer and therefore in participation with God in God's own Triune life. In this communion, the human knower is raised up through the statements of Scripture to a knowledge of God that grasps the Trinitarian whole (Father, Son, and Holy Spirit) of that which has been revealed by Christ, elicits a personal knowing that is interpersonal and inclusive of the creature, and results in true *theologia*, real knowledge of God in God's own Trinitarian reality. This is nothing less than the gracious participation of redeemed existence proleptically enjoyed by faith, and mediated under the aid and guidance of Scripture.[48]

Characteristically, it is to Athanasius that Torrance turns for the foundation of his doctrine of human participation in the divine. In particular, he looks to Athanasius's treatment of the *enousios logos* and *enousios energeia*. *Enousios logos* refers to the Word/Reason inherent in the *ousia*, or being, of God; *enousios energeia* refers to the activity or movement of power inherent in the *ousia*.[49] God's Logos inheres in God's own being eternally, and that Logos has become

---

46. Torrance, *The Mediation of Christ*, 2nd ed. (Edinburgh: T&T Clark, 1992), 26.

47. This is strikingly, and not surprisingly, similar to the mystical experience of *theosis* in the theology of Gregory Palamas. See Mantzaridis, "The Moral Aspect of Deification," in *The Deification of Man*, 61–85. Cf. 63–64.

48. Richardson, "Revelation, Scripture, and Mystical Apprehension of Divine Knowledge," 193–94.

49. Torrance, *The Ground and Grammar of Theology* (Charlottesville: University of Virginia Press, 1980), 151.

incarnate in Jesus Christ. Through Jesus Christ we have noetic access into the being of God, into God's divine intelligibility or Logos. Likewise, if God's *energeia*, or "act," inheres in God's being, and that act has taken the form of Jesus Christ in the incarnation, so that he is identical with the action of God, then we know God in accord with the acts of God's being, consistent with God's activity in disclosing the divine self to us.[50]

Two important implications follow. First, God's being as Logos means that God's being is speaking being. Hence there can be no thought of knowing God in God's mute being, for apart from the Word there is no such god (thus rejecting a tenet of Latin mysticism). Second, God's *energeia* inheres in God's being. This means that God's being is in God's act and God's act is in God's being, thus rejecting a tenet of Eastern apophaticism and accepting a major tenet of Barth's theology, namely his actualism.[51] It naturally follows that what the Greek patristic theologians termed *theopoiesis* or *theosis* is essentially the consubstantial self-giving of God to humankind through Christ and in his Spirit.[52] This leads Torrance to affirm: "In virtue of his divine reality and presence incarnate within mankind he acts upon people in an utterly divine and creative way, making them partake of himself through grace and thus partake of God. θεοποιησις [*theopoiesis*] or θεωσις [*theosis*] was used to describe the unique act of God incarnate in Jesus Christ, but act which inheres in his divine being and is inseparable from it."[53]

Thus we can see a basic difference between Torrance's theology and Eastern Orthodoxy. The *homoousion* means that God reveals himself not simply through his impersonal energies but in a very real way through his personal essence: in the incarnation God gives *God's own self* in grace.[54] Unlike Palamite divinization, *theosis* in the pro-Nicene theologians represents communion through Jesus Christ in the Spirit. Torrance insists that in Jesus Christ we know God. Torrance does not, however, contend that we may know all

---

50. Torrance, *The Ground and Grammar of Theology*, 151–52. This is one of the reasons why Torrance rejects the Eastern Orthodox distinction between the essence and energies of God. The identity of the being and act of God in Christ Jesus will not allow this.

51. Ibid., 152–53.

52. Torrance, *The Trinitarian Faith: The Evangelical Theology of the Ancient Catholic Church* (Edinburgh: T&T Clark, 1995),139.

53. Ibid., 139.

54. See, for instance, Torrance's critique of Palamism for its strong distinction between the procession and the mission of the Spirit, which "drive[s] a wedge between the inner life of God and his saving activity in history," in Torrance, *The Christian Doctrine of God: One Being Three Persons*(Edinburgh: T&T Clark, 1996), 187.

there is to know about God. Properly speaking we may *apprehend* God, but never *comprehend* God. In expressing this apophatic reticence,[55] Torrance acknowledges the place of mystery in his theology alongside those elements of mysticism that are clearly evident.

THE MYSTERY OF KNOWING GOD

Given that Torrance has argued that theologians must find a place in their inquiry into the knowledge of God for *mystical theology*,[56] one may be forgiven for thinking that Torrance adopts a notion of Eastern mysticism.[57] However, Torrance is not prepared to have his theology characterized as "mystical" in any preconceived way: "I am not concerned at all with what textbooks on mysticism or mystical theology are concerned.... What I am concerned with in theology is *humility before God*, not with some special or esoteric way of thinking!... The fact is that I do not work with any so-called mystical tradition. Nor do I operate with some mystical theology, but simply endeavour to try to show that at certain crucial and decisive points where humility in thinking, or, if you like, some form of apophatic thinking, is in place."[58]

In responding to claims that he espouses a form of mysticism, Torrance once remarked, "I find the word 'mystical' rather strange, for I have very rarely spoken of mysticism or of mystical knowledge."[59] This leads us to ask directly: How exact is Torrance's definition of mysticism, and what is it he rejects so rigorously? In addressing the latter of these questions, Richardson identifies the following aspects of mysticism rejected by Torrance: "First and foremost, it means that there is no mystical knowing of God apart from or beyond Christ

---

55. "Apophatic" is used in a weak sense, not in the stronger or literal sense of much Eastern Orthodoxy. Vladimir Lossky, *Orthodox Theology: An Introduction*, trans. I. and I. Kasarcodi-Watson (1978; reprint Crestwood, NY: St. Vladimir's Seminary Press, 2001), 13.

56. Torrance, *Reality and Scientific Theology* (Edinburgh: Scottish Academic, 1985), 123.

57. James Houston in a Regent College lecture called Torrance an evangelical mystic (J. M. Houston, "Traditions of Spirituality—A Historical Overview: Lecture Two: 'Reflections on Mysticism—How Valid is Evangelical Mysticism?'" lecture at Regent College, Vancouver, 1990, cited in Yeung, *Being and Knowing*, 191), as did Kurt Richardson, "Revelation, Scripture, and Mystical Apprehension of Divine Knowledge," in *The Promise of Trinitarian Theology: Theologians in Dialogue with T. F. Torrance*, ed. E. M. Colyer (Lanham, MD: Rowman & Littlefield, 2001),185–203.

58. Torrance, "Thomas Torrance Responds," in *The Promise of Trinitarian Theology: Theologians in Dialogue with T. F. Torrance,*ed. E. M. Colyer (Lanham, MD: Rowman & Littlefield, 2001), 328–29.

59. Ibid., 324. What Torrance takes Richardson to mean is that "mystical" really means intuitive knowledge, or non-logical knowing that arises under the constraint of reality upon the mind, as was typified by the scientific work of Albert Einstein and James Clerk Maxwell. This definition Torrance is prepared to accept, but not the label "mysticism."

. . . . Second, the gnostic path of mystic speculation is also closed in that its metaphysical pattern simply does not correspond to whom God truly is as known in Jesus Christ . . . . Finally, the classical philosophical path that is determined to place the impersonal cosmos and its ultimate forces and truths ahead of the personal and living God as revealed in Scripture is also a mystical path bypassed by Torrance."[60]

Mysticism can be characterized quite simply as a search for an experience of immediacy with God.[61] One could go further and say that true *Christian* mysticism, if it is to be Christian at all, is a direct consequence of a doctrine of the Trinity.[62] This form of mysticism would appear to be entirely congruent with Torrance's theology, in that the mystic is not content to know about God but longs for communion with and participation in the life of the triune God.[63] According to Louth, the very heart of mysticism is "the search for God, or the ultimate, for His own sake, and an unwillingness to be satisfied with anything less than Him; the search for immediacy with this object of the soul's longing."[64] Important in this definition is the essential place union with God occupies. The French reformist theologian Jean Gerson (1363–1429) defined mystical theology as an "experiential knowledge of God attained through the union of spiritual affection with Him. Through this union the words of the Apostle are fulfilled: 'He who clings to God is one spirit with Him' (1 Cor 6.17)."[65] Dennis Tamburello draws several important points from this. First, this definition of mysticism rejects any interpretation that would argue that "a soul loses itself and its creaturely being and receives true divine being, so that it is no longer a creature nor does it see and love God through creaturely existence."[66]

---

60. Richardson, "Revelation, Scripture, and Mystical Apprehension of Divine Knowledge," 193.

61. See for instance: Andrew Louth, *The Origins of the Christian Mystical Tradition: From Plato to Denys* (Oxford: Clarendon, 1981), xv.

62. This is the basic position of James Houston in "Spirituality and the Doctrine of the Trinity," in *Christ in Our Place: The Humanity of God in Christ for the Reconciliation of the World: Essays Presented to Professor James Torrance*, ed. T. A. Hart and D. P. Thimell (Exeter: Paternoster, 1981), 48–69. See B. Demarest, *The Cross and Salvation* (Wheaton, IL: Crossway, 1997), 340–41.

63. In line with Torrance's thought, Houston, "Spirituality and the Doctrine of the Trinity," 67, concludes that "A real knowledge of God can only be participatory knowledge . . . . Since God exhausts all our definitions of himself, and indeed overturns them when we try to put him within them, we can only seek by his Spirit to 'know him' as the Reality and Substance that *is*."

64. Louth, *The Origins of the Christian Mystical Tradition*, xv.

65. Selections from *A Deo exivit, Contra curiositatem studentium*, and *De mystica theologia speculative*, 64–65, cited in D. E. Tamburello, *Union With Christ: John Calvin and the Mysticism of St. Bernard* (Louisville: Westminster John Knox, 1994), 11. Gerson's definition reflects a genuine medieval usage of the term and also brings out the focus on "union with God" that is central to mysticism.

This immediately rules out any notions of a literal "essential union" between creature and Creator. Second, union with God always has a noetic component. While the mode of mystical union will always be experiential, it is no less than an experiential knowledge that is in view.

It is well known that the formative period for mysticism in Christian history was the first five centuries. It is not coincidental that the first five centuries were also the formative period for theology; mysticism and theology have often been bound together, particularly within patristic theology. Athanasius and Gregory of Nyssa are prime examples of those who express both. Considering the importance Torrance affords Athanasius within the history of Christian thought, Torrance's supposed aversion to all forms of mysticism is somewhat surprising. One would have at least expected Torrance to side with a nuanced mystical theology in the Alexandrian-Nicene tradition. Apparently in his haste to correct what he perceived to be false forms of mysticism, Torrance tended to emphasize noetic union to the relative neglect of mystical and spiritual union. In so doing, Torrance actually undermined his attempt to construct a truly relational ontology through participatory knowledge. He thus weakened his attempt at a thoroughly christocentric, Trinitarian, and unified scientific dogmatics.

In light of Louth's and Gerson's definitions of mysticism, it is obvious that Torrance is not rejecting *these* forms of mystical apprehension. By rejecting mysticism *tout court,* Torrance's articulation of the Christian life, theology, and spirituality is weakened if not obfuscated. This leads me to conclude that Torrance has adopted a partial and inaccurate definition of mysticism, which leads him to an *a priori* exclusion of mystical elements within his own theology at precisely the points at which it should be most evident, and, I may add, most helpful.

Torrance speaks of knowledge of God that is sacramental in nature. By "sacramental" knowledge Torrance means the truth of God that is communicated to us in the form of mystery (*mystērion*).[67] Torrance adopts the concept of mystery in theology from Barth. "By 'mystery' Barth does not refer to anything a-logical or irrational, but on the contrary to full, complete and self-sufficient rationality, the rationality of God, who is so fully rational that he does

---

66. Ibid., 11.
67. Torrance uses the category of mystery on numerous occasions in his published works: Torrance: *Conflict and Agreement in the Church, Vol. 1: Order and Disorder* (London: Lutterworth, 1959), 265; *Conflict and Agreement in the Church, Vol. 2: The Ministry and the Sacraments of the Gospel* (London: Lutterworth, 1960), 82–92; *Theological Science*(reprint, Edinburgh: T&T Clark, 1996), 149–50; and *Reality and Evangelical Theology*(Philadelphia: Westminster, 1982), 140–45.

not need to be interpreted in terms of anything outside of himself."[68] Torrance adds, "'Mystery' of this kind expresses the objective depth of rationality . . . . . Mystery means that our knowledge contains far more than we can ever specify or reduce to clear cut, that is, delimited, notions or conceptions, and is concerned with a fullness of meaning which by its very nature resists and eludes all attempts to reduce it without remainder, as it were, to what we can formulate or systematize."[69] This form of mystery elicits recognition, reverence, openness of mind, and wonder.[70] However, Torrance fails to recognize that mystery of this kind is inherently Christian *mysticism*.

Torrance wants to preserve the ontological gulf between God and humanity and yet maintain the relational unity of the two in Jesus Christ, and rightly so. This, however, is best achieved not by a rejection of mysticism, but (as is the case in Athanasius and Gregory of Nyssa) by a rejection of *non-Christian* senses of mysticism. In rejecting forms of mysticism incompatible with the gospel, Torrance could have made good use of the language and reality evident within some forms of a distinctly Christian mysticism and affirmed certain strands of the Christian tradition that he tended to pass over with undue haste.

Like Barth before him, Torrance sees the mystery of God's self-revelation in Jesus Christ as the heart of Christian theology. According to Barth, God is made known as the One who is unknowable.[71] In line with Rahner, there are three fundamental mysteries of Christian theology: the mystery of the Trinity, the incarnation, and the divinization of humanity in grace and glory.[72] We see in these three mysteries a direct parallel to the concerns of Torrance, the essence of whose theology may tentatively be stated as the mystery of the Trinitarian God who loves us in Christ by the Spirit and calls us to participate in this mystery through Christ by the Spirit. For this reason, mystical themes are clearly present throughout Torrance's theology.

---

68. Torrance, *Karl Barth: An Introduction to His Early Theology, 1910–1931* (Edinburgh: T&T Clark, 2000), 82.

69. Torrance, *Theological Science*, 150.

70. See Torrance, *Space, Time and Resurrection* (Edinburgh: Handsel, 1976), 193.

71. "God Himself veils Himself and in the very process—which is why we should not dream of intruding into the mystery—unveils Himself." Karl Barth, *Church Dogmatics*, I/1, trans. G. W. Bromiley, ed. G. W. Bromiley and T. F. Torrance, 2nd ed. (Edinburgh: T&T Clark, 1975), 192. Through the incarnation this unveiling through veiling takes place. One is reminded of Luther's comments of the theology of the cross and the *Deus absconditus*. See G. O. Forde, *On Being a Theologian of the Cross* (Grand Rapids: Eerdmans, 1997).

72. Karl Rahner, *Theological Investigations, Vol. IV: More Recent Writings*, trans. K. Smyth (London: Darton, Longman and Todd, 1974), 73.

Yeung argues that a fuller treatment of the concept of mystery within Torrance's theology would reduce his tendency toward over-intellectualism.[73] While the charge of over-intellectualism may not in fact be accurate,[74] Yeung's call for a more sustained treatment of mystery within Torrance's work is welcome, and his own work contributes to addressing this lacuna. However, Yeung does not distinguish Torrance's definition of illegitimate, namely Platonic (*Mystik*), forms of mysticism from legitimate Athanasian mysticism that sees the path to wonder and awe following knowledge, not bypassing it (*Mysticismus*). In Torrance's modifying and guarding his language about mysticism, we are reminded of Barth's reticence toward mysticism as well when he states that we should never use the term mysticism "unless we state precisely what we have in view when we speak of 'mysticism'—and it would have to be a mysticism *sui generis* in this context."[75] Taking into account what it is precisely that Torrance wants to affirm and what it is precisely he wishes to reject, one may tentatively suggest that Torrance is a mystical theologian—*sui generis*.[76]

---

73. J. H-K. Yeung, *Being and Knowing: An Examination of T. F. Torrance's Christological Science*(Hong Kong: China Alliance, 1996), 192.

74. I am reminded of the similar charge against Calvin that his theology was purely noetic and intellectual. With Dowey I note the similarities to Torrance's work: "one of the most common rebukes leveled against Calvin is that he overintellectualized the Christian faith. Some of the sting of this rebuke—some, if not all—will be removed when we discover what Calvin meant by knowledge, particularly knowledge of God. The word knowledge, we may say in anticipation and in apparent contradiction, is not purely noetic in Calvin's theology, and therefore its ubiquity is not *ipso facto*evidence of an intellectualized faith." Edward A. Dowey, *The Knowledge of God in Calvin's Theology* (New York: Columbia University Press, 1952), 3.

75. Karl Barth, *Church Dogmatics*,IV/3.2, trans. G. W. Bromiley, ed. G. W. Bromiley and T. F. Torrance (Edinburgh: T&T Clark, 1961), 539.

76. What Richardson styles "mystical realism." Kurt Richardson, "Revelation, Scripture, and Mystical Apprehension of Divine Knowledge," in *The Promise of Trinitarian Theology: Theologians in Dialogue with T. F. Torrance*, ed. E. M. Colyer (Lanham, MD: Rowman & Littlefield, 2001), 195.

6

Integrative Theology
God, World, Humanity

A central feature of Torrance's dogmatics is the integrated nature of his thought. This feature makes Torrance's work systematic, in the sense that each of the theological loci in his dogmatics is coordinated and offers a comprehensive and coherent body of knowledge. A failure to understand this feature of his work accounts for a number of misunderstandings of his dogmatics by some, and a failure to perceive the profound depths of his theology by others. In this chapter I examine his integrated and coordinated concepts of God, the world, and humanity in order to illustrate this central point and to explore one area of his thought that has received little attention to date in the scholarly literature.

GOD AND CREATION

Christian discussions regarding creation are not new; they are central to theological discourse. Theologians throughout the Great Tradition have sought to articulate the relationship between the Creator and the creation and have done so in a bewildering variety of ways. Many of these presentations have been insightful and rewarding exercises, while others have been either too speculative to be of any lasting significance to the Christian community or, more often, have been *a*theological. By *a*theological I mean they lack sufficient foundation in Scripture or are christologically anemic.[1] More recently, with the turn to science, many theologians have sought to rearticulate the Creator-creature relationship, this time using scientific categories and insights. Many have done so to good effect, while others have tended to capitulate theology to science in a way that results in a "God-of-the-gaps" cosmology. As we have

---

1. As one example, see my critical review of Christopher Southgate, "Review Article: *The Groaning of Creation: God, Evolution, and the Problem of Evil*," *American Theological Inquiry* 3 (2010): 108–13.

seen, throughout his long publishing career of over 600 works, Torrance sought to construct a scientific theology. In so doing, he sought to clarify the Creator-creature relationship in detail.

While Torrance is clearly a major force on the contemporary theological landscape, his work is relatively unexamined in terms of its potential for both development and critique. With this in mind, a study of Torrance's doctrine of creation and how it is related to redemption provides a window into his theology as a whole and in turn invites further critique and development. This chapter attempts to do this by examining his oft-repeated phrase that "creation is proleptically conditioned by redemption." In order to bring out the distinctive contribution Torrance makes in this area, his work is brought into dialogue with that of Wolfhart Pannenberg, one who also worked long and hard to develop the theological link between God and the world.

A TRIADIC COMPLEX OF RELATIONS

Fundamental to a doctrine of creation is the assumption that, as Torrance begins his work *Reality and Evangelical Theology*, "It is distinctive of Christian theology that it treats of God in his relation to the world and of God in his relation to himself, not of one without the other."[2] Torrance makes it clear that Creator and creation must be thought of in vital relation to each other. More specifically, "Our evangelical commitment to Jesus Christ 'through whom and for whom the whole universe has been created,' as Paul expressed it, will not allow us to divorce redemption from creation, but compels us to give the empirical reality of the created order its full and proper place in theological interpretation of divine revelation, especially in the incarnate form and reality in Jesus Christ."[3] The nature of the specific form of this relationship between creation and redemption is the all-important issue at hand.

Torrance envisages a realist theology as operating within a triadic structure. The specific form this complex of relations takes for Torrance is that of God—world—humanity. It is not simply God—humanity, as has so often been the case in formal, especially evangelical, theology; nor is it God—world, as is so often apparent in many of the contemporary ecological approaches.[4]

---

2. Torrance, *Reality and Evangelical Theology* (Philadelphia: Westminster, 1982), 21.

3. Ibid., 11.

4. Ibid., 25. Within Reformed theology there has always been an attempt to relate God, humanity, *and the world* together. One example is clearly evident in discussions over the re-creation or renewing of the earth at the eschaton, which Jürgen Moltmann has taken up with such vigor. See *The Trinity and the Kingdom*, trans. M. Kohl (San Francisco: Harper & Row, 1981); and *The Spirit of Life: A Universal Affirmation*, trans. M. Kohl (Minneapolis: Fortress, 1992).

We cannot speak of God except within the world in which God has placed us, and the world of which humanity is, by divine creation, a primary constituent element. Hence anthropology and creation are not two independent loci of theology; rather, a doctrine of creation is the locus of anthropological reflection. Put another way, anthropology is a focus of the doctrine of creation. As a concise summary we read: "Theologically speaking, man and the universe belong together and together constitute what we mean by 'world', the world in its relation to God."[5]

Following similar lines of inquiry, Wolfhart Pannenberg states in the opening of the second volume of his *Systematic Theology*:

> The doctrine of creation traces the existence of the world to God as its origin by moving from the reality of God to the existence of a world. It does so by means of the concept of divine action. Only thus do we arrive at the definition of the divine origin of the world as creation. The world is the product of an act of God. To say this is to make a momentous statement about the relation of the world to God and of God to the world. If the world has its origin in a free act of God, it does not emanate by necessity from the divine essence or belong by necessity to the deity of God. It might not have existed. Its existence is thus contingent. It is the result and expression of a free act of divine willing and doing. Unlike the Son, it is not in eternity the correlate of God's being as the Father.[6]

This approach becomes all the more evident when humanity is considered in light of the eternal Word of God who became incarnate and is identified as the one through whom creation exists. In this way, Jesus Christ becomes central to our doctrines of creation and anthropology. Given this triadic relation of God—world—humanity, we must examine the role of creation through the specific sort of relations that exist between such a complex of relations. With Pannenberg we may affirm, "Creating is simply the first step in an economy of divine action that includes and expresses God's relation to the world in all its aspects."[7] Pannenberg is thinking specifically of creation as it relates to reconciliation, redemption, and consummation. Eastern Orthodoxy evidences hints in the same direction when, for example, Panayiotis Chrestou states: "The world and man had a definite destiny in God's creations, namely, to partake of

---

5. Torrance, *Reality and Evangelical Theology*, 25.
6. Wolfhart Pannenberg, *Systematic Theology*, vol. 2 (Grand Rapids: Eerdmans, 1994), 1.
7. Ibid., 2:8.

the goodness and glory of God, which is possible only through communion with him."[8] Dumitru Stăniloae, another Orthodox theologian, expresses it thus: "The human being cannot exist apart from his relationship with nature. The three together make an inseparable whole: I-Thou-Nature."[9] This moves both Chrestou and Stăniloae beyond Barth's I-thou notion (via Buber) of constitutive relationality toward the "exocentrism" of Pannenberg[10] and the Trinitarian doctrine of creation found in the work of Torrance.

TRINITARIAN CREATION

We must specifically ask how Creator and creation are related to one another. Creation is a work of the triune God in which all three persons have a distinctive part to play; thus it will help to analyze the Trinitarian basis of creation in order to clarify the purpose of creation. In order to present a Trinitarian account of creation, Torrance accepts and expounds the formula derived from Basil that states that creation is *from* the Father, *through* the Son, and *in* the Holy Spirit.[11] He then offers his own creative insights in order to extend this formula and the theology it seeks to express.

According to Torrance, "The fact that God is always Father, not always Creator, but *became* Creator, means that it is precisely *as Father* that he is Creator."[12] From this axiom Torrance derives certain Trinitarian corollaries. As Torrance phrases it, "it is then of this one God in his intrinsically *homoousial* and *perichoretic* relations as Father, Son and Holy Spirit, that we are to think of him as Sovereign Creator."[13] From this basis, we may work out the relative

---

8. Panayiotis Chrestou, *Partakers of God*(Brookline, MA: Holy Cross Orthodox Press, 1984), 41.

9. Dumitru Stăniloae, *The Experience of God: Orthodox Dogmatic Theology, Vol. 2: The World: Creation and Deification*, trans. and ed. I. Ionita and R. Barringer (Brookline, MA: Holy Cross Orthodox Press, 2000), 198.

10. See F. LeRon Shults, "Constitutive Relationality in Anthropology and Trinity: The Shaping of the Imago Dei Doctrine in Barth and Pannenberg," *NZST* 39 (1997): 304–22.

11. See Basil, *De Spiritu Sancto* 16:37–40. This has become a standard theological way of describing the creating work of the triune God in recent theology. For a similar exploration, see Stanley J. Grenz, *Theology for the Community of God* (Carlisle: Paternoster, 1994), 133–39; Colin E. Gunton, *The Triune Creator: A Historical and Systematic Study*(Grand Rapids: Eerdmans, 1998); Torrance, *The Christian Doctrine of God: One Being Three Persons*(Edinburgh: T&T Clark, 1996), 203–4; and *Theology in Reconstruction*(Eugene, OR: Wipf and Stock, 1996), 221.

12. Torrance, *The Christian Doctrine of God*, 209. Torrance's conception of the relations that exist between God—God and God—world has certain affinities to Pannenberg. Like Pannenberg, Torrance works out a thoroughly Trinitarian framework for the creation and finds the basis of the creation not in any external act of God confined to the economy, but in the perichoretic being of God in the immanent Trinity. Pannenberg, *Systematic Theology*(Grand Rapids: Eerdmans, 1994), 2:20–35.

distinctions in God's threefold activity, appropriate to the persons of the Father, Son, and Holy Spirit in relation to the Pauline doxology of 2 Cor. 13:14: "The grace of the Lord Jesus Christ, and the love of God, and the fellowship of the Holy Spirit, be with you all."

The activity of God the Father is one of love that is *ecstatic* both in the intra-Trinitarian relations and in God's external acts in the economy of creation. The reason for creation is traced back to the love of God. It is of the nature of God to will to exist for others, and it is out of this divine love that the rational order of the creation is to be understood. "It is this Holy Lawful Divine Love that constitutes the ultimate invariant ground of all rational and moral order in the created universe, and it is under its constraint that all physical and moral laws functioning within the universe operate and are in the last resort to be recognised and formulated."[14] The order inherent in creation is a result, according to Torrance, of the prior love of God. Love therefore is a constituent element of contingent creation universally, not just of human creation specifically.

From this basis in the divine love of the Father comes the purpose of the created realm, most vividly epitomized in the ability of human beings to return God's love for them in a fitting response of love for God. "It belongs in particular to the role of man and woman whom God has created after his own image, and made the crown of his creation, to bear witness to that Glory and serve the purpose of God's wonderful Love."[15] It is important to note, however, that men and women are to gather up the praises of *all* creation, not simply that of their own kind. There is something in or about the universe that must be fulfilled, completed, or perfected, and this perfection, or better, maturity, can come about in no other way than by glorifying the Creator God as *Father*. To acknowledge a Creator is one step, but it is not the highest step, as we have seen in our prior discussion on natural theology. To acknowledge the Creator specifically as the *Father* of the eternal Son by the Holy Spirit is central to Torrance's conception of creational maturity. Properly speaking, however, the Father is only the Father of our blessed Lord Jesus Christ. For men and women to know and call God *Father* is, therefore, not simply to know God as Creator, but to know God through the intimate relationship that only properly exists with the Son by the Spirit. But this is to anticipate the future development of a participation in the Father-Son relationship by the

---

13. Torrance, *The Christian Doctrine of God*, 212. Cf. Elmer M. Colyer, *How To Read T. F. Torrance: Understanding His Trinitarian and Scientific Theology* (Downers Grove, IL: InterVarsity, 2001), 162.

14. Ibid., 213.

15. Ibid.

Spirit, which Torrance develops as a consequence of his doctrine of creation, something already touched upon in Torrance's mystical theology in chapter five.[16]

The economic activity of God the Son proceeds in tandem with that of God the Father, albeit in a distinctive way. The Son incarnate in Jesus Christ is the Word and Wisdom of God, the one through whom all that is has come to be and who sustains the creation itself. He is the one who has imparted to the universe its rational order and has come to restore it to the law of God's divine love. Scripture paints a grand picture of the reordering of a fallen world in or through the incarnate Son as *omnipotent grace*. In the identity and mission of Jesus Christ the purposes of God for all of creation, especially humanity, are realized. "Through his cross and resurrection the incarnate Saviour penetrated into the ontological depths of creation where in death created being borders upon non-being, and set it upon an altogether new basis, that of Grace in the triumph of God's Holy Love in what the Bible speaks of as a new heaven and a new earth."[17] The goal of creation is thus conceived as a communion with the triune God.[18]

By this means the interrelation between Christology and soteriology on the one hand, and eschatology and cosmology on the other, is achieved. A new, redeemed humanity necessitates a new, redeemed cosmology. Both are inherent to the creation and to the goal of creation. Not only are men and women to commune with God, to become one with God in an appropriate relationship, but so too is the entire creation; the cosmos as a whole is drawn into a relationship with God, albeit in a distinctive way. In the first creation account in Genesis the earth and all that is in it is described as "good" (Gen. 1:25)—good because it is able to perform the function for which it was created. However, it is only after the creation of humanity—male and female—that creation is said to be "*very* good" (Gen. 1:31).

The perfect human, and the one to whom the title "very good" most appropriately belongs, is of course Jesus Christ. Colossians 1:15-20 establishes the fact that creation is from Christ and for Christ, while Phil. 2:5-11 highlights the fact that Christ alone is the one worthy of exaltation, and given the "name which is above every name." The confession that the Son is the principle or rationale of creation means that he exemplifies the proper relation of creation to the Creator. The response that creatures owe to the Creator is based in

---

16. See further in Myk Habets, *Theosis in the Theology of Thomas Torrance*, Ashgate New Critical Thinking in Religion, Theology and Biblical Studies (Farnham: Ashgate, 2009).

17. Torrance, *The Christian Doctrine of God*, 214.

18. Thomas F. Torrance, "The Atoning Obedience of Christ," *MTSB* (Fall 1959): 65–66.

the response of the Son to the Father. And once again, this response has its foundation in the intra-Trinitarian relationship, which in turn is exemplified in the incarnate Word, Jesus of Nazareth.

The activity of the Holy Spirit as Creator in union with the Father and Son also takes on a distinctive cast—that of transcendent and unlimited freedom as the *Spiritus Creator*. Torrance envisions the work of the Spirit as creating communion when he writes that "in his outgoing Love and ungrudging Grace God irreversibly binds the created universe to his own Existence and his own Existence to the universe."[19] This is not to imply a pantheistic or panentheistic vision of the relation between God and the world. The creature is always contingent on the Creator as appropriate to creaturely reality. The Holy Spirit binds creation and creatures to God through a holy communion (*koinōnia*), upholding and sustaining creaturely existence beyond its own power in an open-ended relation toward God in whom its true end and purpose is lodged. In Nicene fashion, we may assert the Holy Spirit is "the Lord and Giver of Life," and it is through the presence of the Spirit that we live and move and have our being in God.

As a way of summarizing the distinctive ways in which the triune God creates, Torrance writes:

> The supreme end for which God has designed his creation and which he activates and rules throughout all his relations with it is the purpose of his Holy Love not to live for himself alone but to bring into being a creaturely realm of heaven and earth which will reflect his glory and within which he may share with others the Communion of Love which constitutes his inner Life as Father, Son and Holy Spirit. It is in the incarnation of God's beloved Son in Jesus Christ, and in our sharing in that relation of the Son to the Father through the Holy Spirit, that the secret of the creation, hidden from the ages, has become disclosed to us.[20]

In a summary of the triune creation, Stanley Grenz concurs: "The creation of the world comes as the outflowing of the eternal love relationship within the triune God. More specifically, the Father who eternally loves the Son creates the world in order that it might share in his existence and with the intent that the world reciprocate his love after the pattern of the Son's love for the Father."[21]

---

19. Torrance, *The Christian Doctrine of God*, 217.
20. Ibid., 218. Torrance goes on to quote in full Eph. 1:3-14.
21. Grenz, *Theology for the Community of God*, 138.

Along with more recent trends in theology, the Trinitarian conception of creation outlined above is able to give space to the Spirit as the one who brings creation to its destined end or *telos*.[22] This implies that the Spirit is the *Spiritus Vivificans* who works not only in the church but also throughout the entire world, bringing order out of chaos as in the first creation account, and bringing all things to their providential end—communion with God.

THE "REORDERING" OF CREATION

We may now move beyond the Trinitarian *how* of creation to an investigation of the *purpose* of creation. It is here that Torrance contributes significant and insightful resources for the church, and it is precisely this area that many other accounts of creation simply fail to address. This investigation may be done through an examination of the concept of ordering and reordering and an exploration of the axiom that "creation is proleptically conditioned by redemption."[23] With this phrase there is a direct and explicit link between God the Father as Creator and the person and work of the Son and Spirit in the economy. This is not to be understood simply as a Trinitarian conception of creation; rather, it speaks to the issue of *purpose*. Christology actually conditions the creation in the first place, proleptically influencing its very reality. Our vision of creation must be here, as elsewhere, a christocentric one. Creation is not only *through* Christ, but also *for* Christ. [24] In the incarnation, redemption intersects and overlaps with creation in such a way that all of history is encompassed by Christ and his kingdom. Purpose is deliberately built into creation from the beginning and, as with human beings so with creation itself, perfection is anticipated from the very beginning. Yet this perfection will not come about mechanistically or "naturally," but rather through divine grace—through Christ. As opposed to many other Christian-scientific accounts

---

22. See the seminal essay of D. Lyle Dabney, "Starting with the Spirit: Why the Last Should Now be First," in *Starting with the Spirit*, Task of Theology Today II, ed. S. Pickard and G. Preece (Adelaide: ATF, 2001), 3; and Torrance, "The Atoning Obedience of Christ."

23. See for instance, Torrance, "Introduction," in *The School of Faith: The Catechisms of the Reformed Church*, trans. and ed. with Introduction by T. F. Torrance (London: James Clarke, 1959), ciii; *The Christian Doctrine of God: One Being Three Persons* (Edinburgh: T&T Clark, 1996), 204; *The Trinitarian Faith: The Evangelical Theology of the Ancient Catholic Church* (Edinburgh: T&T Clark, 1995), 102.

24. Alister E. McGrath, *A Scientific Theology, Volume 1: Nature* (Grand Rapids: Eerdmans, 2001),193, perceptively notes: "The Christian understanding of creation leads directly to the conclusion that there is a correspondence – the degree of which requires clarification – between the works of God and the being of God. Creation and redemption are not merely interconnected within the economy of salvation; they can each be argued to embody the character of God."

that tend to leave Christology out of the equation in any meaningful way, this is one of Torrance's more enduring legacies to the church: a robust articulation of the centrality of Christ to a doctrine of creation.

We see this theme echoed within the theology of Torrance's patristic hero, Athanasius, who repeatedly emphasized the connection between creation and redemption. According to Athanasius, the purpose of the incarnation was not only the restoration of humanity but of the whole created order. Accordingly, "It is, then, proper for us to begin the treatment of this subject by speaking of the creation of the universe, and of God its Artificer, that so it may be duly perceived that the renewal of creation has been the work of the self-same Word that made it at the beginning. For it will appear not inconsonant for the Father to have wrought its salvation in Him by Whose means He made it."[25] Athanasius, and in turn Torrance, is adamant on this score: without Christ, creation makes little sense and has no inherent purpose. As Kimlyn Bender has written, "To speak of creation is therefore implicitly yet intentionally to speak not first of a cosmology but of a relation between God and the world."[26] Understood in light of the incarnation, the Creator-creature relationship becomes clear. This insight impels Torrance to adopt the idea that the incarnation proleptically conditions creation, and not the other way around.[27]

In harmony with Athanasius, Torrance adopts a "scientific" approach to theology and considers redemption in terms of the relationship between theology and the natural sciences and the mutuality of their commitment to *order*.[28] As a result of the fall, creation's order has been corrupted, resulting in a radical *disorder*.[29] Torrance argues that atonement can be seen in terms of a *reordering* of creation. This applies to the entire creation, not simply

---

25. Athanasius, *On the Incarnation* 1.4, *NPNF2* 4:273.

26. Kimlyn J. Bender, "Christ, Creation and the Drama of Redemption: 'The Play's the Thing..,'" *SJT* 62 (2009): 150.

27. This does raise the issue regarding the primacy of Christ and supralapsarian Christology, for which one may consult Myk Habets, "On Getting First Things First: Assessing Claims for the Primacy of Christ," *NBf* 90 (2009): 343–64.

28. See Torrance, *Divine and Contingent Order* (reprint, Edinburgh: T&T Clark, 1998), 113–28.

29. Torrance takes up many of Calvin's insights regarding the emphasis on the present disorder of creation as a result of the fall. See Susan Schreiner, *The Theatre of His Glory: Nature and the Natural Order in the Thought of John Calvin* (Durham, NC: Labyrinth, 1991), 97–111.

to humanity.[30] Torrance notes how the universe requires "redemption from disorder":

> In Christian theology that redemption is precisely the bearing of the cross upon the way things actually are in our universe of space and time. It represents the refusal of God to remain aloof from the disintegration of order in what he has made, or merely to act upon it 'at a distance.' It is his decisive personal intervention in the world through the incarnation of his Word and love in Jesus Christ. In his life and passion he who is the ultimate source and power of all order has penetrated into the untouchable core of our contingent existence in such a way as to deal with the twisted force of evil entrenched in it, and thereby to bring about an atoning reordering of creation.[31]

By means of the life of Christ, and especially his resurrection, order was achieved out of disorder.[32] In a similar way to Irenaeus, Torrance considers redemption to entail the restoration of the God-given order in which the cosmos came into being. "Redemption is thus the restoration of humanity, in order that humanity may play its defined role . . . in the restoration of the universe as a whole."[33] Once more the themes of God—world—humanity are kept in creative balance and arrangement.

Because creation is purposive it, no less than human beings, has a *telos*: "Somehow it is not just man who has fallen but the whole created order along with him, so that we may not isolate our understanding of human evil from natural evil, or moral evil from material evil, the pain and suffering of human being from the suffering and misery, the pain and travail of the whole creation."[34] From this Torrance draws the conclusion that "real redemption from the power of human sin and guilt involves a radical change in the material world and calls for the complete redemption of the created order."[35] As with

---

30. An interesting account of the original ordering of creation can be found in Vladimir Lossky, *Orthodox Theology: An Introduction*, trans. I. and I. Kasarcodi-Watson (1978; reprint Crestwood, NY: St. Vladimir's Seminary Press, 2001), 63–70, in which men and women are described as the "summit" and "principle" of creation, the beings to whom is entrusted the ordering of creation.

31. Torrance, *The Christian Frame of Mind:?Reason, Order, and Openness in Theology and Natural Science* (Colorado Springs: Helmers & Howard, 1989), 103. This "disorder" is not simply natural but also extends to moral disorder.

32. Torrance, *Divine and Contingent Order*, 138.

33. Alister E. McGrath, *T. F. Torrance: An Intellectual Biography* (Edinburgh: T&T Clark, 1999), 227.

34. Torrance, *The Christian Doctrine of God*, 226.

35. Ibid.

human beings, the physical creation is created for a *telos*, the new heaven and new earth (Rev. 21:1-5; 22:1-5).[36] Torrance's principle is that "God does not abandon his creation when he has saved man, for all creation, together with man, will be renewed when Christ comes again."[37]

What will this redemption applied to nature look like, beyond merely saying "new heaven and new earth"? One can only speculate based upon the scant biblical references. The outcome, if we accept this grandiose vision of the cosmic consequences of redemption, is that harmony, freedom, and contingency will reach its ultimate fulfillment. Alongside these familiar themes we could go beyond what Torrance has stated to a picture he might also agree with—the perfection of the beauty, artistry, and fecundity of the entire creation. John of Patmos could speak of golden streets, foundations of precious stones, and walls of costly jewels (Rev. 21:19). The natural scientist could perhaps speak of balanced ecosystems, the extinction of extinction itself, and the ordered-yet-free, harmonious-yet-new fulfillment of the natural order. Clearly, we have left behind Newton's mechanistic world or Thomas Moore's Utopia[38] and have entered the land of biblical eschatology. It is a place where God walks with creation in perfect harmony, where the sun has no need to shine for God's presence is manifest in Christ, and where all of creation finds its fulfillment and "rest" in God (Heb. 4:1-11; 1 John 3:19). In Torrance's words:

> God made the creation for such a communion that it might sing His praises and reflect in gladness and joy His loving kindness and glory. Hence the restoration of creation involves the restoration of creation to communion and fellowship with Him in which the peace of God reigns over all, the joy and gladness in God the Father fills the whole of creation. Thus in reconciliation of atonement it is not only with obedience and justice that we have to do, but with the worship and adoration of creation, in which it faithfully reflects the Father's glory and love.[39]

---

36. See Torrance, *Space, Time and Resurrection* (Edinburgh: Handsel, 1976), 155, where this point is made and we are pointed to Karl Barth's *Church Dogmatics*, III/3, trans. G. W. Bromiley and R. J. Ehrlich, ed. G. W. Bromiley and T. F. Torrance (Edinburgh: T&T Clark, 1960), §49, pages 58–288, in which the doctrine of creation and its continuous preservation under the lordship of Christ is discussed.

37. Torrance, *Space, Time and Resurrection*, 155.

38. Along with Moore we could add the utopian visions of Marx, Engels, Bloch, Marcuse, and Levitas. See H. H. Kögler, "Utopianism," in *The Oxford Companion to Philosophy*, ed. T. Honderich (Oxford: Oxford University Press, 1995), 892–93. Clearly the biblical view of the consummation of the world and the entire eschatological vision is inherently *non*-utopian in a literal sense.

39. Torrance, "The Atoning Obedience of Christ," *MTSB* (Fall 1959): 66.

From this principle of reordering Torrance affirms a cosmic extension of redemption, with special emphasis on the redemption of the natural order. The order of redemption "reaches back to the original order of creation and far transcends it in the amazing purpose of the divine love, as the order, of the new creation."[40] Redemption is not an interference with or interruption of the created order, but is a healing or restoration of a damaged (disordered) creation.

Creation is thus, in Calvin's famous words, the theater for God's glory.[41] It is a theater, to extend the metaphor, upon which the drama of redemption is being played out, one day to reach its final act under divine grace. This *theatrum Dei* serves the twofold purpose of glorifying God the Creator and leading God's creation to glorify God. Torrance writes, "The whole of creation is a mirror, a theatre, a world of signs, which God uses in fulfilment of His Covenant relations with men, as the tools and instruments of His Word."[42] Creation and redemption share a mutual history. This presupposes a central axiom, that "creation is conditioned by redemption."[43]

THE NON-LINEAR NATURE OF GOD'S DEALINGS WITH CREATION

How creation is proleptically conditioned by redemption requires some specific elaboration.[44] Torrance maintains that "the incarnation is to be understood as completing the work of creation and of consummating its contingent relation to God. Thus in a certain sense the creation is to be thought of as proleptically conditioned by redemption."[45] Torrance makes this statement amidst a discussion of the contingent nature of creation. Colyer helpfully attempts to

---

40. Torrance, *Conflict and Agreement in the Church, Vol. 2: The Ministry and the Sacraments of the Gospel* (London: Lutterworth, 1960),15. Torrance provides more background to this "new creation" in "The Doctrine of Order," *CQR*160 (1959): 21–36.

41. Calvin, *The Institutes of the Christian Religion*, trans. H. Beveridge (London: James Clarke, 1953), 1.5.8, cf. 1.6.2; 1.14.20; 2.6.1; 3.9.2.

42. Torrance, "Introduction," in *The School of Faith: The Catechisms of the Reformed Church*,trans. and ed. with Introduction by T. F. Torrance (London: James Clarke, 1959), liii.

43. See Torrance, *The Christian Doctrine of God,*204.

44. The idea derives from many of the Fathers, most especially Athanasius in whose work the essential connection between creation and redemption is repeatedly emphasized. See Athanasius, *On the Incarnation*, 1.2 (*NPNF*2 4:272). For a concise overview see P. E. Hughes, *The True Image: The Origin and Destiny of Man in Christ* (Grand Rapids: Eerdmans, 1989), 276–80. We also read that Torrance heard of the idea from H. R. Mackintosh; see Torrance, "Introduction," in *The School of Faith: The Catechisms of the Reformed Church*,trans. and ed. with Introduction by T. F. Torrance (London: James Clarke, 1959), ciii.

45. Torrance, *The Trinitarian Faith: The Evangelical Theology of the Ancient Catholic Church* (Edinburgh: T&T Clark, 1995),102.

summarize his thought on the proleptic nature of creation in the following way: "What Torrance intends, I believe, is that God's ultimate *telos* for creation from the beginning is revealed and actualised in the incarnation, death and resurrection of Christ, a *telos* in which all creation comes to share in the eternal communion of love that God is. This is the ultimate goal of both redemption and creation. It is actually realized in redemption after the Fall, and it is a *telos* that proleptically conditions the creation."[46]

Such a theology has previously been suggested in the Great Tradition, but never worked out with as much acumen as it is by Torrance. Spjuth notes Torrance's application of the hypostatic analogy to creation, such that "the whole universe of creaturely existence" is brought into relationship to the redemption of Christ (the covenant) and thus is appointed to reflect God's glory. Citing Torrance, Spjuth comments, "Here there is a covenanted correspondence between the creation and the Creator."[47] Accordingly, the whole of creation lives by this hypostatic relation to the covenant in a form of created correspondence (analogy).

In Pannenberg we find echoes remarkably similar to Torrance when he writes that "the incarnation cannot be an external appendix to creation nor a mere reaction of the Creator to Adam's sin. From the very first it is the crown of God's world order, the supreme concretion of the active presence of the Logos in creation."[48] And Pannenberg is right. While Torrance does not share Pannenberg's eschatology, nor does he articulate God's so-called "becoming" in the same way, they both share this central conviction: creation is not something unrelated to the incarnation or related simply by some "mistake" on the part of humanity (or worse, a mistake on the part of God!) by which God had to "rescue" creation by means of sending the Son. What Torrance and Pannenberg so convincingly articulate is a doctrine of creation wedded to and subordinate to a doctrine of incarnation so that Christ comes to have first place in everything. In so doing, both theologians provide a christologically robust doctrine of creation that is lacking in many of the scientific treatments of creation by

---

46. Elmer M. Colyer, *How To Read T. F. Torrance: Understanding His Trinitarian and Scientific Theology* (Downers Grove, IL: InterVarsity, 2001),164, n. 34.

47. Roland Spjuth, *Creation, Contingency and Divine Presence: In the Theologies of Thomas F. Torrance and Eberhard Jüngel*(Lund: Lund University Press, 1995),40, citing Torrance, "Introduction," *The School of Faith*, li.

48. Wolfhart Pannenberg, *Systematic Theology,*vol. 2 (Grand Rapids: Eerdmans, 1994), 64. While Pannenberg comes at this from eschatological premises drastically different from those of Torrance, they do share, at this point at least, a remarkable correspondence. See Pannenberg, *Theology and the Kingdom of God*, ed. R. J. Neuhaus (Philadelphia: Westminster, 1969), 67.

pseudo-Redemption and creation thus imply one another, with redemption conditioning creation. After the fall the world is in such a precarious state that the incarnate Son unites its creatureliness to himself in order to save it. Without the incarnation, neither humanity nor creation more generally could reach its intended *telos*. In Torrance's work on the resurrection under the subtitle "the cosmic range of eschatology," we read that "the range of Christ's mighty acts in incarnation, reconciliation and resurrection apply to the whole universe of things, visible and invisible. The whole creation falls within the range of his Lordship, as he works out his purpose by bringing redemption together with creation, and actualizing the holy will of the Father in everything."[49] Christ is central to creation as a whole, not simply to humanity. And this applies to creation in general, not simply to creation after the fall. Creation's *telos* is bound up with the Christ who was crucified before the foundation of the world.

Through the incarnation of the Son of God, in God's taking on human nature, God transfers our creaturely contingent existence into God's own experience, so that Jesus Christ secures the origin and end of creation in his own eternal being.[50] For Torrance, such logic is central to redemption—the participation of men and women in Christ, along with the summing up of all things in Christ: "For by Him all things were created, both in the heavens and on earth, visible and invisible, whether thrones or dominions or rulers or authorities—all things have been created through Him and for Him. He is before all things, and in Him all things hold together" (Col. 1:16-17). With "all things" we must include the entire animate and inanimate creation.

Like Torrance, Pannenberg also works out the cosmic consequences of redemption and builds this around the centrality of Christ whose incarnation conditions creation. It will be useful to compare his articulation of this theme with that of Torrance. In a simple but profound statement Pannenberg summarizes the relation between God and the world: "From the standpoint of Christian theology the participation of creatures in the Trinitarian fellowship of the Son with the Father is the goal of creation."[51] Pannenberg "proves" his point above by applying the christological test: "we see this plainly in the incarnation of the divine Logos in Jesus of Nazareth. For the goal of the event was that all might be reconciled in him (Col 1.20; cf. Eph 1.10)."[52] Importantly,

---

49. Torrance, *Space, Time and Resurrection*(Edinburgh: Handsel, 1976), 155.
50. Torrance, *The Trinitarian Faith*,102.
51. Pannenberg, *Systematic Theology*, 2:73, 137–38. Pannenberg applies this principle not only to humans but to all other creatures as well. What separates humans from other creatures is the fact that "only at the human stage in the sequence of creaturely forms did express distinction come to be seen between God and all creaturely reality" (2:138).

Pannenberg does not restrict redemption to the realm of human creatures but to the whole of creation. In a theological exposition of Rom. 8:19-30, Pannenberg relates the redemption of the human person to that of creation itself, a creation that waits longingly for the manifestation of divine sonship in the human race. "If, however," Pannenberg concludes, "this suffering [the result of the fall] is overcome by the adoption of humans into the filial relation of Jesus to the Father, the relation of nonhuman creatures to their Creator thereby also comes to fulfilment."[53]

In a complex but important discussion of the Trinitarian origin and act of creation, Pannenberg advances a thesis for the contingent but free existence of human persons as predicated on the self-distinction of the Son from the Father. His argument brings together many of the emphases already highlighted, but also enables us to go further than perhaps Torrance does at this point.

> On the Christian view creation can be thought of as God's free act because it does not derive from a necessity that flows one-sidedly from the Father, nor from a mistake of the *Pneuma*, but from the free agreement of the Son with the Father through the Spirit in the act of the Son's self-distinction from the Father, insofar as we have here the transition from the self-distinction of the Son from the Father within the unity of deity to self-distinction from the Father as the one God, and thus to the otherness of a creaturely existence, which is the form of the existence of the Son only in the man Jesus. Thus the Son is the origin of creaturely existence not only as the principle of distinction and self-distinction but also as the link with that which is thus distinct. As in the intratrinitarian life of God the self-distinction of the Son from the Father is the condition of his unity with the Father through the Spirit, so creatures are related to their Creator by their distinction from God and to one another by their distinctions from one another.[54]

Pannenberg continues to apply this logic when he writes:

> In his linkage with the Spirit the Son acts in creation as the principle not merely of the distinction of the creatures but also of their interrelation in the order of creation. In this sense, too, he is the

---

52. Pannenberg, *Systematic Theology*, 2:73.
53. Ibid., 2:73.
54. Ibid., 2:31–32, cf. 2:63.

Logos of creation. He gathers the creatures into the order that is posited by their distinctions and relations and brings them together through himself . . . for participation in his fellowship with the Father. But this takes place only through the Spirit, for the creative work of the Son is linked at every point to that of the Spirit.[55]

What Pannenberg is speaking about in terms of the self-distinction of the eternal Son has affinities with Torrance's discussion on the unfolding of creation, the close connection between creation and redemption, and creation being proleptically conditioned by redemption. While Pannenberg and Torrance do not share a common cosmology they do have enough in common that each may inform the other's work in this area, as I have attempted to do here.

Contemporary theologies of creation consistently point to the Trinitarian act of creation but rarely move on to include the Trinitarian purposes for creation. Torrance and Pannenberg provide ample evidence of what a genuine Christian doctrine of creation requires when articulated in a Trinitarian way.[56] In such a theology Christ remains central as the God-man, and sufficient space remains for the constitutive role of the Holy Spirit in creation, redemption, and eschatology. What is required in theologies of creation today is for theologians and scientists alike to appreciate the force of a statement like Torrance's—"creation is proleptically conditioned by redemption"—in order to tease out the profound implications such a theology has both for dogmatics and science. Torrance encourages theologians to return to a method of inquiry known as *kata physin*, a concept introduced in earlier chapters.

The essential formulation of this was expressed in the great ecumenical creeds of Christendom at Nicaea and Constantinople, formalized in what Torrance describes as the "linchpin of this theology"—the *homoousion*—the confession that Jesus Christ the incarnate Son is of one being or of one substance with God the Father. This is crucial to a truly scientific Christian theology because it provides a realist basis for knowledge of God. Pro-Nicene theology thus gave basic shape to the doctrine of the Trinity and to the intrinsic grammar of Christian thought. The *homoousion* is also what shapes a Christian doctrine of creation, as we have seen.

---

55. Ibid., 2:32.

56. Other outlines worthy of mention include Kathryn Tanner, *God and Creation in Christian Theology: Tyranny or Empowerment?* (Oxford: Blackwell, 1988) and John Webster, "Trinity and Creation," *IJST* 12 (2010): 4–19.

In this manner Torrance moves from method or epistemology to doctrinal and dogmatic material. Jesus Christ reveals very God of very God. God is in God's own being what God is as God's revealing Word and saving act toward us. Through Christ and the Spirit we are given access to God as God is in God's very self. This access to God is, in part, in the form of knowledge of God as God is in God's self, in God's internal relations as Father, Son, and Holy Spirit. The epistemological strength of the *homoousion* works here with full force, for it represents the consubstantial relation between Jesus Christ, the Word made flesh, and God. As the image of God, identical with God's reality, knowledge of the incarnate Son through the Holy Spirit has a unique and controlling finality in knowledge of God.[57]

A Christian doctrine of creation entails an articulation of the relations between God—world—humanity, not simply between God—humanity, as has unfortunately so often been the case. Torrance, and to a lesser extent Pannenberg, develop a Trinitarian conception of God the Creator in which creation is conditioned by redemption, resulting in the reordering of creation from its current state of disorder. Christ is thus central to a Christian view of creation no less than to a Christian view of human redemption. The redemption of men and women occurs in space-time, in the world—a contingent world that is utterly dependent upon God, and a world that, like men and women, also awaits a final redemption. This worldly redemption is inextricably bound to the incarnate Christ, to his image bearers, and to the cosmos God has created and continues to sustain.

---

57. Torrance, *The Ground and Grammar of Theology* (Charlottesville: University of Virginia Press, 1980), 40.

7

Christocentric Theology
The Fallen Humanity of the Son of God

While interest in the historical figure of Jesus of Nazareth is as old as the Gospels themselves (and even before, of course!) contemporary Christology shows a decided concern with the specific issue of the humanity of Jesus, and with it, a reconsideration of his human nature.[1] Torrance is no exception in this wider discussion. While not directly interested in the psychology of Christ, or entering into the "quests" for the historical Jesus (something he was highly critical of), Torrance was concerned to highlight the reality of Jesus' humanity and its *theological* consequences. A direct corollary of Torrance's doctrine of the vicarious humanity of Christ is the rather contentious and often debated issue regarding the relation of the Holy Son of God to our fallen and sinful humanity. Torrance approached this question specifically on a number of occasions and alluded to it on many more.[2] The central issue I address here is how Torrance

---

1. See M. Hellwig, "Re-Emergence of the Human, Critical, Public Jesus," *TS* 50 (1989): 466–80. D. M. Rogich, *Becoming Uncreated: The Journey to Human Authenticity: Updating the Spiritual Christology of Gregory Palamas*(Minneapolis: Light and Life, 1997), 166, is surely right when he remarks, "There seems today to be a Docetism in reverse: a race to see who can proclaim the 'full' humanity of Jesus to the point of ascribing to him not only suffering, doubt, and temptation, but also, as Hans Küng claims, 'the possibility of error.'" The quote comes from H. Kung, *On Being a Christian* (London: Collins, 1977), 449. I. Davidson, "Theologizing the Human Jesus: An Ancient (and Modern) Approach to Christology Reassessed," *IJST* 3 (2001): 129–30, provides further evidence of this scholarly commitment to the humanity of Jesus evident in contemporary theology.

2. For example: Thomas F. Torrance, *Scottish Theology from John Knox to John McLeod Campbell*(Edinburgh: T&T Clark, 1996); *The Doctrine of Jesus Christ: Auburn Lectures 1938–39*(Eugene, OR: Wipf and Stock, 2002), 121–30; "The Atonement: the Singularity of Christ and the Finality of the Cross: The Atonement and the Moral Order," in *Universalism and the Doctrine of Hell*,ed. N. M de S. Cameron (Carlisle: Paternoster, 1992; Grand Rapids: Baker, 1992), 237–39.

answers the question of whether Christ's humanity was of the fallen stock of Adam or of some pristine celestial origin, untouched by the sin of Adam.[3]

Once theologians were pilloried for considering Christ as having a fallen human nature. In the Church of Scotland this was perhaps never more so than when, on March 13, 1833, Edward Irving was found guilty of heresy and deposed from the ministry largely for his espousal of such a view.[4] Just over 100 years later, the Church of Scotland would have a moderator who believed and openly taught the same doctrine! This moderator was Thomas Torrance. In so doing, Torrance believed himself to be appealing to a much older Scottish tradition, a position that has been seriously challenged.[5]

What Torrance meant by the assumption of a fallen or sinful humanity, and what importance this doctrine plays in his dogmatics will be the focus of the chapter, and we shall pursue such questions in critical dialogue with a number of contemporary scholars who take exception to such a theology.

THE HISTORY OF A DOCTRINE

A brief history of how theologians have sought to construe the humanity of Christ is in order before we consider Torrance's contribution to the topic in detail. We will see that Torrance's views were not formed in a vacuum, and that he was developing a theology that has been held within the tradition since the early church. Only when such a historical understanding is achieved

---

3. Throughout the history of Christian thinking the normative status of humanity has most often been ascribed to Adam and Eve in their prelapsarian condition rather than to the humanity of Jesus Christ in his incarnation. This chapter is a continuation of that discussion in many respects, as we examine how Christ could be true man and yet also enter the world with a postlapsarian human nature like the rest of us in order to redeem us. For an overview of the central theological issues, see the excellent work *Persons, Divine and Human*, ed. C. Schwöbel and C. E. Gunton (Edinburgh: T&T Clark, 1991).

4. See the history of the controversy in C. Gordon Strachan, *The Pentecostal Theology of Edward Irving*(London: Darton, Longman and Todd, 1973).

5. Donald Macleod, "Dr. T. F. Torrance and Scottish Theology: A Review Article [*Scottish Theology from John Knox to John McLeod Campbell*, 1996]," *EvQ*72 (2000): 57–72, see especially 68–71. Also one may listen to a discussion between Torrance and Macleod over the work *Scottish Theology*: Donald MacLeod, "Review of Scottish Theology by Tom Torrance," Tape 198; Thomas Torrance, "Reply to Donald Macleod," Tape 199; and "Thomas Torrance and Donald Macleod Dialogue," Tape 200 (Edinburgh: Rutherford House, 1999, http://tapesfromscotland.org/Rutherfordhouseaudio.htm). The other major contemporary critic of this position from within Reformed theology is Oliver D. Crisp, "Did Christ Have a *Fallen* Human Nature?" *IJST*6 (2004): 270–88; *Divinity and Humanity: The Incarnation Reconsidered*(Cambridge: Cambridge University Press, 2007), 162–206; "Was Christ Sinless or Impeccable?" *ITQ*72 (2007): 168–86; and *God Incarnate: Explorations in Christology*(London: T&T Clark, 2009), 122–36.

will Torrance's contribution to the issue of the fallen humanity of Christ be appreciated.

PATRISTIC VIEWS CONSIDERED

The literature of the patristic era relating to the humanity of Christ is almost unanimous in understanding that it was essential for Jesus to become what we are in order for fallen human persons to become partakers of God.[6] This common belief was encapsulated by the phrase, "What is not assumed is not healed,"[7] a phrase that summarizes the soteriological principle employed by the Fathers: only if Jesus assumed a humanity equivalent with the fallen race of Adam could Jesus' death and resurrection heal and save that humanity.[8] Irenaeus expressed this clearly when he referred to Jesus as "the Word of God, our Lord Jesus Christ, who did, through His transcendent love, become what we are, that He might bring us to be even what He is Himself."[9] The question to be asked is this: Did this soteriological phrase assert that Jesus assumed a *fallen* or sinful human nature or not?

ATHANASIUS (AND TORRANCE) ON DIVINE AGENCY

The dominant concept of the Alexandrian Christology that Torrance is so heavily influenced by is that the divine Word or eternal Son determines the human life of Jesus directly or immediately, rather than indirectly by means of the Holy Spirit. With Irenaeus, Athanasius posited a very real and direct union of God with humanity in the person of Christ.[10] The Arian counter-claim was that if the Logos is truly God, the Gospel portrait of Christ does not

---

6. Just some examples include Irenaeus, *Adversus haereses*,3.18.7 (*ANF* 1:890–91) and Cyril of Jerusalem, *Catechesis,* 12.15 (*NPNF*2 7:223). Two exceptions would include Clement of Alexandria, *Stromata,* 6.9 (*ANF* 2:998–1002) and Hilary of Poitiers, *De Trinitate*,10.23–25 (*NPNF*2 8:505–8).

7. Literally: "For that which He has not assumed He has not healed; but that which is united to His Godhead is also saved." Gregory of Nazianzus, *Ep*.101 (*NPNF*2 7:830).

8. See the unpacking of this phrase by Maurice Wiles, "The Unassumed is the Unhealed," *RelS* 4 (1968): 47–56.

9. Irenaeus, *Adversus haereses,* 5, pref. (*ANF* 1:1047–48). Torrance provides extensive support from the Fathers for the belief that Christ assumed a fallen human nature in his incarnation. See Torrance, *The Trinitarian Faith*, 161–68. Thomas G. Weinandy, *In the Likeness of Sinful Flesh: An Essay on the Humanity of Christ*(Edinburgh: T&T Clark, 1993), 21–38, comes to the same conclusions from his reading of patristic Christology. Macleod disagrees completely. According to his reading the Fathers merely meant Christ assumed a human nature, will, soul, and mind in contrast to the threat of Apollinarianism. See Donald Macleod, "Christology," in *Dictionary of Scottish History and Theology,*ed. D. F. Wright, D. C. Lachman, and D. E. Meek (Edinburgh: T&T Clark, 1993), 175, and *The Person of Christ*(Leicester: Inter-Varsity, 1998), 224–25.

fit.¹¹ The Gospel witness is that Christ hungered, thirsted, evidenced emotions, and showed intellectual ignorance, even cognitive dissonance from God his Father. These are not traits of God but of a creature. The Arians (and much of the early church) assumed that the Logos was the sole real subject in Jesus, or alternatively, that Jesus was simply the Logos with a body.¹²

In *Orations Against the Arians,* book three, Athanasius seeks to answer these difficulties and so posits a difference between the "Logos in himself" and the "Logos in the incarnate state." Athanasius allows for the humanity of Jesus as evidenced in the Gospels, manifestly sharing the Arians' view of the person of Jesus but not their view of the Logos.¹³ However, when it came to accounting for the humanity of Jesus Christ in the Gospels, he had problems. Athanasius does not dismiss the humanity of Christ; on the contrary, he includes passage after passage where he takes it seriously. ¹⁴ However, he has no conceptual basis in which to fully justify the full humanity of Christ. While certainly not a Docetist or Apollinarian, he could not adequately account for Jesus' human nature.¹⁵ As Gunton remarked, "While it is unfair . . . to charge Athanasius with anticipations of Apollinaris, his language is undoubtedly guarded at times . . . . To that extent, Sellars is justified in commenting that the humanity of

---

10. And so rejected Origen's emanationism. Thomas G. Weinandy, *Does God Change? The Word's Becoming in the Incarnation*(Petersham, MA: St. Bede's, 1985), 14–16.

11. Athanasius, *Contra Arianos,* 3.37 (*NPNF2*4:1009–10). The Arians asked "How could he (Logos), being God, become man?"

12. This is an extreme form of Logos-sarx Christology. The Logos takes the place of the soul and is united to the flesh in such a way that it becomes the principle of Jesus' existence.

13. Weinandy, *Does God Change?* 21–38.

14. *Contra Arianos,* 1.46ff.; 2.10ff. (*NPNF2* 4:859–60; 899–900).

15. Because Athanasius held that the Logos was incarnated he insists, against the Arians, that all the human attributes must be predicated of him. The fact that Athanasius held unswervingly to the true humanity and true divinity of Jesus is not in question. His ability to speak of these two is seriously questioned. Athanasius, *Contra Arianos,*3.32, 34 (*NPNF2*4:1004–5; 1006–7). The Athanasian scholar Alvyn Pettersen notes a lack of detail about the incarnation, or the humanity of Christ. He writes, "Athanasius treats the incarnation, at times, almost in passing, in that his main interest is God's wholly gracious salvation of humanity, secured through the incarnation." A. Pettersen, *Athanasius* (London: Geoffrey Chapman, 1995), 109. He can also speak of Athanasius's Christology as "somewhat Docetic," 105 (cf. 121). However, Pettersen accounts for this lack of interest in the specifics of the human life of Christ in this way: "Athanasius is not primarily concerned with the anthropology of the incarnation; his interest is the 'why' rather than the 'what' of Christ's humanity," 105, and again, "In his [Christ's] dispelling ignorance, lightening suffering and conquering death, there is the divinising of everyone in Christ. What superficially may appear to be inchoate Docetism is in fact pervasive soteriology," 126. See the helpful discussion of Athanasian "Docetism" or lack thereof in K. Anatolios, *Athanasius: The Coherence of his Thought* (London: Routledge, 1998), 70–73.

Jesus lacks historical particularity in Athanasius. It is not that the saviour is less than human: he took a body 'of no different sort from ours', and Athanasius's soteriological teaching depends upon it. It is rather that there is relative lack of interest in what we might call the lineaments of the human story."[16]

As I will show, Torrance's Christology suffers from the same deficiency, or at least "lack of interest" at this point. This is largely because Torrance self-consciously seeks to work primarily with the third and highest level of theology—the ontological—rather than the lowest level, the evangelical. It is evangelical theology, thus understood, that is most concerned with the details of the Gospel story concerning the particulars of the human life of Christ, his psychology, and history. Torrance is concerned with the humanity of God as a theological principle, the *homoousios,* and what this means for theology. While this explains Torrance's minimal treatment of the details of Jesus' human life on earth, it does not excuse it.

In discussing Athanasius's high view of Christ's real humanity, Torrance includes many direct quotations where Athanasius states that Christ received a true human nature like ours. He does this in order to show that Athanasius believed Christ assumed a fallen human nature like ours.[17] In so doing, Torrance acknowledges that his view of Athanasius's Christology is at odds with what he calls the "familiar text books."[18] While we concede that Athanasius did make space for the humanity of Jesus as *homoousios* with us, we still conclude that he was unable to adequately account for the two natures in the one person under his Christological construct.[19] The same basic problem is found within Torrance's theology.

Weinandy observed that "the real problem resides in Athanasius's inability to state in one consistent conceptual framework both the ontological nature of the union and the distinction that must necessarily be made in order to ensure the integrity of the Logos, and of the humanity."[20] This is well stated. The crux of the problem, as Kelly rightly highlights, is whether Athanasius holds that

---

16. Colin E. Gunton, "Two Dogmas Revisited: Edward Irving's Christology," *SJT* 41 (1988): 359.

17. Torrance, *Theology in Reconciliation: Essays Towards Evangelical and Catholic Unity in East and West*(reprint, Eugene, OR: Wipf and Stock, 1997), 151–56.

18. See the helpful historical review of the issues in Kelly M. Kapic, "The Son's Assumption of a Human Nature: A Call for Clarity," *IJST* 3 (2001): 154–66, who includes useful material from contemporary Eastern Orthodox theologians as well.

19. Alan Spence comes to the same conclusions in his essay "Christ's Humanity and Ours: John Owen," in *Persons, Divine and Human,* ed. C. Schwöbel and C. E. Gunton (Edinburgh: T&T Clark, 1991), 77–81.

20. Weinandy, *Does God Change?* 22. Aloys Grillmeier, *Christ in Christian Tradition,* vol. 1 (Atlanta: John Knox, 1975), 314–15, chronicles a similar line.

Christ's humanity includes a human rational soul or regards the Logos as taking the place of one.[21] It is beyond doubt that Athanasius did not think Christ lacked a true human soul (Apollinarianism), but despite Athanasius's best attempts at a *communio idiomatum*, and the fact that he nowhere explicitly refuses a human soul to Christ, he never brings out its theological significance.[22] Because of his failure to give adequate space to the human soul of Christ, Athanasius appears incapable of accounting for the ignorance, emotions, agony, and suffering of Jesus, even taking into account his argument about the difference between the Logos in himself and as incarnate.[23] As Spence surmises, "This brief analysis of Athanasius's Christology is instructive in that it highlights the inherent difficulty faced by any theory which would emphasise the Word's role in directly determining the humanity of Jesus."[24] Torrance's Christology, by emphasizing similar themes, suffers from many of the same problems.[25] Despite these problems, however, Torrance's construal of the fallen humanity of Christ is currently the most viable due to, in Kelly Kapic's words, its "massive compilation of evidence."[26]

---

21. John N. D. Kelly, *Early Christian Doctrines*, 4th ed. (London: A&C Black, 1977), 286–87. It is not that Athanasius refused Christ a human soul. He clearly states with reference to John 1:14 that the Logos became man and did not just enter man (*Contra Arianos*, 3.30). The issue is his inability due to the Logos Christology to develop this insight meaningfully and in harmony with his Christology.

22. See, for instance, Athanasius, *Contra Arianos*, 3.31, 35, 57 (*NPNF2*4:1003–4; 1007–8; 1009–10). Grillmeier, *Christ in Christian Tradition*, 1:313, discusses Athanasius's appropriation of the term and why he sought to use it in his Christology. Khaled Anatolios argues that Athanasius's Christology has been unfairly criticised as Docetic because in seeking to see the active human agency of Christ which gives significant place to the human soul of Christ, Kelly, Hanson and others fail to see the "crucial fact that in Athanasius's anthropology the human relation to the divine is characterized by receptivity rather than active agency, and so the way Athanasius takes Christ's humanity seriously is precisely to attribute such receptivity to him as central to his full humanity (c.f., CA 1:45, 1:48)." Khaled Anatolios, *Athanasius: The Coherence of his Thought* (London: Routledge, 1998), 2.

23. Grillmeier, *Christ in Christian Tradition*, 1:308–26, comes to the same conclusion. However, Grillmeier is also quick to state that this does not make Athanasius an Arian nor an Apollinarian. While all three work from a Logos/sarx model, only Athanasius keeps his model "open for an explicit doctrine of the soul of Christ. That of Apollinarius is closed," (ibid., 25). We could add Arius to the list. Reaching the same conclusions is Weinandy, *Does God Change?* 24–25.

24. Spence, "Christ's Humanity and Ours," 78.

25. For a discussion of Torrance's reading of Athanasius and his detractors, including J. Quasten, A. Grillmeier, R. P. C. Hanson, and M. Wiles, see Graeme Redding, *Prayer and the Priesthood of Christ in the Reformed Tradition* (Edinburgh: T&T Clark, 2003), 13–72.

26. Kapic, "The Son's Assumption of a Human Nature," 159.

ANSELM'S CHRISTOLOGY

In the medieval period it was Anselm who specifically addressed the issue of the fallen nature of Jesus, making it one of the central features of his work *Cur Deus Homo*.[27] Anselm makes it patently clear that since it was a human that sinned, only a human could redeem humanity; however, this could not be achieved, as humanity is now in a sinful state. This necessitated God's intervention, for only God is without sin. Anselm believed this created the situation in which God alone could make "satisfaction" for sin but none but a human ought to do this.[28] Only a person who is both God and human could overcome this dilemma.

Within Anselm's soteriology we see two constituent features: first, Jesus had to possess a humanity derived directly from the (sinful) root of Adam;[29] second, Jesus must have been sinless, for only a perfect and sinless life of obedient humanity could make true satisfaction to the Father. Jesus thus possessed a fallen humanity and yet he remained sinless. These two features directly reflect the consistent teaching of the Fathers. Of course, Anselm added his own accents to this teaching, most notably in the fact that he did not think Jesus had to die but that he chose to.[30] The specifics of Anselmian theology will not detain us here, other than to note these constituent features of his soteriology, and through him, Torrance's also.[31]

---

27. Anselm, "Why God Became Man," in *A Scholastic Miscellany: Anselm to Ockham*, ed. and trans. E. R. Fairweather, The Library of Christian Classics (Philadelphia: Westminster, 1956), 100–183.

28. Anselm, *Cur Deus Homo*, 2.6. Cf. 1.11; 1.23. On Anselm's use of *satisfactio, iustitia,*and *debitum* see S. Rodger, "The Soteriology of Anselm of Canterbury, An Orthodox Perspective," *GOTR* 34 (1989): 32–37.

29. While Anselm does not state that Christ assumed a "sinful" humanity, I think it is clearly implied in his rhetoric.

30. This is developed in Anselm, *De Conceptu Virginali et de Originali Peccato*. See *St. Anselm: Basic Writings*, trans. S. N. Deane (La Salle: Open Court, 1968). For a critique of Anselmian soteriology from a patristic and Eastern Orthodox perspective see Rodger, "The Soteriology of Anselm of Canterbury," 19–43. According to Rodger, Anselm overstressed to the point of Nestorianism the human agency of Christ in offering atonement for sin. Anselm on many occasions throughout *Cur Deus Homo* implies that the man Jesus is the subject of the actions of the *Deus-homo*, thereby confusing person and nature. John McIntyre develops similar criticisms in his *St. Anselm and His Critics: A Reinterpretation of the Cur Deus Homo* (London: Oliver and Boyd, 1954), 170.

31. I echo the thought of Weinandy at this point, who, in critiquing Anselm's position, argued, "Here we want to be more Anselmian than Anselm." See his treatment in Thomas G. Weinandy, *In the Likeness of Sinful Flesh: An Essay on the Humanity of Christ*(Edinburgh: T&T Clark, 1993), 39–46. I am greatly indebted to Weinandy's work throughout this chapter.

THOMISTIC EXPLANATIONS

Following Anselm, Aquinas also directly addressed this question.[32] He used three arguments to maintain the assumption of the sinlessness of the Savior within a fallen humanity. First, Aquinas adopts the soteriological principle of Jesus' "fallen" humanity. He recognized with Anselm that if fallen humanity were to be saved then one like us ought to offer proper satisfaction to the Father, while remaining sinless. Second, true restoration of human dignity could only be achieved by one who felt directly the indignity of a fallen nature and conquered it. Finally, the power of God is manifest in the obedient human life of Jesus. For Aquinas, Christ is different from the rest of fallen humanity in that the Son assumed a humanity tainted by sin, but he did not assume original sin and did not sin himself.[33] In this way, Aquinas offers a thoroughly orthodox answer to Christ's relation to sin.

Although he never acknowledges Aquinas in this discussion, Torrance develops many of these themes in his own treatment of the issue. Christians have universally believed Christ was sinless. Christ was free from original sin, as well as being free from actual or personal sins, defined as evil acts freely committed that involve moral responsibility and require divine forgiveness.[34] This belief has consistent conciliar support in the Chalcedonian Definition's statement that Christ was like us in all things except sin.

So far, we have established the fact that Christ assumed a human nature of the same kind as the rest of fallen humanity (a postlapsarian nature). While many would not use the language of sinful humanity when applied to Jesus Christ, the basic understanding within Chalcedonian Christology is that the *homoousios* means, if nothing else, that Christ is like us in all respects *except* without personal sin. However, theologians have not been able to establish convincingly how we are to understand Christ's fallen humanity and sinless personality. The best Athanasius could do was to say Jesus was sinless due to the divine nature, being the person of the eternal Word.

JOHN OWEN ON CHRIST AND THE SPIRIT

As Torrance is a Reformed theologian, it is useful to see how he "fits" within that history. From within the Reformed tradition several thinkers have sought to deal with Christ's assumption of a fallen humanity, including John Owen,

---

32. Thomas Aquinas, *Summa theologica*, 3.4.6. Cf. *Summa contra gentiles*, 4.30, 28.
33. Ibid., 3.15.1, 2–4.
34. H. P. Owen, "The Sinlessness of Jesus," in *Religion, Reason, and the Self: Essays in Honour of Hywel D. Lewis*, ed. S. R. Sutherland and T. A. Roberts (Cardiff: University of Wales Press, 1989), 119–28.

Jonathan Edwards, and Edward Irving. Because of the similarity between the positions of Owen and Irving, we shall examine their proposals first before analyzing the theology of Edwards.

But first, given Calvin's importance for Reformed theology, we may ask if he addressed this question at all. Bruce McCormack examined sixteenth- and seventeenth-century Reformed thought on the issue and concluded that Calvin rejected the dominant view of the time (as typically upheld by Menno Simons) that women are without seed, thus the virgin conception ensured Christ's sinlessness. Instead, Calvin upheld the view, later developed by Owen, that "we make Christ free of all stain not just because he was begotten of his mother without copulation with man, but because he was sanctified by the Spirit that the generation might be pure and undefiled as would have been true before Adam's fall."[35] McCormack also sees the same theology worked out in the work of Ursinus.[36] Unlike Owen, neither Calvin nor Ursinus considered the sanctifying work of the Spirit to be progressive or "in a processive fashion through the acts of obedience carried out by the God-man through the course of his life."[37] What they share in common with Owen is that the agent who healed the human nature was not the Logos directly but the Holy Spirit.

John Owen (1616–1683) sought to provide an answer to the problem by examining the agency of the Holy Spirit in the incarnation.[38] This was a move of genius (not to mention biblical fidelity!) on Owen's part, and offers great promise for resourcing this entire discussion. Owen attempted to present Christ as the Scriptures do, as the archetype of Christian existence, continually empowered, comforted, and sanctified by the Holy Spirit. He argued that the eternal Son of God assumed human nature into personal union with himself, but—and this was the distinctive insight of his Christology—he held that all

---

35. Calvin, *Institutes*, 2.13.4, cited in Bruce L. McCormack, "For Us and Our Salvation: Incarnation and Atonement in the Reformed Tradition," *GOTR* 43 (1998): 295–300.

36. Ibid., 296.

37. Ibid.

38. Through the encouragement of Colin Gunton, Alan Spence has become one of the standard interpreters of Owen today. See Spence, "Christ's Humanity and Ours: John Owen," in *Persons, Divine and Human*, ed. C. Schwöbel and C. E. Gunton (Edinburgh: T&T Clark, 1991), 75–76; "Incarnation and Inspiration: John Owen and the Coherence of Christology," (PhD dissertation, Kings College, London, 1989), subsequently published as *Incarnation and Inspiration: John Owen and the Coherence of Christology* (London: T&T Clark, 2007); and "John Owen and Trinitarian Agency," *SJT* 43 (1990): 157–73. Also see another of Gunton's previous students, Graham W. P. McFarlane, *Why Do You Believe What You Believe About The Holy Spirit?*(Carlisle, UK: Paternoster, 1998), 94–110; and Colin E. Gunton, "The Church: John Owen and John Zizioulas on the Church," in *Theology Through the Theologians: Selected Essays 1972–1995* (Edinburgh: T&T Clark, 1996), 187–205.

direct divine activity on that assumed human nature was that of the Holy Spirit.[39] As we have seen, prior to this time it was held that the Logos, the Son, determined the human life of Jesus directly, rather than indirectly through the Holy Spirit.[40]

According to Owen, the Holy Spirit accomplished the initial sanctification of Jesus Christ in the womb, and Jesus was filled with grace *according to the measure of his receptivity*.[41] This forms an important step in Owen's argument. As Jesus Christ was a divine creation in the womb by the Holy Spirit, so Jesus Christ was also filled with the Holy Spirit from conception in order that Christ's human nature would not fall prey to the human condition—the propensity to sin (Isa 11:1-3). Owen does not mean to say that upon conception and initial sanctification the Son was filled with *all* grace and *all* knowledge, rather that "the soul of Christ, from the first moment of its infusion, was a subject capable of a fullness of grace, as unto its habitual residence and in-being, though the actual exercise of it was suspended for a while, until the organs of the body were fitted for it."[42] In addition, the Spirit carried on the work of progressive sanctification.[43]

Owen is content to read Scripture at face value and give full weight to the man Jesus, growing in grace and knowledge (Luke 2:40, 52). He writes, "His divine nature was not unto him in the place of a soul, nor did it immediately operate the things which he performed, as some of old vainly imagined; but being a perfect man, his rational soul was in him the immediate principle of all his moral operations even as ours are in us."[44] Owen is advocating here the view that Jesus Christ is, in his words, *autokineton*—a self-determining spiritual principle, fully self-conscious and, as a creature, open and responsive to God, not immediately determined by the Logos. If this were not so then Christ would not be truly human.[45]

The experience of God for the man Jesus is indirect, being as it is through the Holy Spirit, and it is thus voluntary rather than natural.[46] In Christ there is both continuity with humanity and discontinuity, for after all, he is the God-

---

39. Spence, "Christ's Humanity and Ours," 75–76.

40. Owen sought to defend this position from Scripture, raising extensive testimony in support. John Owen, "Work of the Holy Spirit with Respect unto the Head of the New Creation—the Human Nature of Christ," in *The Works of John Owen*, ed. W. H. Goold (reprint, London: Banner of Truth, 1966), 3:159–88.

41. Ibid., 3:168 (emphasis mine).

42. Ibid., 3:169.

43. Ibid.

44. Ibid.

45. See Spence, "Christ's Humanity and Ours," 82–83.

man. As the eternal Word, Christ was privy to the entire counsel and wisdom of the Father from all ages. However, as a human Christ restricted himself to the mediation of that knowledge and wisdom through the Holy Spirit. Hence, Christ stood in continuity with the prophets of old as they were inspired by the Holy Spirit to both foretell and forthtell the things of God. What distinguishes the revelation in Christ from that of these prophets is "the infinite excellency of his person above theirs,"[47] due to Christ's person being the everlasting Son.[48]

EDWARD IRVING'S PENTECOSTAL THEOLOGY

Owen's christological insights on this issue were not taken up significantly until the work of Edward Irving (1792–1834).[49] Irving's distinctive contribution to this discussion is that he elaborates the role of the Holy Spirit in the life of Christ and does so in Trinitarian fashion: "Irving believed that to rely solely on the Son's divinity as the solitary source of holiness within the humanity of Jesus bordered on Docetism or Monophysitism."[50] According to Irving, the Holy Spirit is active in the life of Christ from conception to resurrection. The soul of Christ was anointed with the Holy Spirit, and it was this union that enabled Jesus to resist the devil and live a sinless life. As with Owen before him, in order to account for the divine and human in the one person of the incarnate Son Jesus Christ, Irving sought to identify the place of the Spirit within the incarnation.[51]

---

46. This is worked out in Owen's exegesis of Hebrews, especially Heb. 5:7. John Owen, *An Exposition of the Epistle to the Hebrews*, ed. W. H. Goold (reprint, Grand Rapids: Baker, 1980), 4:507.

47. Ibid., 3:31.

48. This is fully consistent with the traditional doctrine of the *enhypostasia* and the *anhypostasia*. For an overview see Richard A. Muller, *Dictionary of Latin and Greek Theological Terms* (Grand Rapids: Baker, 1985), 35, 103. In this way Owen argues for an ontological uniqueness to Christ, not just a functional one.

49. Although nowhere does he indicate an awareness of Owen's Christology. Gunton asks this very question, "Did Irving read Owen?" and answers: "There seems little reason why he should not have done." Gunton, "Two Dogmas Revisited: Edward Irving's Christology," *SJT* 41 (1988): 375. Gunton then asks the more important question of "why neither Owen nor Irving has been read seriously during the last century and a half." It would appear Gunton forgot about Barth and Torrance! A contemporary of Irving's, Thomas Erskine (1788–1870), also put forward a similar position. See his *The Brazen Serpent, or Life Coming Through Death* (Edinburgh: Waugh & Innes, 1831), and Trevor A. Hart, *The Teaching Father: An Introduction to the Theology of Thomas Erskine of Linlathen* (Edinburgh: Saint Andrew, 1993).

50. Thomas G. Weinandy, *In the Likeness of Sinful Flesh: An Essay on the Humanity of Christ* (Edinburgh: T&T Clark, 1993), 59.

51. See Edward Irving, *The Collected Writings of Edward Irving*, ed. G. Carlyle (London: Alexander Strachan, 1865).

Christ was not merely filled with the Holy Spirit; the Spirit was the author of Christ's bodily existence. For Irving, like Owen, the Spirit was united to the human soul of Jesus and so, because of his presence and control of the soul, Jesus was tempted but never assented to an evil suggestion.[52] According to this account, the soul is the central location of the incarnation: the Son unites himself to a human soul, which is assumed (but not replaced) by the Holy Spirit. The Holy Spirit possesses and anoints the soul, but it is the Son who wields the Spirit.

JONATHAN EDWARDS'S SPIRIT CHRISTOLOGY

The many recent studies on Edwards and his theology reveal one consistent theme: the centerpiece of his theology was the glory of God, something from which all else emanated. It is also universally recognized that Edwards was a Reformed theologian, although the exact influences on his thought are still a topic of debate.[53] A final feature gaining unanimity in recent scholarship is Edwards's radical commitment to a doctrine of Christ's humanity that depended upon the Holy Spirit for its explanation. Owen and Irving both agreed that the Logos is in union with the man Jesus, not immediately but through the Spirit. As Holmes states, "Edwards agreed with Owen and anticipated Irving."[54]

Edwards's theology evidences three essential unions: Trinitarian, christological, and soteriological (*theosis*). The Trinitarian union is the perichoretic union of the three persons in the one being of God in which the Spirit is the bond of love between the three. The soteriological union is specifically the union of God with humanity through the indwelling Spirit. "The intermediate christological identification of God with humanity is a necessary step, even if emphasized less by Edwards."[55] This christological union refers to the hypostatic union of Christ in which divinity is mediated to humanity via the Holy Spirit.

Such are the historical antecedents to the contemporary discussion over the Son's assumption of a human nature, the role of the Spirit in this assumption,

---

52. Along with the soul of Jesus, the will also plays a prominent part in Irving's pneumatic Christology. The Spirit occupies the will of Jesus to superintend it; in this way Jesus is both sinless and remains sinless. See Graham W. P. McFarlane, *Christ and the Spirit: The Doctrine of the Incarnation According to Edward Irving* (Carlisle: Paternoster, 1996),168–72.

53. See W. R. Hastings, "'Honouring the Spirit': Analysis and Evaluation of Jonathan Edwards' Pneumatological Doctrine of the Incarnation," *IJST* 7 (2003): 280–81.

54. Stephen R. Holmes, *God of Grace and God of Glory: An Account of the Theology of Jonathan Edwards* (Grand Rapids: Eerdmans, 2000), 136.

55. Hastings, "Honouring the Spirit," 284.

and the issue over whether or not Christ assumed a fallen humanity. Each of the figures deserves a thorough treatment beyond what has been offered here, but enough has been outlined to show the contours within which a certain strand of the tradition has formed.

CONTEMPORARY PROPOSALS

In the wake of Irving's affirmation that Jesus assumed a sinful human nature, several theologians adopted the idea into their own works. Most notable among these are the Protestant Karl Barth in the first half of the twentieth century and more recently the Roman Catholic scholar Thomas Weinandy.[56] Barth developed what he considered to be a thoroughly orthodox Christology in incorporating this doctrine of the assumption of a fallen human nature of Christ in the incarnation. Citing many authors, including Irving, Barth outlines, in Anselmian fashion, the necessity for Christ to have a fallen human nature in order to redeem fallen humanity. Barth writes, "There must be no weakening or obscuring of the saving truth that the nature which God assumed in Christ is identical with our nature as we see it in the light of the Fall. If it were otherwise, how could Christ really be like us? What concern could we have with Him? We stand before God characterised by the Fall. God's Son not only assumed our nature but He entered the concrete form of our nature, under which we stand before God as men damned and lost."[57] Like Aquinas, he argues that Christ did not inherit original sin while taking on sinful humanity, for "he bore innocently what Adam and all of us in Adam have been guilty of."[58] Other than echo the primary thoughts of Irving, Barth did not make a distinctive contribution to this debate.

Thomas Weinandy's work *In the Likeness of Sinful Flesh: An Essay on the Humanity of Christ*[59] is the most recent and comprehensive study of the doctrine of Christ's assumption of a sinful human nature. Weinandy gives a soteriological reason for insisting that the Son assumed a fallen human nature.

---

56. In his article on the topic, "The Son's Assumption of a Human Nature: A Call for Clarity," *IJST* 3 (2001): 154–66, Kelly Kapic points out that on the continent similar language was being adopted at the time of Irving and more recently by E. Böhl, *Zur Abwehr* (Amsterdam: Scheffer, 1888); cf. Emil Brunner, *The Mediator: A Study of the Central Doctrine of the Christian Faith*, trans. Olive Wyon (Philadelphia: Westminster, 1947), esp. in his development of "incognito" on pages 328–54.

57. Barth, *Church Dogmatics* I/2, trans. G. T. Thomson and Harold Knight, ed. G. W. Bromiley and T. F. Torrance (Edinburgh: T&T Clark, 1956), 153.

58. Barth, *CD* I/2, 152. Barth deals with this issue on pages 152–58.

59. Thomas G. Weinandy, *In the Likeness of Sinful Flesh: An Essay on the Humanity of Christ* (Edinburgh: T&T Clark, 1993).

He believes, like the Fathers before him, that "ultimately, our salvation is unconditionally dependent upon the Son's assuming a humanity disfigured by sin and freely acting as a son of Adam."[60] With Aquinas, Weinandy affirms that Jesus did not assume original sin and did not himself sin. Jesus did not inherit interior moral concupiscence or the "fomes" of sin. This meant that Christ's death was efficacious inasmuch as he was the sinless man who defeated the power of the devil and of sin in the body of Adam as the Son obedient to the Father in the power of the Holy Spirit.

Like the authors we have already mentioned, and along with Torrance, Weinandy acknowledges the correctness of the principle "the unassumed is the unhealed," and takes this to mean the assumption of a fallen humanity by Christ in the incarnation.[61] By Jesus' possession of a "sinful humanity," "sinful flesh," or "sinful human nature," Weinandy means, "While he never sinned personally, or . . . had an inner propensity to sin (concupiscence), nonetheless his humanity was of the race of Adam and he experienced, of necessity, many of the effects of sin which permeate the world and plague human beings—hunger and thirst, sickness and sorrow, temptation and harassment by Satan, being hated and despised, fear and loneliness, even death and separation from God. The eternal Son of God functioned from within the confines of a humanity altered by sin and the Fall."[62]

According to Weinandy, this doctrine of the assumption of a fallen humanity by Jesus is "the inherent and indispensable Christological prolegomenon to soteriology."[63] This is no understatement, especially as the doctrine functions within the Christology of Weinandy and also, it can be said, of Torrance himself.

This brief survey on the sinful humanity of Christ highlights some important points germane to our investigation of Torrance's dealing with the issue. We may conclude that, far from being a peculiarly Scottish oddity, this doctrine can be shown to be a part of the Great Tradition from the patristic era to today. From early on there has been consistent and universal belief in the

---

60. Ibid., 19.

61. Weinandy does not merely read this directly from the patristic texts, as they often do not state in simple terms that Jesus assumed a sinful human nature. However, through comprehensive citation Weinandy does show how the "form" of humanity Christ assumed was understood by the patristic theologians to be equivalent to the human nature of Adam's postlapsarian children, including a sinful human nature. Here Weinandy's use of patristic sources is more judicious than that of Torrance, as he not only asserts what this or that writer meant but illustrates, shows counterproposals, and provides arguments as to why his interpretation is the most fitting.

62. Ibid., 18.

63. Ibid., 68.

personal sinlessness of Jesus. For soteriological reasons there has been an equal emphasis on the fact that Christ had to assume a real human nature like ours in order for atonement and reconciliation to occur. At this point disagreements arise. Some of the main issues brought up in this debate are: Was this human nature like ours postlapsarian or prelapsarian? If it was a postlapsarian nature, then how could Christ not incur personal guilt?

Another common feature of this debate is that apart from Owen and Irving, no theologian has been able to provide a suitable explanation as to how Christ could assume a sinful human nature and yet remain sinless.[64] It is not simply in showing *that* Christ assumed a fallen or sinful human nature that these works are deficient, but in giving a theological articulation of *how* it could be so. The fact of an assumed fallen nature is developed in each of the works canvassed, but the dynamics and theological foundation for this doctrine are not adequately addressed. It is a live debate, and one that Torrance wades into with his usual enthusiasm and theological acumen.

Torrance's Christology

What is Torrance's contribution to this discussion? In the 1938 Auburn Lectures, Torrance addressed this question specifically and framed it in this way: "Does not the Lord Jesus in his vicarious humiliation take upon himself *our* humanity, *fallen* humanity, and yet without sin?"[65] Torrance's reply is an assured "yes": Yes, Christ did assume the fallen humanity of the human race, not some pristine humanity like that which existed before the fall. Torrance stated this plainly in his 1992 lecture to Princeton theological students:

> We must not flinch from the statement of St. Paul in the Epistle to the Romans (8.3) that the Son of God came among us in the concrete likeness of sinful flesh . . . . Nor must we try to water down St. Paul's statement that Christ was made sin for us, although he knew no sin (2 Cor 5.21) . . . many people in the West have found this soteriological principle rather difficult and have preferred to think of Christ as having taken upon himself human nature as it came from

---

64. While Weinandy's thesis is strong on historical and biblical support for the fact of an assumption of a sinful humanity, what he does not provide in this otherwise excellent treatment is critical reflection on such dialogue partners as Irving, Barth, and von Balthasar—nor indeed T. F. Torrance, whom he cites appreciatively. Weinandy, *In the Likeness of Sinful Flesh*, 30, n. 25.

65. Torrance, *The Doctrine of Jesus Christ: Auburn Lectures 1938–39*(Eugene, OR: Wipf and Stock, 2002), 121.

the hand of God before the fall, but that is to separate the incarnation from reconciliation, the person of Christ from his saving work.[66]

An example of one who takes these same texts to mean Christ assumed a prelapsarian human nature is Philip Hughes. He writes:

> The humanity that died in Adam must be created anew and journey afresh toward the goal for which it was originally created. This new beginning is made a reality in the last Adam whose human nature assumed at Bethlehem was the exact equivalent of the first Adam's human nature received from God . . . thus affirming the solidarity with our race in its entirety . . . . . 'The second man' entered our world just as did 'the first man,' without sin and in the freedom of a relationship of direct communion with the Father. The starting point was the same for both.[67]

The position of Hughes is arguably a mediating one between what Torrance is advocating, namely, that Christ assumed a fallen human nature, and what much of contemporary popular Christology assumes, namely, that Christ assumed a humanity mingled with his divinity. Hughes constructs it this way: "But first the man of heaven had to establish his own righteousness in mortal conflict with the devil, so that, victorious, he could go to Calvary and cancel our condemnation by bearing our sins in his own body as the spotless Lamb of God. The requirements for the second Adam, therefore, were that, like the first Adam, he should be truly man, he should be truly innocent, he should be truly tested, and that, unlike the first Adam, he should be truly victorious in his encounter with the power of evil."[68] Hughes's position will no doubt prove appealing to much contemporary Christology but certainly not to Torrance.[69]

According to Torrance, "flesh" in the Pauline sense of the word often refers to the actual form of our humanity under the fall, and Scripture asserts

---

66. Torrance, *Preaching Christ Today* (Grand Rapids: Eerdmans, 1994), 58–59.

67. Philip E. Hughes, *The True Image: The Origin and Destiny of Man in Christ* (Grand Rapids: Eerdmans, 1989), 330.

68. Ibid., 331.

69. Torrance considers this position to be the one that was adopted by the Latin Fathers and became received orthodoxy in the West. Torrance traces the idea that Christ assumed some neutral humanity back to the "rather dualist Tome of Leo sent to the Council of Chalcedon." See Torrance, *Karl Barth: Biblical and Evangelical Theologian* (Edinburgh: T&T Clark, 1990), 203. This resulted in the "Latin Heresy," which Torrance so often rails against. Torrance, "Karl Barth and the Latin Heresy," *SJT* 39 (1986): 476–77.

that Christ assumed human, fallen, and sinful flesh.[70] "That must mean that the flesh he assumes is not to be thought of in some neutral sense, but as really *our* flesh. He has come to redeem *us*, to destroy our sin in human flesh; and therefore he becomes what we are that he might raise us up to where he is."[71] While Torrance clearly uses the theme of *theosis* here, he is appealing to the patristic notion of the "wonderful exchange," whereby Christ becomes what we are so that we may become what Christ is. For Torrance, such an understanding necessitates that we understand the Son's assumption of a fallen human nature. Torrance referred to this fallen, sinful flesh as the "House of Bondage," which Christ's obedience turned into the "House of God," the place where God dwells.[72]

James Torrance affirms the same concept when he commends Athanasius's teaching that Christ is the Great Physician of our humanity. Christ does not stand over against us, diagnosing our sickness and prescribing a remedy; rather, he becomes the patient and assumes the very humanity that is in need of redemption. "That was why these fathers did not hesitate to say, as Edward Irving the Scottish theologian in the early nineteenth century and Karl Barth in our own day have said, that Christ assumed 'fallen humanity' that our humanity might be turned back to God in him by his sinless life in the Spirit, and, through him, in us."[73]

In order to make some sense of this point we must, along with Herman Ridderbos, insist that "in approaching the Pauline doctrine of sin, we must not orient ourselves in the first place to the individual and personal, but to the redemptive-historical and collective points of view."[74] In light of such Pauline texts as Rom. 8:3; 2 Cor. 5:21; 2 Cor. 8:9, and Phil. 2:6 we must view sin as the supra-individual mode of existence in which one shares before we see it as an individual act. By viewing sin in this Pauline way, we can more fully see how it was that Christ could "be sin for us" (2 Cor. 5:21), that is, assume a sinful human

---

70. See his brief New Testament survey in "The Atoning Obedience of Christ," *MTSB* (Fall 1959): 67. Torrance is here supported by such exegesis as is found in C. E. B. Cranfield, *A Critical and Exegetical Commentary on the Epistle to the Romans*, vol. 1, International Critical Commentary (Edinburgh: T&T Clark, 1975), 379–82; C. H. Dodd, *The Epistle of Paul to the Romans* (New York: Harper & Row, 1959), 119–20; R. E. Brown, J. Fitzmyer, and R. E. Murphy, eds., *The New Jerome Biblical Commentary* (Englewood Cliffs, NJ: Prentice Hall, 1990), 822; and Vincent P. Branick, "The Sinful Flesh of the Son of God (Rom 8.3): A Key Image of Pauline Theology," *CBQ* 47 (1985): 246–62.

71. Torrance, *The Doctrine of Jesus Christ*, 121.

72. Torrance, "The Atoning Obedience of Christ," 73–74.

73. James B. Torrance, "The Vicarious Humanity of Christ," in *The Incarnation: Ecumenical Studies in the Nicene-Constantinopolitan Creed A.D. 381*, ed. T. F. Torrance (Edinburgh: Handsel, 1981), 141.

74. Herman Ridderbos, *Paul: An Outline of His Theology* (Grand Rapids: Eerdmans, 1975), 91.

nature, and yet remain perfectly sinless. This goes some way to countering the oft-heard charge reflected by Crisp, for example, that the notion that Christ had a fallen but not sinful human nature is incoherent.[75] By "sinful human nature," it is clear that Crisp means the person is sinful and thus guilty. This is clearly not the way Torrance uses such language.

In Christ's own body, specifically his "body of flesh," God's redemption and reconciliation take place. It is God who reconciles the world to God's own self "in Christ" (2 Cor 5:18-19). While slightly overstating his case, Branick is surely on the right track when he affirms, "Christ here is not so much the agent of redemption but rather the place of redemption because he himself was redeemed from the curse and subjection to the Law."[76]

In discussing the sinlessness of Christ, Torrance makes it clear that as God, Jesus Christ could not sin. Torrance recognizes a real temptation, but at the same time the assurance that victory was bound to be won. Christ assumed human nature, not a human person (*anhypostasis*). Christ assumed the possibility of being tempted, but he did not assume the corrupted personality spoiled by original sin, that is, the necessity of falling in temptation. In agreement with a Cyrillian soteriology, Torrance affirms: "There can be no thought here of the Son of God becoming contaminated by our sinful flesh, for while he certainly assumed sinful flesh from the lump of our fallen humanity, he healed and sanctified it at the same time, by condemning sin in the flesh and by imparting to what he assumed the virtue of his own holy life."[77]

Which of the traditional positions is then to be adopted concerning Christ: *posse peccare*("possible to sin"), *posse non peccare*("possible not to sin"), *non posse peccare*("not possible to sin"),or *non posse non peccare*("not possible not to sin")?[78] Like the Alexandrian Christology from which Torrance draws upon so deeply, he finds the answer to lie in a true consideration of the person of Christ. The person of Christ is divine, and hence what pertains to God eternally applies to Christ temporally. This is a clear departure from both Owen's and Irving's lines

---

75. Crisp, "Did Christ Have a *Fallen* Human Nature?" *IJST* 6 (2004): 271–72.

76. Branick, "The Sinful Flesh of the Son of God," 260. Branick overstates his case when he posits a case for the Gnostic language of the "redeemed Redeemer" (260–61). It would be better to say, "Christ here is *not only* the agent of redemption *but also* the place of redemption because he himself was redeemed from the curse and subjection to the Law." This provides the force of Paul's definitive statement, "If Christ has not been raised your faith is futile, and you are still in your sins" (1 Cor. 15:17).

77. Torrance *Theology in Reconciliation: Essays Towards Evangelical and Catholic Unity in East and West*(reprint, Eugene, OR: Wipf and Stock, 1997), 169 (see n. 3 for bibliographical details to Cyril's work).

78. Torrance, *The Doctrine of Jesus Christ*, 125. For definitions see Muller, *Dictionary of Latin and Greek Theological Terms* (Grand Rapids: Baker, 1985), 136–38, 176, 200, and 230.

of argument on this issue. In what would become a hallmark of his theology, Torrance adopted an *a posteriori* approach to this question as early as 1938–39 and concluded that Christ "was not able to sin because we see that he did not sin."[79] This immediately excludes the first position, *non potuit non peccare* ("he was not able not to sin"). The second and third views, *potuit peccare* ("able to sin") and *potuit non peccare* ("able not to sin"), are also immediately ruled out by Torrance as they both indicate that Christ approached sin neutrally. This is clearly not the case if the divine personality of Christ is to be taken seriously (*enhypostasis*). God is not neutral in the face of sin, but is wholly opposed to it![80] The final position, *non potuit peccare*, is the only one possible according to the logic of Torrance's argument. Jesus was unable to sin, "not only because he did not sin but because he was of such a nature, in being One with the Word, that he would not have sinned."[81] Sin is a turning away from God, it is rebellion against the love of God, and it is the autonomy of self in contradistinction to reliance on the Creator.[82] As Jesus is the Word incarnate, and God cannot turn against God, so the Son cannot be autonomous from the Father or the Spirit. Hence, according to Torrance, the temptations of Christ were real, indeed more real than for any other human being, but the victory was certain.[83]

Unlike Calvin, Ursinus, Owen, Edwards, and Irving, nowhere so far has Torrance introduced a discussion about the role of the Holy Spirit in the

79. Torrance, *The Doctrine of Jesus Christ*, 126. In his essay on the patristic phrase "the unassumed is the unhealed," Wiles shows how the Greek Fathers worked with this same methodology specifically in formulating this phrase when he writes: "The logical connection is presumably that 'assuming' is a necessary causative factor in producing 'healing'; but in at least its initial employment in theology, the epistemological order was the other way round. It was rather the conviction of full salvation which came first and which (on the basis of this principle) led on to the conviction of the divine Son's assuming a full humanity." Wiles, "The Unassumed is the Unhealed," *RelS* 4 (1968): 48.

80. Torrance points out that a neutral freedom would amount to caprice. Torrance also includes at this point a brief discussion on the "freedom" that bondage to God brings, and entertains a Reformed perspective on the freedom and bondage of the will. Torrance, *The Doctrine of Jesus Christ*, 127–28.

81. Torrance, *The Doctrine of Jesus Christ*, 128.

82. For Torrance, autonomy of the self is the very antithesis of humanity; it is inhumanity. As Jesus was the True Human, the Real Man, then rebellion and sin has no place in his being. The same thought is offered by Rogich, *Becoming Uncreated: The Journey to Human Authenticity: Updating the Spiritual Christology of Gregory Palamas* (Minneapolis: Light and Life, 1997), 168. When commenting on Palamite Christology he writes, "Jesus does not have to sin in order to prove his [mettle] as a human being. To sin means that a human being is inhuman, not more authentically human."

83. Similar conclusions are drawn by such eclectic sources as: Alfred Edersheim, *The Life and Times of Jesus the Messiah* (Peabody, MA: Hendrickson, 1993), 208; Leon Morris, *The Lord from Heaven; A Study of the New Testament Teaching on the Deity and Humanity of Jesus* (Grand Rapids: Eerdmans, 1958), 51–52; and John F. Walvoord, "The Impeccability of Christ," *BibSac* 118 (1961): 195–202.

incarnation nor specifically in the doctrine of Christ's sinful humanity. To date, Torrance has relied solely on the Athanasian/Alexandrian line of reasoning that the divinity of the person of the eternal Son is holy and sinless and so this is how Christ could assume fallen humanity and yet remain personally sinless. Unlike Irving, Torrance consistently maintains, with Cyril, that Christ came "in the likeness of sinful flesh" but not in sinful flesh. By such a statement he does not mean to imply that Christ's identification with fallen humanity is merely external or accidentally related, but rather that the Son took up our human nature into a real or physical and hypostatic union with himself so that "it was precisely one who was unlike us who was made like us, so that in being made like us he remained one who is also unlike us."[84] This is the doctrine of *henosis* that so complements the doctrine of *theosis* in both the Fathers and in Torrance. Christ became one with us (*henosis*) in the depths of our fallen human condition, yet without ceasing to remain perfect in his divinity, in order to make us one with the Father as Christ is one with the Father.[85]

INCARNATIONAL ATONEMENT

As we would expect, Torrance incorporates into this discussion a specific stress on the notion of an incarnational atonement when he explicitly links incarnation and atonement.[86] Torrance argues strongly that if the incarnation of the Son was not an incarnation of sinful, fallen human nature, then it was no real saving incarnation at all. At best, if the Son was incarnated into a perfected or "ideal" human nature, then the doctrine of atonement could only be formulated in terms of an "external transaction of a merely judicial and legalist kind."[87] This is the result, if Torrance is to be believed, of an

---

84. Torrance, *Theology in Reconciliation,*169. This goes some way in answering some of the criticisms of this phrase and its development put forward in the latter half of the Wiles essay, "The Unassumed is the Unhealed," 47–56.

85. Torrance, *Theology in Reconciliation*, 173, and Torrance, "Incarnation and Atonement: *Theosis* and *Henosis* in the Light of Modern Scientific Rejection of Dualism," *Society of Ordained Scientists,*Bulletin No. 7, Edgeware, Middlesex (Spring 1992): 8–20.

86. Crisp's real difficulty with the notion of the Son's assumption of a fallen human nature is found in his rejection of the idea of an incarnational atonement. See Crisp, "Kathryn Tanner (1954–): On Incarnation as Atonement," in *Revisioning Christology: Theology in the Reformed Tradition*(Farnham: Ashgate, 2011), 111–32, where Tanner is the object of his critique. Such an *a priori*commitment necessitates Crisp's rejection of any notion of the Son's assumption of a fallen human nature.

87. Torrance, "Incarnation and Atonement: *Theosis* and *Henosis* in the Light of Modern Scientific Rejection of Dualism," *Society of Ordained Scientists,*Bulletin No. 7, Edgeware, Middlesex (Spring 1992): 13.

instrumentalist reading of the incarnation in which the vicarious human life of the Word is discounted or given minimal treatment.

> I believe that it is very crucial for us to hold this truth, that the Savior took our fallen Adamic humanity upon him, but we must add that in the very act of taking it he was at work redeeming and sanctifying it in himself.... Hence we must think of his incarnating and atoning activities as interpenetrating one another from the very beginning to the end of his oneness with us. Otherwise the humanity of Christ has to be thought of only in an instrumentalist way, and the atonement can be formulated only in terms of external moral relations or legal transactions.[88]

According to Torrance, the view that in the incarnation the Son took, not our actual nature, but a human nature untouched by sin and guilt, can be seen throughout Latin theology. This view gave rise to the notion of the Immaculate Conception, and to a doctrine of atoning transaction thought out in external terms.[89] We have had occasion to see that Torrance has committed himself to rooting out any merely external or forensic categories in his Christology; this discussion is no exception. In fact, it provides a good framework from which Torrance can launch his attack upon "the Latin heresy."[90]

Greek theology, according to Torrance's reading of the tradition, rejected all notions of an external or instrumental atoning transaction. It took to heart Paul's non-dualist approach, insisting that in the incarnation the Son of God took upon himself our actual sinful existence and redeemed and healed it from the inside out, so to speak. "In Christ our fallen Adamic humanity was recreated

---

88. See Torrance, *Preaching Christ Today*(Grand Rapids: Eerdmans, 1994), 59.

89. Torrance labels this a dualistic, anti-Pauline approach. Torrance, "The Atonement: The Singularity of Christ and the Finality of the Cross: The Atonement and the Moral Order," in *Universalism and the Doctrine of Hell*,ed. N. M de S. Cameron (Carlisle: Paternoster, 1992; Grand Rapids: Baker, 1992), 238–39.

90. In an interesting if not convincing postscript to his monograph, Weinandy argues for the traditional Roman Catholic view of the Immaculate Conception and seeks to show how it is compatible with the doctrine of Christ's assumption of a sinful human nature. See Weinandy, *In the Likeness of Sinful Flesh: An Essay on the Humanity of Christ*(Edinburgh: T&T Clark, 1993), 153–56. Equally interesting is the suggestion of at least one Eastern Orthodox priest that the doctrine of the Immaculate Conception may be a means of rapprochement between Roman Catholics and the Eastern Orthodox. See Rogich, *Becoming Uncreated: The Journey to Human Authenticity: Updating the Spiritual Christology of Gregory Palamas*(Minneapolis: Light and Life, 1997), 163–64, and n. 73. Such notions would be as unacceptable to Torrance as they are to me.

and through his vicarious obedience as the Son of God become man it was restored to perfect filial relation to the Father."[91]

What Torrance asserted throughout his career is that the incarnation and atonement inhere in one another completely.[92] If this is truly taken seriously, then the Word had to have assumed an identical human nature to the heirs of Adam *after the fall*. This results in the saving work of Christ being seen in a twofold way, as the act of God *toward* humanity, and as the act of humanity *toward* God but, and this is crucial, within the *one person* of Jesus Christ the incarnate Son of God. As Torrance once argued: "Our salvation depends entirely upon the downright act of God in Jesus Christ and the Holy Spirit. If Christ and the Spirit are not themselves true God of true God and completely one with the Father, then we are not saved, but we can be saved only by the act of God himself."[93] It is this that compels Torrance to forcefully assert the Son's assumption of a fallen human nature.

In order to explain the humanity the Son assumed, Torrance writes:

> He was very man, our Brother. In him the Holy Son of God was grafted on to the stock of our fallen human existence, and in him our mortal and corrupt human nature was assumed into union with the Holy Son of God, so that in Jesus, in his birth and sinless life, in his death and resurrection, there took place a holy and awful judgment on our flesh of sin, and an atoning sanctification of our unholy human existence. It was through such atonement that God in all his Godness and holiness came to dwell in the midst of mortal, sinful man.[94]

The assumption of a fallen human nature Torrance considers to be essential to a full doctrine of atonement. Because union with God is through the human

---

91. Torrance, "The Atonement: The Singularity of Christ," 238.

92. In this, Torrance is at once being thoroughly patristic and thoroughly Reformed. In his essay "For Us and Our Salvation: Incarnation and Atonement in the Reformed Tradition," GOTR 43 (1998): 281–316, McCormack helpfully surveys the history of Reformed thought and shows the parallels between sixteenth- and seventeenth-century Reformed Christology and that of the Seventh Ecumenical Council and patristic Christology. While heavily reliant on Barth, McCormack's one reference to Torrance could have been multiplied many times to highlight the same point. Torrance undoubtedly understands and stands within Reformed orthodoxy, perhaps nowhere more strongly than in his articulation of the implications of the *anhypostasia/enhypostasia*, and the two natures–one person doctrines within Christology.

93. Torrance, "Incarnation and Atonement," 13.

94. Torrance, *Theology in Reconstruction* (Eugene, OR: Wipf and Stock, 1996), 241.

nature of the incarnate Christ, then Christ's nature had to be fallen in order to redeem fallen nature for human persons to participate in Christ. By this means the inner life of the Holy Trinity is extended to include human nature in and through Jesus Christ. This is possible, according to Torrance, because of the atonement that took place in Christ. For, having redeemed fallen human nature, the Holy Spirit may dwell in the midst of mortal sinful humanity. "This is the way that the divine love has taken to redeem man, by making him share in the holy power in which God lives his own divine life."[95] Finally Torrance introduces the Holy Spirit into the discussion, but only as an appendix in the traditional fashion, to assert that the Holy Spirit applies to us what Christ won for us in his life, death, and resurrection.

THE UNASSUMED IS THE UNHEALED

It will be observed that Torrance, like Athanasius, Gregory Nazianzen, and the other theologians already surveyed in this section, adopts the patristic soteriological axiom, "The unassumed is the unhealed."[96] By this phrase Torrance intends that Christ assumed a sinful, fallen humanity and redeemed it in his life and death. The question to be asked is, has Torrance interpreted this phrase correctly? This phrase is common among the early Fathers of the church—for example, Hippolytus, Tertullian, and Origen[97]—but it was Gregory Nazianzen who gave it its classical and definitive form.[98] By means of this axiom the church has consistently proclaimed and defended the full humanity of Christ. Originally a defense against Apollinarianism, the phrase states that Christ took upon himself a true material body, human soul, mind, and will.[99] Apollinaris rejected the idea that Christ possessed a human will, for the will or mind was thought to be the seat of sin. By rejecting Apollinarianism,

---

95. Ibid.

96. Torrance, "Incarnation and Atonement: *Theosis* and *Henosis* in the Light of Modern Scientific Rejection of Dualism," *Society of Ordained Scientists,*Bulletin No. 7, Edgeware, Middlesex (Spring 1992): 12. Torrance treated this again in another 1992 publication, "The Atonement: The Singularity of Christ and the Finality of the Cross: The Atonement and the Moral Order," in *Universalism and the Doctrine of Hell,*ed. N. M de S. Cameron (Carlisle: Paternoster, 1992; Grand Rapids: Baker, 1992), 237–39; and in his 1996 work *The Christian Doctrine of God: One Being Three Persons* (Edinburgh: T&T Clark, 1996), 250. In addition, Torrance works this theological phrase into numerous articles and chapters, especially *Karl Barth: Biblical and Evangelical Theologian*(Edinburgh: T&T Clark, 1990), 103–5, 160, 202–5, and 231–34.

97. See Aloys Grillmeier, *Christ in Christian Tradition*, vol. 1 (Atlanta: John Knox, 1975), 52, 115, 148.

98. See *Ep.*101 and *Or.* 1.13; 13.21 (*NPNF*2 7). The phrase was of course used by Athanasius and after him Cyril of Alexandria. Torrance provides extensive references to all these thinkers throughout chapter four of his *Theology in Reconciliation: Essays Towards Evangelical and Catholic Unity in East and West*(reprint, Eugene, OR: Wipf and Stock, 1997), 139–214.

Athanasius, the Cappadocians, and Torrance himself contend that Christ assumed a human will subject to the fall and redeemed the human mind by means of this assumption.[100] Torrance concludes, along with Weinandy, that this can only equate to a sinful or fallen human nature being assumed by the eternal Word. The Word became all that we are in order to make us all that he is.[101] The comment by Holmes on this phrase is certainly reflective of Torrance's own position: "The derivation from this of Christ's assumption of fallen human nature is uncomplicated." [102]

In response to Apollinaris's claims that the Logos became flesh without assuming a human mind, for a human mind is the locus of sin, Athanasius contended that if Christ did not have a human mind then Christ had not assumed complete or real human nature. Lacking a human mind would deprive Christ of our human experiences of birth, growth, death, pain, anguish, distress, and temptation.[103] This would disqualify Christ from being a priest, and so his mediatorial office is undermined if not utterly contradicted. Athanasius also considered this to be a rejection of the *homoousios* doctrine—if Christ was not man in the wholeness of our humanity, then Christ was something else. As something else, he could not atone for our sins.[104] Torrance is convinced that in rejecting Apollinarianism Athanasius, by means of the phrase we are considering, affirms that true emancipation from original sin and the power of death were taken up into Christ and so were defeated and atoned for.[105]

---

99. Torrance makes much of the mind of Christ, especially in worship. See his 1972 lecture to the Church Service Society of the Church of Scotland "The Mind of Christ in Worship: The Problem of Apollinarianism in the Liturgy," in *Theology in Reconciliation*, 139–214.

100. Torrance traces this idea immediately back to Barth, to whom he attributes this as one of his most significant contributions to evangelical theology. Torrance, *Karl Barth: Biblical and Evangelical Theologian*, 104, 202–5, citing in support Barth, *Church Dogmatics* I/2, trans. G. T. Thomson and Harold Knight, ed. G. W. Bromiley and T. F. Torrance (Edinburgh: T&T Clark, 1956), 151.

101. Torrance considers the Cappadocians as taking even more seriously than Athanasius the Pauline teaching that Christ took upon himself fallen human nature, "the flesh of sin," "the body of death," while at the same time sanctifying and recreating it. Torrance, *Theology in Reconciliation*, 155.

102. Holmes, *God of Grace and God of Glory: An Account of the Theology of Jonathan Edwards* (Grand Rapids: Eerdmans, 2000), 137.

103. This is all developed in Athanasius, *Contra Apollinarium*, 1.2, 5, 10, 15; 2.8, 17.

104. Torrance is so committed to an incarnational atonement that he can write of Christ's assumption of a human soul and mind that "it is indeed precisely in this area that the essential work of redemption took place, where the inward and outward man are one and inseparable, and where Christ's redeeming work was no less a work of his soul than a work of his body." Torrance *Theology in Reconciliation*, 149.

105. On various notions of original sin, including a Reformed view, see Crisp, "Did Christ Have a Fallen Human Nature?" *IJST* 6 (2004): 272–84. Crisp maintains that any articulation of Christ's assumption of a fallen human nature necessarily entails a reformulated doctrine of original sin that

Torrance considers Apollinarianism, both ancient and modern, to be nothing other than "another gospel,"[106] primarily because it cuts away the atonement as the "reconciling exchange" of Christ.[107] That is, Apollinarianism is nothing other than a rejection of salvation, according to Torrance, and the consequence of this rejection is the destruction of true worship because there is no real relation between God and the human soul, or between the will of God and the will of humanity, in and through the rational soul and will of Christ. Torrance summarizes the situation as follows:

> In allowing no room for the mental and moral life of Jesus as man and in denying to him authentic human agency in his saving work, it left no place for the vicarious role of the human soul and mind and will of Jesus in the reconciling 'exchange' of like for like in the redemption of man. And by destroying his representative capacity, it had no place for his priesthood or human mediation in our worship of the Father, and by the same token it took away the ground for any worship of God with our human minds. A mutilated humanity in Christ could not but result in a mutilated Christian worship of God.[108]

What Torrance sees as evident within patristic Christology is that the phrase "the unassumed is the unhealed" equates to the following: to be healed is to be deified, therefore humanity must first have been "assumed" into special hypostatic relation with the Word and in that act divinized.[109] The phrase is intimately linked to the doctrine of *theosis* in the early church and was seen as a central formula for accounting for how *theosis* occurs. The logic behind this is that divinization is thought to be the ultimate goal of humankind (something

---

accounts for the place of original guilt. Torrance never enters into the details of this aspect of the argument; however, it is clear that according to Torrance Christ did not inherit or assume any original guilt, just original corruption in his human nature. For a complementary account of original sin see Habets, "'Suffer the little children to come to me, for theirs is the kingdom of heaven.' Infant Salvation and the Destiny of the Severely Mentally Disabled," in *Evangelical Calvinism: Essays Resourcing the Continuing Reformation of the Church,*ed. Myk Habets and Robert Grow (Eugene, OR: Pickwick, 2012),287–328, especially 308–15.

106. Torrance, *Theology in Reconciliation*, 148.

107. Ibid., 150. Torrance is reliant upon a theological exegesis of Athanasius's work, especially *Contra Apollinarium*, 1.17.

108. Ibid., 150.

109. This is the conclusion Wiles, "The Unassumed is the Unhealed," *RelS* 4 (1968): 55, comes to with regard to the patristic theologians.

Torrance also terms "worship").¹¹⁰ This provides an understanding of salvation in which a logically necessary first step is a prior divinization of human persons by the assumption of humanity into a relationship with God of a distinct, hypostatic nature in Christ.¹¹¹ This is precisely the way Torrance constructs his accounting of salvation as the following highlights:

> If the incarnate Son through his birth of the Virgin Mary actually assumed our flesh of sin, the fallen, corrupt and enslaved human nature which we have all inherited from Adam, then the redeeming activity of Christ took place within the ontological depths of his humanity in such a way that far from sinning himself, he condemned sin in the flesh and sanctified what he assumed, so that incarnating and redeeming events were one and indivisible, from the very beginning of his earthly existence to its end in his death and resurrection.¹¹²

A VICARIOUS FALLEN NATURE

For Torrance, "We cannot think of Christ's becoming flesh in a sense which would separate his flesh from ours, and yet we cannot think of his flesh as corrupt in the sense of Irving."¹¹³ Torrance maintains that Christ has entered sinlessly into our corrupt and fallen humanity in order to redeem us. He maintains that there are not two *separate* natures in Christ (a Nestorian mistake); there are two natures, but they are united *hypostatically* in the one incarnate

---

110. Torrance, "The Mind of Christ in Worship: The Problem of Apollinarianism in the Liturgy," in *Theology in Reconciliation*, 139–214. His brother James Torrance works from a similar construct and also makes much of the necessity of the fallen human nature of Christ and its association with Christian worship. See his "The Vicarious Humanity of Christ," in *The Incarnation: Ecumenical Studies in the Nicene-Constantinopolitan Creed A.D. 381*, ed. T. F. Torrance (Edinburgh: Handsel, 1981), 127–47.

111. Wiles, "The Unassumed is the Unhealed," 47–56, recognizes the logic of this early Christology but rejects its use today, arguing that φαρμακον, or healing/medicinal imagery, is merely one of a number of analogies used for salvation. As an analogy it is useful, but only to a point. Analogies he briefly mentions other than the medical include the juridical and the sacrificial. Wiles does not appear to give enough weight to the uniqueness of Christ and his relationship with both God and humanity, and so downplays the vicarious and mediatorial ministry of Christ. For a contemporary elaboration on the analogy of healing as salvation see John de Gruchy, "Salvation as Healing and Humanization," in *Christ in Our Place: The Humanity of God in Christ for the Reconciliation of the World: Essays Presented to Professor James Torrance*, ed. T. A. Hart and D. P. Thimell (Exeter: Paternoster, 1981), 32–47.

112. Torrance, "Incarnation and Atonement," 12.

113. Torrance, *The Doctrine of Jesus Christ: Auburn Lectures 1938–39*(Eugene, OR: Wipf and Stock, 2002), 122.

person.[114] As a result, the human nature of the incarnate Word is thus holy, not in any sense corrupt. So while the human nature was derived from Mary, from the stock of fallen humanity, it was a *vicarious* humanity that Christ assumed. "In this Union the flesh of Christ becomes Holy though it is a member of humanity under the curse of the law, under the ban of God's wrath. Thus we are to think of Christ's flesh as perfectly and completely sinless in his own nature, and not simply in virtue of the Spirit as Irving puts it."[115] Here Torrance clearly eschews Irving's unique contribution to this discussion—the sanctifying work of the Holy Spirit on Jesus at conception.

According to Torrance, Christ did not have original sin because his person (*he!*) was divine.[116] However, Christ entered fallen humanity and chose to live within the confines and conditions of corrupt humanity *vicariously*.[117] Christ freely came under the same judgment and condemnation as we did, not because

---

114. This form of reasoning has a long history within the Reformed tradition, arising out of the initial debates with the Lutheran construction of a *communicatio idiomatum*. As with the best of Reformed scholarship, Torrance knows the distinction between persons and natures and how to hold the two together in a thoroughly Chalcedonian way. McCormack is helpful here in presenting two points about Reformed orthodoxy: "The first is that for a Christology to be 'Reformed,' it must affirm the principle that the two natures remain distinct and their properties unimpaired after the union . . . . Secondly, we have established that the Subject who worked out our redemption is the God-man in his divine-human activity." McCormack, "For Us and Our Salvation: Incarnation and Atonement in the Reformed Tradition," *GOTR* 43 (1998): 294.

115. Torrance, *The Doctrine of Jesus Christ*, 122.

116. Crisp's otherwise excellent article, "Did Christ Have a *Fallen* Human Nature?" *IJST* 6 (2004): 270–88, limits discussion to *natures* rather than opening it up to *persons*. Torrance's construction of the doctrine moves from nature to person; it is this movement that lends coherence to his thought and distinguishes his own point of view from that of Irving.

117. Once again Torrance is echoing a staple of Reformed orthodoxy, that "to be made sin" in 2 Cor. 5:21 means that the sin and guilt of the world is *imputed* to the Son, a judicial act whereby the God-man is made liable for our sins and judged in our place. See Calvin, *The Institutes of the Christian Religion*, trans. H. Beveridge (London: James Clarke, 1953), 2.16.5–6. While Torrance would not stress the juridical aspects of this exchange, the imputed or vicarious nature of it is certainly highlighted. Luther himself asserted in more direct fashion that Christ assumed a sinful human nature, not some neutral humanity. He spoke of Christ as the "greatest sinner" (*maximus peccator*) because he bears the sins of all human beings *in a real manner* in the human nature he has assumed. Luther goes beyond Reformed orthodoxy at this point, insisting that the real manner goes beyond a mere imputation of sins to Christ to his real assumption of these sins. While Christ himself is innocent, he assumes the sins of all humans. The corollary of Christ as the greatest sinner is Christ as the "greatest person" (*maxima persona*); Christ is every sinner. This leads Luther to posit Christ as the "only sinner," an idea that is foundational for his doctrine of atonement. See Luther's *Lectures on Galatians*, 1535, in *Luther's Works*, 26:281, cited in T. Mannermaa, "Justification and *Theosis* in Lutheran-Orthodox Perspective," in *Union With Christ: The New Finnish Interpretation of Luther*, ed. C. E. Braaten and R. W. Jensen (Grand Rapids: Eerdmans, 1998), 29–31.

he sinned, but because in his union he loved us even unto death and did *not* sin! Torrance's argument hangs on the concept of a vicarious assumption of human nature in its fallenness and sin. Christ did not, according to this logic, inherit sin *naturally,* and so he had no sin nature or the stain of original sin, as do all other children of Adam. However, through an assumption of human nature in its postlapsarian condition, Christ could remain guilt-free while still assuming a *vicarious* fallen and sinful human nature.[118] As noted above, when Torrance was applying Cyril's Christology to this discussion, this is how Christ can be both like and unlike us in the incarnation. We note Kruger's comment that "in an unpublished sermon on Rom. 12:1-2 Torrance says, following Irenaeus, that he likes to think of the Son's assumption of our fallen humanity in the light of Jesus' healing of the leper, when 'instead of becoming leprous himself, he healed the leper . . . . Jesus had taken our leprous humanity upon himself, but . . . instead of becoming a leper himself he healed and transformed our leprous human nature.'"[119] This is a clear illustration of Torrance's position.

Consequently, Torrance disagrees with Irving's Christology at this point because it would imply that Christ would have to atone for his own sin as well as for the world. This would be impossible, for it requires a sinless sacrifice to atone for the sinful. If we adopt Torrance's position, the human nature of Jesus Christ is not guilty of original sin (how can a nature be guilty?) and hence does not need to be atoned for. However, the person of the eternal Son took to himself, freely and vicariously, a postlapsarian human nature and lived under the conditions of corrupt humanity. In that humanity like ours, he redeemed the flesh, defeated the curse, and restored human nature to a right standing with God in the power of the Holy Spirit. This is Torrance's innovation in the debate, and one that has little weakness in its basic orientation. It is also the point that is not addressed in the critical accounts of the issue offered by Kapic, Crisp, or Macleod.

Torrance further articulated how Christ remained sinless despite vicariously assuming a fallen human nature in his 1976 work *Space, Time and Resurrection* when he wrote:

---

118. Torrance is here thoroughly patristic and in line with the Fathers when he attributes sin to the person-hypostasis and not, as Augustine (and the Western tradition since) did, to essence or nature. This accounts for why Christ could assume the likeness of sinful flesh (nature) and yet remain sinless (person). Again the *an/enhypostatic* couplet is playing its part in the hinterland of Torrance's Christology.

119. C. Baxter Kruger, "The Doctrine of the Knowledge of God in the Theology of T. F. Torrance: Sharing in the Son's Communion with the Father in the Spirit," *SJT* 43 (1990): 372, n. 19. The sermon can be found in The Thomas F. Torrance Manuscript Collection, Special Collections, Princeton Theological Seminary Library, Box 38, "Handwritten notes, Romans 12.1–3."

Although he assumed our fallen and corrupt humanity when he became flesh, in assuming it he sanctified it in himself, and all through his earthly life he overcame our sin through his righteousness, our impurity through his purity, condemning sin in our flesh by the sheer holiness of his life within it.[120]

Torrance goes on to say that this is precisely why death could not hold Christ, for there was no sin in him that allowed it to subject him to corruption. Death had nothing in Christ, for he had already passed through its clutches by the perfection of his holiness.[121] In short, "He triumphed over the grave through his sheer sinlessness."[122] Torrance concludes with the clear statement, "The resurrection is thus the resurrection of the union forged between man and God in Jesus out of the damned and lost condition of men into which Christ entered in order to share their lot and redeem them from doom."[123]

Throughout Torrance's discussion of the assumption of the vicarious fallen human nature of Christ the anhypostatic/enhypostatic couplet is being applied. This is a fundamentally important move in his construction. According to Torrance, the passive obedience of Christ is more related to the doctrine of the *anhypostasia*, while the active obedience of Christ is more related to the doctrine of the *enhypostasia*. While treating the *theologoumenon* in this way is a theological novelty, Torrance does not mean to imply any separation of these terms or strict delineation between them and the work of Christ. Rather, he considers the work of Christ from different aspects using these terms. Through the active obedience of Christ, his sinless human life of obedience to the Father, Christ "appropriated for and into our human nature the eternal Life of God."[124] This is the enhypostatic aspect of the incarnation. In his passion, Christ propitiated God and expiated sin, making union and communion with God a reality. This is the anhypostatic aspect of the incarnation. Torrance develops these themes further, as illustrated in an essay on the cross and atonement:

> The atoning mediation of Christ is thus to be expounded in terms of the *internal* relations between Christ and God and between Christ and all mankind. The expiatory and propitiatory activity of the Mediator, while deriving from the innermost being of God, is

---

120. Torrance, *Space, Time and Resurrection* (Edinburgh: Handsel, 1976), 53.
121. Ibid.
122. Ibid., 53–54.
123. Ibid., 54.
124. Ibid., 55.

fulfilled within the ontological depths of our fallen, enslaved, depraved and guilt-laden human existence, that is, in and through the oneness of God with us in our actual condition embodied in the incarnate existence of the Mediator.[125]

Torrance wants us to understand that Christ's incarnation is itself integral to redemption. The assumption of a sinful human nature provides the explanation as to how this can be so. Atoning mediation is first achieved within the hypostatic union itself and is then applied to fellow human beings. We participate in what Christ has already achieved, not independently of Christ. Christ is not simply a moral trailblazer, or external example, but the Mediator, Immanuel—God with us and us with God.[126] Christ "took upon himself our twisted, lost and damned existence, with all its wickedness, violence and abject misery, and substituted himself for us in the deepest and darkest depths of our perdition and godlessness, all in order to save and redeem us through the atoning sacrifice of himself."[127] At this point in Torrance's essay he again echoes the *mirifica commutatio*: "And such is the astonishing grace of the Lord Jesus Christ who, though he was rich, for our sakes became poor that we might be made rich in him—the blessed reconciling exchange summed up in the New Testament term *katallage*."[128]

Conclusion

It remains to draw some conclusions from the various threads we have been weaving throughout this chapter. In a series of articles, Donald Macleod would have us believe that Torrance has merely appropriated Irving's theology in asserting the assumption of a fallen humanity in the incarnation.[129] But is this really true? To answer in the affirmative would be too simplistic. Torrance does

---

125. Torrance, "The Atonement: The Singularity of Christ and the Finality of the Cross: The Atonement and the Moral Order," in *Universalism and the Doctrine of Hell*, ed. N. M de S. Cameron (Carlisle: Paternoster, 1992; Grand Rapids: Baker, 1992), 236.

126. This is the common theological tension between the One and the Many. See for instance Colin E. Gunton, *The One, the Three, and the Many: God, Creation and the culture of Modernity*, The Bampton Lectures 1992 (Cambridge: Cambridge University Press, 1993).

127. Torrance, "The Atonement: The Singularity of Christ," 236–37.

128. Ibid., 237. For a Reformed background to the link between incarnation and atonement on the one hand, and the *mirifica commutatio* and *theosis* on the other hand, consult McCormack, "For Us and Our Salvation," 281–316.

129. Macleod, "Christology," in *Dictionary of Scottish History and Theology*, ed. D. F. Wright, D. C. Lachman, and D. E. Meek (Edinburgh: T&T Clark, 1993), 175. Macleod claims that Torrance "went on to reintroduce to Scotland the peculiar Christology of Edward Irving," and so Macleod calls this the

speak of Irving as providing some useful resources showing that Jesus assumed a fallen human nature. In this, Irving and Torrance are at one. However, Torrance is at odds with Irving in how they sought to account for this assumed nature. Throughout his theology, Torrance wished to avoid the Ebionite and docetic extremes that could result from a consideration of the vicarious humanity of Christ. Of those advocating an Ebionite Christology, Torrance mentions Irving as holding that the sinlessness of Christ was due to the indwelling Holy Spirit, not to Christ's own person.[130] On the docetic side, Torrance suggests that certain notions of the deification of Christ's human nature are to be ruled out. What then is Torrance's position on the matter, if not Ebionite or docetic?

The problem with Irving's treatment of this issue is that he makes the Holy Spirit the decisive factor, to the *relative neglect* of the hypostatic union. In Torrance's opinion, this is a grave mistake. While the Holy Spirit is integral to Jesus' life, and especially here to his sinlessness, it is also due to the hypostatic union that Jesus was sinless and so did not have any need to die for his own sins. While Christ's humanity was capable of sin and rebellion, Christ was not simply the substance of a human nature as are the rest of the sons of Adam. Christ had another nature (to use Chalcedonian language), the divine nature, which was not only sinless but incapable of sinning.[131] Torrance realized this essential problem with Irving's Christology and sought to counter it with a stress on the assumption of a *vicarious* fallen human nature in the incarnation. However, it is certainly the case that Torrance went too far in the direction of Alexandrian Christology and all but forgot about the atoning work of the Holy Spirit in the entire life of Christ, despite his occasional caveats.

In an article addressing the imbalances of both Alexandrian Christology and attempts to find the "historical Jesus," Colin Gunton stated that "the need is for an incarnational christology which will yet do full justice to the historical particularity of Jesus and the detailed lineaments of his story."[132] His solution: "I want to suggest that the area where we should look is our understanding of the

---

"Irving-Torrance theory" (175). See the longer discussion in *Jesus Is Lord: Christology Yesterday and Today* (Fearn, Ross-shire: Christian Focus, 1998), 125–34 and 221–30.

130. Despite the confusing explanation of Macleod when in his article he states that "Irving completely repudiated the idea that the human nature of Christ was sanctified at birth by the power of the Holy Spirit." Macleod, "Christology," 175.

131. See the helpful analogy provided by Thomas V. Morris, *The Logic of God Incarnate* (Ithaca: Cornell University Press, 1986), 15–17, cited in Crisp, "Did Christ Have a *Fallen* Human Nature?" *IJST* 6 (2004): 285.

132. Gunton, "Two Dogmas Revisited: Edward Irving's Christology," *SJT* 41 (1988): 361.

place of pneumatology in Christology."[133] Bruce McCormack suggests the same solution when he writes, "The 'sin nature' each of us has is a function of our primal decision to agree with Adam's rebellion. Through his life of obedience, Christ refused to make that primal decision his own. That he did not do so cannot be explained on the basis of the hypostatic union alone; the work of the Spirit has to be appealed to to make the conception fully coherent. That is, the Spirit who brought together divine and human nature in the Virgin's womb was the One who continually empowered the God-man in his life of obedience."[134]

Gunton and McCormack couldn't have been more correct. What John Owen and Edward Irving provide is a consideration of the active role of the Holy Spirit in the incarnation. Athanasius and Torrance both make significant space in their respective theologies for the Holy Spirit at the Trinitarian level; however, they fail to fully develop their pneumatology in any adequate way into Christology and soteriology. The same can be said for Barth himself. The insights of Owen and Irving provide pointers for a possible solution to the deficiencies in Torrance's doctrine of the Son's assumption of a fallen human nature. While Irving leaned too heavily on the empowering presence of the Holy Spirit in the incarnation, as Torrance pointed out, Torrance did not incorporate the Spirit nearly enough in his overemphasis on the eternal Word as the direct divine activity on the assumed human nature. More so than Irving, Torrance makes it clear not only why, but also how, the Word could assume a fallen human nature and not incur personal guilt. As we have seen, he achieves this through use of the notion of an assumption of a vicarious fallen human nature hypostatically united to the eternal Son.

Torrance's account of Christ's fallen human nature is constructive and suggestive. But like Athanasius, Torrance fails to construct a Christology that adequately explains the functional relation between the Word, or divine nature, and the humanity of Jesus. In this regard, Torrance would have done better to inquire further into the implications of his own theology and to work out in greater detail what this means, especially in regard to pneumatology. This is something his own Reformed tradition does very well, particularly in the work

---

133. Ibid.

134. McCormack, "For Us and Our Salvation: Incarnation and Atonement in the Reformed Tradition," *GOTR* 43 (1998): 314, n. 53. McCormack sees in the theology of Karl Barth this understanding of Christ's assumption of a fallen human nature. It is precisely the weakness of Torrance's own theology that he did not allow enough space for a consideration of the place pneumatology should play. Had he followed his *Doktorvater* Karl Barth in this matter also, his position would have been more coherent and convincing, despite the fact that even Barth did not go far enough either!

of Calvin, John Owen, and Edward Irving, as Gunton, Spence, and others have recently pointed out.

Torrance's work should not, however, be understood as positing anything like a physical theory of the atonement in which human persons are automatically saved on the basis of the incarnation. That would amount to a necessary universalism, a position Torrance repeatedly rejected.[135] Against instrumentalist readings of the incarnation, Torrance repeatedly emphasized the biblical material that has Christ grow in knowledge or praying for grace for himself. In this, Torrance achieved his goal of dispelling all forms of Apollinarianism from his Christology.

---

135. Torrance's soteriology vis-à-vis a physical theory of atonement is discussed in Habets, *Theosis in the Theology of Thomas Torrance,* Ashgate New Critical Thinking in Religion, Theology and Biblical Studies (Farnham: Ashgate, 2009), 52, 57–59.

Postscript: Torrance for the Twenty-First Century

In Torrance's Christology we see a dogmatic, systematic, biblical, and orthodox theologian at work. Torrance was never a mere commentator on the Great Tradition, nor was he a blind follower of luminaries from that tradition such as Barth. Rather, Torrance was a constructive theologian of retrieval who worked as a contemporary with the greatest Christian minds of the faith. Shoulder to shoulder with them, as it were, he sought to witness to the truth of God in Christ. In his work, one is invited into a conversation that requires two things: patient listening and informed contribution.

Torrance keenly understood that dogmatics is not primarily about answering questions; it is, rather, about faithful witness. No matter how much he might have wished it to be the case at times, his voice was never the last word in theology—only a word seeking harmony with the Word.

Throughout this volume I have sought to listen patiently to Torrance's theology before offering my own account. The best compliment we might pay Professor Torrance today, based on the way he did theology, is to provide our own educated and constructive contributions to the dogmatic enterprise. If we have learned something from his witness, then all the better.

Myk Habets
DSE

Bibliography

Achtemeier, P. Mark. "The Truth of Tradition: Critical Realism in the Thought of Alasdair MacIntyre and T. F. Torrance." *Scottish Journal of Theology* 47 (1996): 355–74.

Alfeyev, Hilarion. *St. Symeon the New Theologian and Orthodox Tradition.* Oxford: Oxford University Press, 2000.

Anatolios, Khaled. *Athanasius: The Coherence of His Thought.* London: Routledge, 1998.

Anselm. "Why God Became Man." In *A Scholastic Miscellany: Anselm to Ockham*, edited and translated by E. R. Fairweather, 100–183. The Library of Christian Classics. Philadelphia: Westminster, 1956.

Anselm. *Anselm: Basic Writings.* Translated by S. N. Deane. La Salle: Open Court, 1968.

Apczynski, J. V. "Torrance on Polanyi and Polanyi on God: Comments on Weightman's Criticisms—A Review Essay [*Theology in a Polanyian Universe: The Theology of Thomas Torrance*, by C. Weightman, 1994; reply, C. Weightman, 35–38]." *Tradition & Discovery* 24 (1997–98): 32–34.

Barr, James. *Biblical Faith and Natural Theology.* Oxford: Clarendon, 1993.

Barth, Karl. *Anselm: Fides Quarens Intellectum: Anselm's Proof of the Existence of God in the Context of his Theological Scheme.* Translated by I. W. Robertson. London: SCM, 1960.

———. *The Christian Life: Church Dogmatics, IV/4: Lecture Fragments.* Translated by G. W. Bromiley. Edinburgh: T&T Clark, 1981.

———. "Church and Culture." In *Theology and Church: Shorter Writings 1920–1928*, translated by L. Pettibone Smith, 334–54. London: SCM, 1962.

———. *Church Dogmatics.* Edited by G. W. Bromiley and Thomas F. Torrance. 4 volumes in 13 parts. Edinburgh: T&T Clark, 1936–75.

Barth, Karl, and E. Brunner. *Natural Theology: Comprising "Nature and Grace" by Professor Dr. Emil Brunner and the reply "No!" by Dr. Karl Barth.* Translated by P. Fraenkel. London: Geoffrey Bles, The Centenary Press, 1946.

Barth, Peter. *Das Problem der natürlichen Theologie bei Calvin.* Munich: C. Kaiser, 1935.

Bartos, Emil. *Deification in Eastern Orthodoxy: An Evaluation and Critique of the Theology of Dumitru Stăniloae.* Carlisle: Paternoster, 1999.

Baxter, Christina. "The Nature and Place of Scripture in the Church Dogmatics." In *Theology Beyond Christendom: Essays on the Centenary of the Birth of Karl Barth*, edited by John Thompson, 33–62. Allison Park, PA: Pickwick, 1986.

Bender, Kimlyn, J. "Christ, Creation and the Drama of Redemption: 'The Play's the Thing . . .'" *Scottish Journal of Theology* 62 (2009): 149–74.

Bloesch, Donald G. *Holy Scripture: Revelation, Inspiration, and Interpretation*. Downers Grove, IL: InterVarsity, 1994.

———. *A Theology of Word and Spirit: Authority and Method in Theology*.Downers Grove, IL: InterVarsity, 1992.

Böhl, Eduard. *Zur Abwehr: Etliche Bemerkungen gegen Professor Dr. A. Kuyper's Einletungu seiner Schrift: "Die Incarnation des Wortes" ("De Vleeschwording des Woords")*.Amsterdam: Scheffer, 1888.

Bouillard, H. *The Knowledge of God*. Translated by S. D. Femiano. New York: Herder and Herder, 1968.

Brand, Chad O. "Is Carl Henry a Modernist? Rationalism and Foundationalism in Post-War Evangelical Theology." *Trinity Journal* 20 (1999): 3–21.

Branick, Vincent P. "The Sinful Flesh of the Son of God (Rom 8.3): A Key Image of Pauline Theology." *The Catholic Biblical Quarterly* 47 (1985): 246–62

Brown, Raymond E., Joseph Fitzmyer, and Roland E. Murphy, eds. *The New Jerome Biblical Commentary*. Englewood Cliffs, NJ: Prentice Hall, 1990.

Brunner, Emil. *The Mediator: A Study of the Central Doctrine of the Christian Faith*. Translated by Olive Wyon. Philadelphia: Westminster, 1947.

Buckley, James J., and William McF. Wilson. "A Dialogue with Barth and Farrer on Theological Method." *Heythrop Journal* 26 (1985): 274–93.

Calvin, John. *The Institutes of the Christian Religion*. Translated by H. Beveridge. London: James Clarke, 1953.

Carvin, W. P. *Creation and Scientific Explanation*. Edinburgh: Scottish Academic, 1988.

Chrestou, Panayiotis. *Partakers of God*.Brookline, MA: Holy Cross Orthodox, 1984.

Chung, Titus. *Thomas Torrance's Mediations and Revelation*.Farnham: Ashgate, 2011.

Clendenin, Daniel B. *Eastern Orthodox Christianity: A Western Perspective*.Grand Rapids: Baker, 1994.

Colyer, Elmer M. *How To Read T. F. Torrance: Understanding his Trinitarian and Scientific Theology*. Downers Grove, IL: InterVarsity, 2001.

———. *The Nature of Doctrine in T. F. Torrance's Theology*.Eugene, OR: Wipf and Stock, 2001.

———. "A Response to Paul Molnar's Essay, 'A Natural Theology Revisited.'" Thomas F. Torrance Theological Fellowship Annual Meeting 2009, unpublished paper, 1–22.

Cranfield, C. E. B. *A Critical and Exegetical Commentary on the Epistle to the Romans*, vol. 1. International Critical Commentary. Edinburgh: T&T Clark, 1975.

Crisp, Oliver D. "Did Christ Have a *Fallen* Human Nature?" *International Journal of Systematic Theology* 6 (2004): 270–88.

———.*Divinity and Humanity: The Incarnation Reconsidered*.Cambridge: Cambridge University Press, 2007.

———. *God Incarnate: Explorations in Christology*.London: T&T Clark, 2009.

———. "Kathryn Tanner (1954–): On Incarnation as Atonement." In *Revisioning Christology: Theology in the Reformed Tradition,*111–32.Farnham: Ashgate, 2011.

———."Was Christ Sinless or Impeccable?" *Irish Theological Quarterly* 72 (2007): 168–86.

Dabney, D. Lyle. "Starting with the Spirit: Why the Last Should Now be First." In *Starting with the Spirit,* edited by S. Pickard and G. Preece, 3–27. Task of Theology Today II. Adelaide: ATF, 2001.

Davidson, Ivor. "Theologizing the Human Jesus: An Ancient (and Modern) Approach to Christology Reassessed." *International Journal of Systematic Theology* 3 (2001): 129–53.

Davies, P. *The Runaway Universe*. London: J. M. Dent & Sons, 1978.

Dawkins, Richard. *The Blind Watchmaker: Why the Evidence of Evolution Reveals a Universe without Design*.New York: W. W. Norton, 1986.

de Gruchy, John. "Salvation as Healing and Humanization." In *Christ in Our Place: The Humanity of God in Christ for the Reconciliation of the World: Essays Presented to Professor James Torrance*, edited by T. A. Hart and D. P. Thimell, 32–47. Exeter: Paternoster, 1981.

Del Colle, Ralph. "'Person' and 'Being' in John Zizioulas' Trinitarian Theology: Conversations with Thomas F. Torrance and Thomas Aquinas." *Scottish Journal of Theology* 54 (2001): 70–86.

Devitt, M. *Realism and Truth*. Oxford: Blackwell, 1984.

Dodd, C. H. *The Epistle of Paul to the Romans*. New York: Harper & Row, 1959.

Dowey, Edward A. *The Knowledge of God in Calvin's Theology*. New York: Columbia University Press, 1952.

———. "The Structure of Calvin's Thought as Influenced by the Two-Fold Knowledge of God." In *Calvinus Ecclesiae Genevensis Custos*, edited by W. Neuser, 135–148. Frankfurt: Peter Lang, 1984.

Dulles, A. "Faith, Church and God: Insights From Michael Polanyi." *Theological Studies* 45 (1984): 537–50.

Edersheim, Alfred. *The Life and Times of Jesus the Messiah*. Peabody, MA: Hendrickson, 1993.

Edwards, Jonathan. "A Divine and Supernatural Light. Immediately Imparted to the Soul by the Spirit of God, Shown to be Both a Scriptural and Rational Doctrine." In *A Jonathan Edwards Reader*, edited by J. E. Smith, H. S. Stout, and K. P. Minkema, 105–23. New Haven: Yale University Press, 1995.

———. *The Works of Jonathan Edwards, Volume 8: Ethical Writings*.Edited by P. Ramsey. New Haven: Yale University Press, 1989.

Fergusson, David. "Types of Natural Theology." In *The Evolution of Rationality: Interdisciplinary Essays in Honor of J. Wentzel van Huyssteen*, edited by F. LeRon Shults, 380–93. Grand Rapids: Eerdmans, 2006.

Fine, A. *The Shaky Game: Einstein, Realism and the Quantum Theory*. Chicago: University of Chicago Press, 1986.

Forde, Gerhard O. *On Being a Theologian of the Cross*. Grand Rapids: Eerdmans, 1997.

Franke, John R. *The Character of Theology: An Introduction to its Nature, Task, and Purpose*.Grand Rapids: Baker, 2005.

Gascoigne, J. "From Bentley to the Victorians: the Rise and Fall of British Newtonian Natural Theology." *Science in Context* 2 (1988): 219–56.

Gelwick, R. "Michael Polanyi—Modern Reformer." *Religion in Life* 34 (1965): 224–34.

Gilkey, L. *Nature, Reality and the Sacred: The Nexus of Science and Religion*. Minneapolis: Fortress, 1993.

———. *Religion and the Scientific Future: Reflections in Myth, Science and Theology*.New York: Harper & Row, 1970.

Gloede, G. *Theologia naturalis bei Calvin*. Stuttgart: Kohlhammer, 1935.

Grenz, Stanley J. *Renewing the Center: Evangelical Theology in a Post-Theological Era*.Grand Rapids: Baker, 2000.

———. *Theology for the Community of God*. Carlisle, PA: Paternoster, 1994.

Grillmeier, Aloys. *Christ in Christian Tradition*, vol. 1. Atlanta: John Knox, 1975.

Grudem, Wayne. *Systematic Theology: An Introduction to Biblical Doctrine.*Grand Rapids: Zondervan, 1994.

Gunton, Colin E. *A Brief Theology of Revelation.* Edinburgh: T&T Clark, 1995.

———. "The Church: John Owen and John Zizioulas on the Church." In *Theology Through the Theologians: Selected Essays 1972–1995.* Edinburgh: T&T Clark, 1996, 187–205.

———. *Enlightenment and Alienation: An Essay Towards a Trinitarian Theology.* Basingstoke: Marshall, Morgan and Scott, 1985.

———. *The One, the Three, and the Many: God, Creation and the Culture of Modernity.*The Bampton Lectures 1992. Cambridge: Cambridge University Press, 1993.

———. *Revelation and Reason: Prolegomena to Systematic Theology.* Edited by Paul. H. Brazier. London: T&T Clark, 2008.

———. *The Triune Creator: A Historical and Systematic Study.*Grand Rapids: Eerdmans, 1998.

———. "Two Dogmas Revisited: Edward Irving's Christology." *Scottish Journal of Theology* 41 (1988): 359–76.

Habets, Myk. "Beyond Henry's Nominalism and Evangelical Foundationalism: Thomas Torrance's Theological Realism." In *Gospel, Truth and Interpretation: Evangelical Identity in Aotearoa New Zealand*, edited by Tim Meadowcroft and Myk Habets, 205–40. Archer Studies in Pacific Christianity. Auckland: Archer Press, 2011.

———. "*Filioque? Nein.* A Proposal for Coherent Coinherence." In *Trinitarian Theology After Barth,*edited by Myk Habets and Phillip Tolliday, 161–202. Eugene, OR: Pickwick, 2011.

———. "On Getting First Things First: Assessing Claims for the Primacy of Christ." *New Blackfriars* 90 (2009): 343–64.

———. "'Reformed Theosis?' A Response to Gannon Murphy." *Theology Today* 65 (2009): 489–98.

———. "Reforming Theosis." In *Theosis: Deification in Christian Theology*, edited by S. Finlan and V. Kharlamov, 146–67. Princeton Theological Monograph Series 52. Eugene, OR: Pickwick, 2006.

———. "Third Article Theology and the *Filioque.*" In *Ecumenical Perspectives on the*Filioque *for the 21st Century*, edited by Myk Habets. London: T&T Clark, forthcoming.

———. "Review Article: *The Groaning of Creation: God, Evolution, and the Problem of Evil.*" *American Theological Inquiry* 3 (2010): 108–13.

———. "Theological Interpretation of Scripture in Sermonic Mode: The Case of T. F. Torrance." In *Ears That Hear: Explorations in Theological Interpretation of the Bible*, edited by Joel Green and Tim Meadowcroft, 44–71. Sheffield: Sheffield Phoenix, 2013.

———. *Theosis in the Theology of Thomas Torrance*. Ashgate New Critical Thinking in Religion, Theology and Biblical Studies. Farnham: Ashgate, 2009.

———. "Theosis, Yes; Deification, No." In *The Spirit of Truth: Reading Scripture and Constructing Theology with the Holy Spirit,* edited by Myk Habets, 124–49. Eugene, OR: Pickwick, 2010.

———. "Walking in *mirabilibus supra me*: How C. S. Lewis Transposes Theosis." *Evangelical Quarterly* 82 (2010): 15–27.

Habets, Myk, and Robert Grow, eds. *Evangelical Calvinism: Essays Resourcing the Continuing Reformation of the Church.* Eugene, OR: Pickwick, 2012.

Hardy, Daniel W. "Thomas F. Torrance." In *The Modern Theologians: An Introduction*, vol. 1, edited by D. F. Ford, 71–91. Oxford: Blackwell, 1989.

Hart, Trevor A. *The Teaching Father: An Introduction to the Theology of Thomas Erskine of Linlathen*. Edinburgh: Saint Andrew, 1993.

———. *Regarding Karl Barth: Toward a Reading of His Theology.* Downers Grove, IL: InterVarsity, 1999.

Hastings, W. R. "'Honouring the Spirit': Analysis and Evaluation of Jonathan Edwards' Pneumatological Doctrine of the Incarnation." *International Journal of Systematic Theology* 7 (2003): 279–99.

Hawking, Stephen W. *A Brief History of Time*. Toronto: Bantam, 1988.

Hebblethwaite, Brian. "*T. F. Torrance: An Intellectual Biography*, A Review." *Scottish Journal of Theology* 53 (2000): 239–42.

Hellwig, M. "Re-Emergence of the Human, Critical, Public Jesus." *Theological Studies* 50 (1989): 466–80.

Michaud, Derek. "Thomas Torrance." In the *Boston Collaborative Dictionary of Western Theology*. http://people.bu.edu/wwildman/bce/torrance.htm.

Henry, Carl F. H. *Frontiers in Modern Theology: A Critique of Current Theological Trends.* Chicago: Moody, 1964.

———. *God, Revelation and Authority*. 6 Vols. Waco: Word, 1976–83.

———. "Presuppositions and Theological Method." Tape 172a, Part 1; Tape 172b, Part 2. Edinburgh: Rutherford House. http://tapesfromscotland.org/Rutherfordhouseaudio.htm.

———. "Reaction and Realignment." *Christianity Today* 20 (July 2, 1976): 30.

Heron, Alasdair I. C. "*Homo Peccator* and the *Imago Dei* According to John Calvin." In *Incarnational Ministry: Essays in Honor of Ray S. Anderson*, edited by C. D. Kettler and T. H. Speidell, 32–57. Colorado Springs: Helmers and Howard, 1990.

———."James Torrance: An Appreciation." In *Christ in Our Place: The Humanity of God in Christ for the Reconciliation of the World: Essays Presented to Professor James Torrance*, edited by T. A. Hart and D. P. Thimell, 1–8. Exeter: Paternoster, 1981.

———. "Karl Barth: A Personal Engagement." In *The Cambridge Companion to Karl Barth*, edited by J. Webster, 296–306. Cambridge: Cambridge University Press, 2000.

———. "T. F. Torrance In Relation to Reformed Theology." In *The Promise of Trinitarian Theology: Theologians in Dialogue with T. F. Torrance*, edited by E. M. Colyer, 31–49. Lanham, MD: Rowman & Littlefield, 2001.

Hesselink, I. John. "A Pilgrimage in the School of Christ: An Interview with T. F. Torrance." *Reformed Review* 38 (1984): 49–64.

Holder, Rodney D. *The Heavens Declare: Natural Theology and the Legacy of Karl Barth*.West Conshohoken, PA: Templeton, 2012.

———."Karl Barth and the Legitimacy of Natural Theology." *Themelios*26 (2001): 22–37.

Holmes, Stephen R. *God of Grace and God of Glory: An Account of the Theology of Jonathan Edwards*. Grand Rapids: Eerdmans, 2000.

Houston, James M. "Spirituality and the Doctrine of the Trinity." In *Christ in Our Place: The Humanity of God in Christ for the Reconciliation of the World: Essays Presented to Professor James Torrance*, edited by T. A. Hart and D. P. Thimell, 48–69. Exeter: Paternoster, 1981.

———."Traditions of Spirituality—A Historical Overview: Lecture Two: 'Reflections on Mysticism—How Valid is Evangelical Mysticism?'" Lecture at Regent College, Vancouver, 1990.

Howe, G. *Die Christenheit im Atomzeitalter: Vortlage und Studien*. Stuttgart: Klett, 1970.

Hoyningen-Huene, P. "Kuhn's Conception of Incommensurability." *Studies in History and Philosophy of Science*53 (1980): 481–92.

Hughes, Philip E. *The True Image: The Origin and Destiny of Man in Christ*. Grand Rapids: Eerdmans, 1989.

Hunsinger, George. *Disruptive Grace: Studies in the Theology of Karl Barth*. Grand Rapids: Eerdmans, 2000.

———. *How to Read Karl Barth: The Shape of His Theology*.Oxford: Oxford University Press, 1991.

———. "Light from Light: From Irenaeus and Torrance to Aquinas and Barth." In *Light From Light: Scientists and Theologians in Dialogue*, edited by G. O'Collins and M. A. Myers, 208–35. Grand Rapids: Eerdmans, 2012.

Irving, Edward. *The Collected Writings of Edward Irving*. Edited by G. Carlyle. London: Alexander Strachan, 1865.

Jaki, S. L. *Cosmos in Transition*. Tucson, AZ: Pachart, 1990.

———. *The Road to Science and the Ways to God*. Chicago: University of Chicago Press, 1978.

Jeon, J. K. *Covenant Theology: John Murray's and Meredith Kline's Response to the Historical Development of Federal Theology in Reformed Thought*. Lanham, MD: University Press of America, 1999.

Kapic, Kelly M. "The Son's Assumption of a Human Nature: A Call for Clarity." *International Journal of Systematic Theology* 3 (2001): 154–66.

Keating James F., and Thomas J. White, eds. *Divine Impassibility and the Mystery of Human Suffering*. Grand Rapids: Eerdmans, 2009.

Kelly, John N. D. *Early Christian Doctrines*,4th ed. London: A&C Black, 1977.

Kernohan, Robert D. "Tom Torrance: The Man and the Reputation." *Life and Work* 32 (1976): 14–16.

Kögler, H. H. "Utopianism." In *The Oxford Companion to Philosophy*, edited by T. Honderich, 892–93. Oxford: Oxford University Press, 1995.

Kreitzmann, N. *The Metaphysics of Theism: Aquinas's Natural Theology in Summa contra Gentiles I*. Oxford: Clarendon, 1997.

Kruger, C. Baxter. "The Doctrine of the Knowledge of God in the Theology of T. F. Torrance: Sharing in the Son's Communion with the Father in the Spirit." *Scottish Journal of Theology* 43 (1990): 366–89.

Kuhn, Thomas S. *The Structure of Scientific Revolutions*. Chicago: University of Chicago Press, 1962.

Lane, Anthony N. S. *John Calvin: Student of the Church Fathers*. Edinburgh: T&T Clark, 1999.

Laudisa, F. "Einstein, Bell and Nonseparable Realism." *British Journal for the Philosophy of Science* 46 (1995): 309–29.

Leplin, J., ed. *Scientific Realism*. Berkeley: University of California Press, 1984.

Leung, Mavis M. "With What is Evangelicalism to Penetrate the World? A Study of Cary Henry's Envisioned Evangelicalism." *Trinity Journal* 27 (2006): 227–44.

Levering, Matthew. *Participatory Biblical Exegesis: A Theology of Biblical Interpretation.*Notre Dame: University of Notre Dame Press, 2008.
Lewis, C. S. "The Weight of Glory." In *Screwtape Proposes a Toast and Other Pieces*, 94–110.London: Fontana, 1965.
Lossky, Vladimir. *In the Image and Likeness of God.*Crestwood, NY: St. Vladimir's Seminary Press, 1985.
———. *The Mystical Theology of the Eastern Church.*Crestwood, NY: St. Vladimir's Seminary Press, 1998.
———. *Orthodox Theology: An Introduction.* Translated by I. and I. Kasarcodi-Watson. 1978; Reprint Crestwood, NY: St. Vladimir's Seminary Press, 2001.
———. *The Vision of God.*Translated by A. Moorhouse. Crestwood, NY: St. Vladimir's Seminary Press, 1973.
Louth, Andrew. *Discerning the Mystery: An Essay on the Nature of Theology.* Oxford: Clarendon, 1983.
———. *The Origins of the Christian Mystical Tradition: From Plato to Denys.* Oxford: Clarendon, 1981.
Macierowski, E. M., and R. F. Hassing. "John Philoponus on Aristotle's Definition of Nature: A Translation from the Greek with Introduction and Notes." *Ancient Philosophy* 8 (1988): 73–100.
Mackenzie, Iain. "Let the Brain Take the Strain (or: The Hail in this Tale Falls Mainly on the Gael)." In *St. Andrews Rock*, edited by S. Lamont, 76–90. London: Bellew, 1992.
Macleod, Donald. "Christology." In *Dictionary of Scottish History and Theology*, edited by D. F. Wright, D. C. Lachman, and D. E. Meek, 172–77. Edinburgh: T&T Clark, 1993.
———."Dr. T. F. Torrance and Scottish Theology: A Review Article [*Scottish Theology from John Knox to John McLeod Campbell*, 1996]." *Evangelical Quarterly*72 (2000): 57–72.
———. *Jesus Is Lord: Christology Yesterday and Today*. Fearn, Ross-shire: Christian Focus, 1998.
———. *The Person of Christ.*Leicester: Inter-Varsity, 1998.
———. "Review of *Scottish Theology* by Tom Torrance." Tape 198. Edinburgh: Rutherford House, 1999. http://tapesfromscotland.org/Rutherfordhouseaudio.htm.
Mannermaa, T. "Justification and *Theosis*in Lutheran-Orthodox Perspective." In *Union With Christ: The New Finnish Interpretation of Luther*, edited by C. E. Braaten, and R. W. Jensen, 25–41. Grand Rapids: Eerdmans, 1998.

Mantzaridis, G. I. *The Deification of Man: St. Gregory Palamas and the Orthodox Tradition*.Translated by L. Sherrard. Crestwood, NY: St. Vladimir's Seminary Press, 1984.

Marley, Alan G. *T. F. Torrance: The Rejection of Dualism*. Nutshell Series 4. Edinburgh: Handsel, 1992.

Mascall, Eric L. *Christian Theology and Natural Science: Some Questions in Their Relations*. London: Longmans, Green, 1956.

———. *Theology and the Gospel of Christ: An Essay in Reorientation*.London: SPCK, 1977.

Maury, P. "La Théologie naturelle d'après Calvin." *The Bulletin de la Soc. de l'Hist. du Protest. Francais* LXXXIV (1935): 267–79.

Maxwell, James Clerk. *A Dynamical Theory of the Electromagnetic Field*. Edinburgh: Scottish Academic, 1982.

McCall, Tom. "Ronald Thiemann, Thomas Torrance and Epistemological Doctrines of Revelation." *International Journal of Systematic Theology* 6 (2004): 148–68.

McClymont, M. J. "Salvation as Divinization: Jonathan Edwards, Gregory Palamas and the Theological Uses of Neoplatonism." In *Jonathan Edwards: Philosophical Theologian*, edited by P. Helm and O. D. Crisp, 136–60. Aldershot: Ashgate, 2003.

McCormack, Bruce L. "For Us and Our Salvation: Incarnation and Atonement in the Reformed Tradition." *The Greek Orthodox Theological Review* 43 (1998): 281–316.

McDowell, John C. "A Response to Rodney Holder on Barth on Natural Theology." *Themelios* 27 (2002): 32–44.

McFarlane, Graham W. P. *Christ and the Spirit: The Doctrine of the Incarnation According to Edward Irving*.Carlisle: Paternoster, 1996.

———. *Why Do You Believe What You Believe About The Holy Spirit?*Carlisle: Paternoster, 1998.

McIntyre, John. *St. Anselm and His Critics: A Reinterpretation of the Cur Deus Homo*. London: Oliver and Boyd, 1954.

McGrath, Alister E. *A Fine-Tuned Universe: The Quest for God in Science and Theology*.Louisville: Westminster John Knox, 2009.

———. *The Foundations of Dialogue in Science and Religion*. Oxford: Blackwell, 1998.

———. *The Genesis of Doctrine: A Study in the Foundations of Doctrinal Criticism*. Oxford: Blackwell, 1990.

———. *The Open Secret: A New Vision for Natural Theology*. Oxford: Blackwell, 2008.

———. *A Passion for Truth: The Intellectual Coherence of Evangelicalism*. Leicester: Apollos, 1996.

———. *The Science of God*. London: T&T Clark, 2004.

———. "Scientific Method and the Reconstruction of Theology: Introducing 'A Scientific Theology.'" Lecture for the John Templeton Oxford Seminars on Science and Christianity, Harris Manchester College. July 24, 2003. http://www.metanexus.net/archives/message_fs.asp?ARCHIVEID=8363.

———. *A Scientific Theology, Volume 1: Nature*. Grand Rapids: Eerdmans, 2001.

———. *A Scientific Theology, Volume 2: Reality*. Grand Rapids: Eerdmans, 2002.

———. *A Scientific Theology, Volume 3: Theory*. Grand Rapids: Eerdmans, 2003.

———. *T. F. Torrance: An Intellectual Biography*. Edinburgh: T&T Clark, 1999.

McKenzie, Ross H. "Emergence, Reductionism and the Stratification of Reality in Science and Theology." *Scottish Journal of Theology* 64 (2011): 211–35.

McMaken, W. Travis. "The Impossibility of Natural Knowledge of God in T. F. Torrance's Reformulated Natural Theology." *International Journal of Systematic Theology* 12 (2010): 319–40.

Mitchell, R. G. *Einstein and Christ: A New Approach to the Defence of the Christian Religion*. Edinburgh: Scottish Academic, 1987.

Molendijk, A. L. "Henirich Sholz-Karl Barth: Een discussie over de wetenschappelijkheid van de theologie." *Nederlands Theologisch Tijdschrift* 39 (1985): 295–313.

Molnar, Paul D. *Divine Freedom and the Doctrine of the Immanent Trinity: In Dialogue with Karl Barth and Contemporary Theology*. London: T&T Clark, 2002.

———. "Natural Theology Revisited: A Comparison of T. F. Torrance and Karl Barth." *Zeitschrift für dialektische Theologie* 21 (2005): 53–83.

———. *Thomas F. Torrance: Theologian of the Trinity*. Surrey: Ashgate, 2009.

Moltmann, Jürgen. *The Spirit of Life: A Universal Affirmation*. Translated by M. Kohl. Minneapolis: Fortress, 1992.

———. *The Trinity and the Kingdom*. Translated by M. Kohl. San Francisco: Harper & Row, 1981.

Moore, Andrew. *Realism and Christian Faith: God, Grammar and Meaning*. Cambridge: Cambridge University Press, 2003.

Morris, Leon. *The Lord from Heaven: A Study of the New Testament Teaching on the Deity and Humanity of Jesus*. Grand Rapids: Eerdmans, 1958.

Morris, Thomas V. *The Logic of God Incarnate*. Ithaca: Cornell University Press, 1986.

Morrison, John D. "Heidegger, Correspondence Truth and the Realist Theology of Thomas Forsyth Torrance." *Evangelical Quarterly* 69 (1997): 139–55.

———. *Knowledge of the Self-Revealing God in the Thought of Thomas Forsyth Torrance*. Issues in Systematic Theology 2. New York: Peter Lang, 1997.

———. "Thomas Torrance's Reformulation of Karl Barth's Christological Rejection of Natural Theology." *Evangelical Quarterly* 73 (2001): 59–75.

Mostert, Christiaan. *God and the Future: Wolfhart Pannenberg's Eschatological Doctrine of God*. London: T&T Clark, 2002.

Muller, Richard A. *Dictionary of Latin and Greek Theological Terms*. Grand Rapids: Baker, 1985.

Munchin, David. *Is Theology a Science? The Nature of the Scientific Enterprise in the Scientific Theology of Thomas Forsyth Torrance and the Anarchic Epistemology of Paul Feyerabend*.Leiden: Brill, 2011.

Myers, Benjamin. "The Stratification of Knowledge in the Thought of T. F. Torrance." *Scottish Journal of Theology* 61 (2008): 1–15.

Nebelsick, H. *Theology and Science in Mutual Modification*. Belfast: Christian Journals, 1981.

Neidhardt, W. J. "Thomas F. Torrance's Integration of Judeo-Christian Theology and Natural Science: Some Key Themes." *Perspectives on Science and Christian Faith* 41 (1989): 87–98.

Newbigin, Lesslie. *The Gospel in a Pluralist Society*. London: SPCK, 1989.

Owen, H. P. "The Sinlessness of Jesus." In *Religion, Reason, and the Self: Essays in Honour of Hywel D. Lewis*, edited by S. R. Sutherland and T. A. Roberts, 119–28. Cardiff: University of Wales Press, 1989.

Owen, John. *An Exposition of the Epistle to the Hebrews*. 7 vols. Edited by W. H. Goold. 1854. Reprint, Grand Rapids: Baker, 1980.

———. "Work of the Holy Spirit with Respect unto the Head of the New Creation—the Human Nature of Christ." In *The Works of John Owen*, edited by W. H. Goold, 3:159–88. 1862. Reprint, London: Banner of Truth, 1966.

Palma, R. J. "Thomas F. Torrance's Reformed Theology." *Reformed Review* 38 (1984): 2–46.

Pannenberg, Wolfhart. *Systematic Theology*,vol. 2. Translated by G. W. Bromiley. Grand Rapids: Eerdmans, 1994.

———. *Theology and the Kingdom of God*. Edited by R. J. Neuhaus. Philadelphia: Westminster, 1969.

———. *Theology and the Philosophy of Science*. Translated by F. McDonagh. London: Darton, Longman and Todd, 1976.
Parker, T. H. L. *Calvin's Doctrine of the Knowledge of God*. 2nd ed. Grand Rapids: Eerdmans, 1959.
Paul, I. *Science and Theology in Einstein's Perspective*. Edinburgh: Scottish Academic, 1986.
———. *Science, Theology and Einstein.* New York: Oxford University Press, 1981.
Peters, Ted. "Theology and Science: Where Are We?" *Zygon* 31 (1996): 323–43.
Pettersen, A. *Athanasius*. London: Geoffrey Chapman, 1995.
Poirier, M. W. "A Comment on Polanyi and Kuhn." *The Thomist* 53 (1989): 259–79.
Polanyi, Michael. *Personal Knowledge: Towards a Post-Critical Philosophy*. Chicago: University of Chicago Press, 1958.
———. "Science and Man's Place in the Universe." In *Science as a Cultural Force*, edited by H. Woolf, 54–76. Baltimore: Johns Hopkins Press, 1964.
———. *The Tacit Dimension*. New York: Doubleday, 1966.
Polanyi, Michael, and Harry Prosch. *Meaning*. Chicago: University of Chicago Press, 1975.
Polikarov, A. "On the Nature of Einstein's Realism." *Epistemologia* 12 (1980): 277–304.
Prenter, R. "Das Problem der natürlichen Theologie bei Karl Barth." *Theologische Literaturzeitung* 77 (1952): 607–11.
Rahner, Karl. *Theological Investigations, Volume IV: More Recent Writings.* Translated by K. Smyth. London: Darton, Longman and Todd, 1974.
———. *The Trinity*. Translated by J. Donceel. New York: Seabury, 1974.
Redding, Graeme. *Prayer and the Priesthood of Christ in the Reformed Tradition*. Edinburgh: T&T Clark, 2003.
Rehnman, S. "Barthian Epigoni: Thomas F. Torrance's Barth-Reception." *Westminster Theological Journal* 60 (1998): 271–96.
Richardson, Kurt. "Revelation, Scripture, and Mystical Apprehension of Divine Knowledge." In *The Promise of Trinitarian Theology: Theologians in Dialogue with T. F. Torrance*, edited by E. M. Colyer, 185–203. Lanham, MD: Rowman & Littlefield, 2001.
Ridderbos, Herman. *Paul: An Outline of His Theology*. Grand Rapids: Eerdmans, 1975.

Rodger, Simeon. "The Soteriology of Anselm of Canterbury, An Orthodox Perspective." *The Greek Orthodox Theological Review* 34 (1989): 19–43.

Rogich, D. M. *Becoming Uncreated: The Journey to Human Authenticity: Updating the Spiritual Christology of Gregory Palamas*.Minneapolis: Light and Life, 1997.

Russell, R. J. "Contingency in Physics and Cosmology: A Critique of the Theology of Wolfhart Pannenberg." *Zygon* 23 (1988): 23–43.

Schreiner, Susan. *The Theatre of His Glory: Nature and the Natural Order in the Thought of John Calvin*. Durham, NC.: Labyrinth, 1991.

Schwöbel, Christoph, and Colin E. Gunton, eds. *Persons, Divine and Human*.Edinburgh: T&T Clark, 1991.

Sholz, H. "Wie ist eine evangelische Theologie als Wisseschaft moglich?" *Zweschen den Zeiten* 9 (1931): 8–53.

Shults, F. LeRon. "Constitutive Relationality in Anthropology and Trinity: The Shaping of the Imago Dei Doctrine in Barth and Pannenberg." *Neue Zeitschrift für systematische Theologie und Religionsphilosophie* 39 (1997): 304–22.

Shuster, Marguerite. "'What is Truth?' An Exploration of Thomas F. Torrance's Epistemology." *Studia Biblica Et Theologia*3 (1973): 50–56.

Sorabji, R. K., ed. *Philoponos and the Rejection of Aristotelian Science*.Ithaca, NY: Cornell University Press, 1987.

Spence, Alan. "Incarnation and Inspiration: John Owen and the Coherence of Christology." PhD dissertation, Kings College, London, 1989.

———. *Incarnation and Inspiration: John Owen and the Coherence of Christology*. London: T&T Clark, 2007.

———. "John Owen and Trinitarian Agency." *Scottish Journal of Theology* 43 (1990): 157–73.

Spjuth, Roland. *Creation, Contingency and Divine Presence: In the Theologies of Thomas F. Torrance and Eberhard Jüngel*.Lund: Lund University Press, 1995.

Stăniloae, Dumitru. *The Experience of God: Orthodox Dogmatic Theology, Volume 2, The World: Creation and Deification*. Translated and edited by I. Ionita and R. Barringer. Brookline, MA: Holy Cross Orthodox, 2000.

Stein, Jock, ed. *Gospel, Church, and Ministry*. Thomas F. Torrance Collected Studies 1. Eugene, OR: Pickwick, 2012.

———. "The Legacy of the Gospel." In *A Passion for Christ: Vision that Ignites Ministry*, edited by G. Dawson and J. Stein, 131–50. Edinburgh: Handsel, 1999.

Strachan, C. Gordon. *The Pentecostal Theology of Edward Irving*.London: Darton, Longman and Todd, 1973.
Strobel, Kyle. "Jonathan Edwards and the Polemics of *Theosis*." *Harvard Theological Review*105 (2012): 259–79.
Strug, C. "Kuhn's Paradigm Thesis: A Two-Edged Sword for the Philosophy of Religion." *Religious Studies* 20 (1984): 269–79.
Sudduth, Michael. *The Reformed Objection to Natural Theology*. Farnham: Ashgate, 2009.
Tamburello, D. E. *Union With Christ: John Calvin and the Mysticism of St. Bernard*.Louisville: Westminster John Knox, 1994.
Tanner, Kathryn E. "Creation and Providence." In *The Cambridge Companion to Karl Barth*, edited by J. Webster, 111–26. Cambridge: Cambridge University Press, 2000.
———. *God and Creation in Christian Theology: Tyranny or Empowerment?* Oxford: Blackwell, 1988.
———. "The Use of Perceived Properties of Light as a Theological Analogy." In *Light from Light: Scientists and Theologians in Dialogue*, edited by G. O'Collins and M. A. Myers, 122–30. Grand Rapids: Eerdmans, 2012.
Thiemann, Ronald. *Revelation and Theology: The Gospel as Narrated Promise*.Notre Dame: University of Notre Dame Press, 1985.
Thorson, W. R. "The Biblical Insights of Michael Polanyi." *Journal of the American Scientific Affiliation* 33 (1981): 129–38
———. "Scientific Objectivity and the Listening Attitude." In *Objective Knowledge: A Christian Perspective*, edited by P. Helm, 59–83. Leicester: Inter-Varsity, 1987.
Torrance, David W. "Thomas Forsyth Torrance: Minister of the Gospel, Pastor, and Evangelical Theologian." In *The Promise of Trinitarian Theology: Theologians in Dialogue with T. F. Torrance*, edited by E. M. Colyer, 1–30. Lanham, MD: Rowman & Littlefield, 2001.
Torrance, James B. "The Vicarious Humanity of Christ." In *The Incarnation: Ecumenical Studies in the Nicene-Constantinopolitan Creed A.D. 381*, edited by T. F. Torrance, 127–47. Edinburgh: Handsel, 1981.
Torrance, Thomas F. *The Atonement: The Person and Work of Christ*.Edited by Robert T. Walker. Downers Grove, IL: IVP Academic, 2009.
———. "The Atonement: The Singularity of Christ and the Finality of the Cross: The Atonement and the Moral Order." In *Universalism and the Doctrine of Hell*, edited by N. M de S. Cameron, 225–56. Carlisle: Paternoster, 1992; Grand Rapids: Baker, 1992.

———. "The Atoning Obedience of Christ." *Moravian Theological Seminary Bulletin* (Fall 1959): 65–81.

———. *Calvin's Doctrine of Man*. London: Lutterworth, 1949.

———. "Christ in the Midst of His Church." In *When Christ Comes and Comes Again*, 101–16. London: Hodder and Stoughton, 1957.

———. *Christ's Words*. Jedburgh: The Unity Press, 1980.

———. *The Christian Doctrine of God: One Being Three Persons*. Edinburgh: T&T Clark, 1996.

———. ?*The Christian Frame of Mind:?Reason, Order, and Openness in Theology and Natural Science*. Eugene, OR: Wipf and Stock, 2010.

———. *Christian Theology and Scientific Culture*. New York: Oxford University Press, 1981.

———. *Conflict and Agreement in the Church, Volume 1: Order and Disorder*. London: Lutterworth, 1959.

———. *Conflict and Agreement in the Church, Volume 2: The Ministry and the Sacraments of the Gospel*. London: Lutterworth, 1960.

———. "The Deposit of Faith." *Scottish Journal of Theology* 36 (1983): 1–28.

———. "The Distinctive Character of the Reformed Tradition." In *Incarnational Ministry: Essays in Honor of Ray S. Anderson*, edited by C. H. Kettler and T. H. Speidell, 2–15. Colorado Springs: Helmers and Howard, 1990.

———. *Divine and Contingent Order*. Reprint, Edinburgh: T&T Clark, 1998.

———. *Divine Meaning: Studies in Patristic Hermeneutics*. Edinburgh: T&T Clark, 1995.

———. *The Doctrine of Grace in the Apostolic Fathers*. Edinburgh: Oliver and Boyd, 1948.

———. *The Doctrine of Jesus Christ: Auburn Lectures 1938–39*. Eugene, OR: Wipf and Stock, 2002.

———. "The Doctrine of Order." *Church Quarterly Review* 160 (1959): 21–36.

———. "The Framework of Belief." In *Belief in Science and in Christian Life: The Relevance of Michael Polanyi's Thought for Christian Faith and Life*, edited by T. F. Torrance, 1–27. Edinburgh: Handsel, 1980.

———. *God and Rationality*. London: Oxford University Press, 1971.

———. *The Ground and Grammar of Theology*. Charlottesville: University of Virginia Press, 1980.

———. "The Ground and Grammar of Theology." Lectures given at Fuller Theological Seminary: Lecture 6, Q & A, 20:54–22:42 minutes (1981). http://www.gci.org/audio/torrance.

———. *The Hermeneutics of John Calvin*. Edinburgh: Scottish Academic, 1988.

———. "'The Historical Jesus': From the Perspective of a Theologian." In *The New Testament Age: Essays in Honor of Bo Reicke*, vol. 2, edited by W. C. Weinrich, 49–64. Macon, GA: Mercer University Press, 1984.

———. "Hugh Ross Mackintosh: Theologian of the Cross." *Scottish Bulletin of Evangelical Theology* 5 (1987): 160–73.

———. "Incarnation and Atonement: *Theosis* and *Henosis* in the Light of Modern Scientific Rejection of Dualism." *Society of Ordained Scientists,* Bulletin No. 7. Edgeware, Middlesex (Spring 1992): 8–20.

———. *The Incarnation: The Person and Life of Christ*. Edited by Robert T. Walker. Downers Grove, IL: IVP Academic, 2008.

———. "Introduction." In *The Incarnation: Ecumenical Studies in the Nicene-Constantinopolitan Creed A.D. 381*, edited by T. F. Torrance, xi–xxii. Edinburgh: Handsel, 1981.

———. "Introduction." In William Manson, *Jesus and the Christian*, 9–14. London: James Clarke, 1967.

———. "Introduction." In *The School of Faith: The Catechisms of the Reformed Church*, translated and edited with introduction by T. F. Torrance, xi–cxxvi. London: James Clarke, 1959.

———. "Intuitive and Abstractive Knowledge: From Duns Scotus to Calvin." In *De Doctrina Ioannis Duns Scoti. Congressus Scotisticus Internationalis. Studia Scholastico-Scotistica 5*, edited by C. Balic, 291–305. Rome: Societas Internationalis Scotistica, 1968.

———. "John Philoponos of Alexandria, Sixth Century Christian Physicist." *Texts and Studies*, vol. 2. London: Thyateira House, 1983: 261–65.

———. *Juridical Law and Physical Law: Toward a Realist Foundation for Human Law*. Eugene, OR: Wipf and Stock, 1997.

———. *Karl Barth: Biblical and Evangelical Theologian*. Edinburgh: T&T Clark, 1990.

———. *Karl Barth: An Introduction to His Early Theology, 1910–1931*. Edinburgh: T&T Clark, 2000.

———. "Karl Barth and the Latin Heresy." *Scottish Journal of Theology* 39 (1986): 461–82.

———. "Kerygmatic Proclamation of the Gospel: *The Demonstration of Apostolic Preaching* of Irenaios of Lyons." *The Greek Orthodox Theological Review* 37 (1992): 105–21.

———. *The Mediation of Christ*. Edinburgh: T&T Clark, 1992.

———. "Michael Polanyi and the Christian Faith—A Personal Report." *Tradition and Discovery: The Polanyi Society Periodical* 27 (2000–2001): 26–32.

———. "My Interaction with Karl Barth." In *How Karl Barth Changed My Mind*, edited by D. K. McKim, 52–64. Grand Rapids: Eerdmans, 1986.

———. "The Place of Michael Polanyi in the Modern Philosophy of Science." *Ethics in Science and Medicine* 7 (1980): 57–95.

———. *Preaching Christ Today*.Grand Rapids: Eerdmans, 1994.

———. "The Problem of Natural Theology in the Thought of Karl Barth." *Religious Studies* 6 (1970): 121–35.

———. *Reality and Evangelical Theology*. Philadelphia: Westminster, 1982.

———. *Reality and Scientific Theology*.Edinburgh: Scottish Academic, 1985.

———. "Reply to Donald Macleod." Tape 199. Edinburgh: Rutherford House, 1999. http://tapesfromscotland.org/Rutherfordhouseaudio.htm.

———, ed. and trans. *The School of Faith: The Catechisms of the Reformed Church*. London: James Clarke, 1959.

———. *Scottish Theology from John Knox to John McLeod Campbell*. Edinburgh: T&T Clark, 1996.

———. *Space, Time and Incarnation*.Edinburgh: T&T Clark, 2005.

———. *Space, Time and Resurrection*.Edinburgh: Handsel, 1976.

———. "'The Substance of the Faith': A Clarification of the Concept in the Church of Scotland," *Scottish Journal of Theology* 36 (1983): 327–38.

———, ed. *Theological Dialogue Between Orthodox and Reformed Churches*,vols. 1 & 2.Edinburgh: Scottish Academic, 1985, 1993.

———. "Theological Realism." In *The Philosophical Frontiers of Christian Theology: Essays Presented to D. M. MacKinnon*, edited by B. Hebblethwaite and S. Sutherland, 169–96. Cambridge: Cambridge University Press, 1982.

———. *Theological and Natural Science*. Eugene, OR: Wipf and Stock, 2002.

———. *Theological Science*.Reprint, Edinburgh: T&T Clark, 1996.

———. *Theology in Reconciliation: Essays Towards Evangelical and Catholic Unity in East and West*.Reprint, Eugene, OR: Wipf and Stock, 1997.

———. *Theology in Reconstruction*. Eugene, OR: Wipf and Stock, 1996.

———. The Thomas F. Torrance Manuscript Collection. Special Collections, Princeton Theological Seminary Library, Box 10, "My Boyhood in China 1913–1927."

———. The Thomas F. Torrance Manuscript Collection. Special Collections, Princeton Theological Seminary Library, Box 10, "Memoir of Visit to Palestine and the Middle East in the Spring."

———. The Thomas F. Torrance Manuscript Collection. Special Collections, Princeton Theological Seminary Library, Box 10, "Student Years—Edinburgh to Basel. 1934–1938."

———. The Thomas F. Torrance Manuscript Collection. Special Collections, Princeton Theological Seminary Library, Box 10, "The Visit by Thomas F. Torrance to Chengdu, the Capital of Sichuan, and to Weichou and Chiang Villages in Wenchuan County, the Upper Min Valley, Sichuan (October 4–18, 1986)," and "Journal of My Visit to Hong Kong, Chengdu and Wenchuan (April 22–June 3, 1994)."

———. The Thomas F. Torrance Manuscript Collection. Special Collections, Princeton Theological Seminary Library, Box 11, "Letters from Thomas F. Torrance to his parents and siblings, from Basel, Switzerland and Berlin, Germany. 1937–1938."

———. The Thomas F. Torrance Manuscript Collection. Special Collections, Princeton Theological Seminary Library, Box 11, "Letters from Thomas F. Torrance to his parents and siblings, from Basel, Switzerland and Berlin, Germany. 1937–1938."

———. The Thomas F. Torrance Manuscript Collection. Special Collections, Princeton Theological Seminary Library, Box 14, "Thomas F. Torrance—Curricula vitae and bibliography (to 1993)."

———. The Thomas F. Torrance Manuscript Collection. Special Collections, Princeton Theological Seminary Library, Box 15, "Program and laureation address from the conferment of the Honorary Doctor of Science to Thomas F. Torrance, Heriot-Watt University. November 12, 1983."

———. The Thomas F. Torrance Manuscript Collection. Special Collections, Princeton Theological Seminary Library, Box 15, "Speech by Duncan Forrester on the occasion of the unveiling of Thomas F. Torrance's portrait by Geoffrey Squire, New College, Edinburgh. October 3, 1991."

———. The Thomas F. Torrance Manuscript Collection. Special Collections, Princeton Theological Seminary Library, Box 19, "Letter from Torrance to Barth dated January 7, 1961."

———. The Thomas F. Torrance Manuscript Collection. Special Collections, Princeton Theological Seminary Library, Box 20, "Beechgrove Church Publications. April 1949."

———. The Thomas F. Torrance Manuscript Collection. Special Collections, Princeton Theological Seminary Library, Box 22, "Science and Theology," with "Theology and Science."

———. The Thomas F. Torrance Manuscript Collection. Special Collections, Princeton Theological Seminary Library, Box 25, "Lectures on Christology: 'The Mystery of Christ.'"

———. The Thomas F. Torrance Manuscript Collection. Special Collections, Princeton Theological Seminary Library, Box 26, "The Mystery of the Kingdom."

———. The Thomas F. Torrance Manuscript Collection. Special Collections, Princeton Theological Seminary Library, Box 29, "Lectures on Ecclesiology (subsequently published as "Le mystere pascal du Christ et l'Eucharistie," *ISTINA* 4 (1975): 404–34)."

———. The Thomas F. Torrance Manuscript Collection. Special Collections, Princeton Theological Seminary Library, Box 29, "The Pascal Mystery and the Eucharist: General Theses," *Liturgical Review* 6 (1976): 6–12)."

———. The Thomas F. Torrance Manuscript Collection. Special Collections, Princeton Theological Seminary Library, Box 29, "The Mystery of Christ (draft)."

———. The Thomas F. Torrance Manuscript Collection. Special Collections, Princeton Theological Seminary Library, Box 38, "Sermon on John 1:9: University Sermon, Leeds, Emmanuel Church, November 15, 1981."

———. The Thomas F. Torrance Manuscript Collection. Special Collections, Princeton Theological Seminary Library, Box 38, "Sermon on John 8:12: Whitekirk, August 31, 1980."

———. The Thomas F. Torrance Manuscript Collection. Special Collections, Princeton Theological Seminary Library, Box 38, "Sermon on 1 John 1:5, 1973."

———. The Thomas F. Torrance Manuscript Collection. Special Collections, Princeton Theological Seminary Library, Box 38, "Handwritten notes, Romans 12.1–3."

———. The Thomas F. Torrance Manuscript Collection. Special Collections, Princeton Theological Seminary Library, Box 39, "'Light' (Kings College Chapel, Aberdeen: February 13, 1977)."

———. The Thomas F. Torrance Manuscript Collection. Special Collections, Princeton Theological Seminary Library, Box 39, "A Faith for Hard Times: The Living Light. Sermon, November 20, 1977."

———. The Thomas F. Torrance Manuscript Collection. Special Collections, Princeton Theological Seminary Library, Box 39, "Light: Its Theology and Physics. Sermon, Lawnswood School, Leeds: November 16, 1981."

———. The Thomas F. Torrance Manuscript Collection. Special Collections, Princeton Theological Seminary Library, Box 39, "The Paschal Mystery of Christ and the Eucharist: General Theses. (New College Lecture)."

———. The Thomas F. Torrance Manuscript Collection. Special Collections, Princeton Theological Seminary Library, Box 40, "Handwritten notes, 'Light and Way.'"

———. The Thomas F. Torrance Manuscript Collection. Special Collections, Princeton Theological Seminary Library, Box 42, "Sermon on Gen 1:1: Alyth, Sept 28, 1941."

———. The Thomas F. Torrance Manuscript Collection. Special Collections, Princeton Theological Seminary Library, Box 75, "The Light of the World: A Sermon. *The Reformed Journal* (December 1988)."

———. *Transformation and Convergence in the Frame of Knowledge: Explorations in the Interrelations of Scientific and Theological Enterprise.* Grand Rapids: Eerdmans, 1984.

———. *The Trinitarian Faith: The Evangelical Theology of the Ancient Catholic Church.* Edinburgh: T&T Clark, 1995.

———. *Trinitarian Perspectives: Toward Doctrinal Agreement.* Edinburgh: T&T Clark, 1994.

———. "Truth and Authority: Theses on Truth." *Irish Theological Quarterly* 39 (1972): 215–42.

———. "What is the Reformed Church?" *Biblical Theology* 9 (1959): 51–62.

Torrance, T. F., and Donald Macleod. "Thomas Torrance and Donald Macleod Dialogue." Tape 200. Edinburgh: Rutherford House, 1999. http://tapesfromscotland.org/Rutherfordhouseaudio.htm.

Trueman, Carl. "Admiring the Sistine Chapel: Reflections on Carl F. H. Henry's *God, Revelation and* Authority." *Themelios* 25 (2000): 48–58.

Vanhoozer, Kevin J. *The Drama of Doctrine: A Canonical Linguistic Approach to Christian Theology.* Louisville: Westminster John Knox, 2005.

———. "Interpreting Scripture Between the Rock of Biblical Studies and the Hard Place of Systematic Theology: The State of the Evangelical (Dis)union." Lecture delivered at "Renewing the Evangelical Mission" Conference held at Gordon-Conwell Theological Seminary (October 13–15, 2009).

Walvoord, John F. "The Impeccability of Christ." *Bibliotheca Sacra* 118 (1961): 195–202.

Ware, Kallistos. "Light and Darkness in the Mystical Theology of the Greek Fathers." In *Light from Light: Scientists and Theologians in Dialogue,* edited by G. O'Collins and M. A. Myers, 131–59. Grand Rapids: Eerdmans, 2012.

———. *The Orthodox Way.* London: Mowbrays, 1979.

Webster, John. *Holiness.* Grand Rapids: Eerdmans, 2003.

———. *Holy Scripture: A Dogmatic Sketch.*Cambridge: Cambridge University Press, 2003.

———. "T. F. Torrance on Scripture." Keynote address at the annual meeting of the T. F. Torrance Theological Fellowship, Montreal, November 6, 2009.

———. "T. F. Torrance on Scripture." *Scottish Journal of Theology*65 (2012): 34–63.

———. "Trinity and Creation." *International Journal of Systematic Theology*12 (2010): 4–19.

Weightman, Colin. *Theology in a Polanyian Universe: The Theology of Thomas Torrance.* New York: Peter Lang, 1994.

Weinandy, Thomas G. *Does God Change? The Word's Becoming in the Incarnation.*Petersham, MA: St. Bede's, 1985.

———. *Does God Suffer?* Edinburgh: T&T Clark, 2000.

———. *In the Likeness of Sinful Flesh: An Essay on the Humanity of Christ.*Edinburgh: T&T Clark, 1993.

Wiles, Maurice. "The Unassumed Is the Unhealed." *Religious Studies* 4 (1968): 47–56.

Willis, E. D. *Calvin's Catholic Christology: The Function of the So-Called Extra Calvinisticum in Calvin's Theology.*Leiden: Brill, 1966.

Wright, N. T. *The New Testament and the People of God.*London: SPCK, 1992.

Yeung, J. H-K. *Being and Knowing: An Examination of T. F. Torrance's Christological Science.*Hong Kong: China Alliance, 1996.

Index of Names and Subjects

Abba, 83
Achtemeier, P. M., 51, 195
Adam, 19, 78, 153, 160–61, 165, 167, 171–72, 174, 180, 184–85, 289–90
Alfeyev, H., 124, 195
Anatolios, K., 162, 164, 195
Anglican, 5, 16, 58
Anselm, 9–10, 25, 42–43, 47, 63, 66, 98, 100, 109, 122, 132, 165–66, 195, 204, 208
Apczynski, J. V., 28, 195
Apostolic, 11, 24, 109, 127, 210–11
Aquinas, T., 9, 39, 63, 67, 88, 126, 132, 166, 171–72, 197, 202
Aristotle, 38–39, 53–54, 203
Atheism, 68, 86
Augustine, 8, 24, 48, 58–59, 66, 186

Barr, J., 72, 195
Barth, K., ix, 4–5, 7–8, 13–16, 21–22, 24–25, 30, 35–39, 42–45, 47, 49, 68, 65–66, 68–76, 78–82, 85–86, 88, 93–94, 98–99, 108–12, 116, 121, 126, 134, 137–39, 144, 151, 169, 171, 173–75, 180–82, 190, 193, 195–96, 199–202, 204–9, 211–13
Bartos, E., 23, 195
Bender, K. J., 149, 196
Bloesch, D. G., 102–3, 115, 196
Böhl, E., 171, 196
Bouillard, H., 76, 87, 196
Brand, C. O., 98–99, 196
Branick, V. P., 175–76, 196
Brown, R. E., 175, 196
Brunner, E., 65, 72–73, 93, 171, 195–96
Buckley, J. J., 74, 196

Calvin, J., 9–10, 14, 16, 19, 47, 58, 65–66, 68–79, 98, 103, 122, 128–31, 136, 139, 149, 152, 167, 177, 186, 191, 195–96, 198, 201–2, 204, 207–8, 216
Calvinism, 9–10, 15, 103, 183, 200
Calvinist, 15, 66
Carvin, W. P., 50, 196
Catholic, 14–16, 33, 48, 53, 58, 69, 76, 92, 107–8, 126, 134, 148, 152, 163, 171, 176, 179, 181, 196, 212, 215–16
Catholicism, 101
Chrestou, P., 143–44, 196
Christocentric, 50, 66, 76, 137, 148, 159, 161, 163, 165, 167, 169, 171, 173, 175, 177, 179, 181, 183, 185, 187, 189, 191
Christological, 9, 14, 16, 24–25, 42, 49, 63, 65–66, 107, 129, 138, 141, 153, 154, 163, 169–70, 172, 206, 216
Christology, xiii, 12, 16–17, 25, 42, 69, 114, 130, 146, 148–49, 159–67, 169–74, 176–80, 183–86, 189–91, 193, 197, 199, 203, 208, 214, 216
Chung, T., 130, 196
Clendenin, D. B., 131, 196
Colyer, E. M., ix, xiv, 4, 6, 8–9, 15, 27–28, 36, 47, 64, 81–83, 99, 109, 123, 132, 135, 139, 145, 152–53, 196, 201, 207, 209
Community, 27, 59, 112, 141, 144, 147, 198
Condemnation/Condemned/Condemning, 69, 77, 174, 176, 184, 185, 187
Consecrate/Consecrated/Consecration, 12, 77, 102, 132
Constantinople, 45, 156

Constantinopolitan, 16, 34, 175, 209
Cosmology, 38–39, 41, 48, 52, 141, 146, 149, 156, 208
Cosmos, 67, 135, 146, 150, 157, 202
Cranfield, C. E. B., 175, 197
Crisp, O. D., 125, 131, 160, 176, 181, 183, 185–86, 189, 197, 204
Curse, 176, 185–186

Dabney, D. L., 148, 197
Damned, 103, 171, 187–88
Darkness, 70, 123, 128, 130, 215
Davidson, I., ix, 159, 197
Dawkins, R., 68, 197
Dawson, G., 3, 208
Death, 14, 54, 57, 78, 80, 83, 102–3, 129, 146, 153, 161–162, 169, 172, 180–82, 184–85, 187
Del Colle, R., 9, 197
Destiny, 92, 143, 152, 174, 183, 201
Devil, 169, 172, 174
Devitt, M., 50, 197
Divinization, 73, 125, 131, 134, 138, 184, 204; deification, 23, 67, 122, 124, 132–33, 144, 189, 195, 199, 200, 204, 208; *theosis*, 67, 73, 107, 122–31, 133–34, 146, 170, 175, 178, 181, 183–84, 186, 188, 191, 199–200, 203, 209, 211
Dodd, C. H., 175, 197
Dostoevsky, F., 58
Dowey, E. A., 65, 77, 139, 198
Dulles, A., 56, 198

Ebionite, 189
Edersheim, A., 177, 198
Edwards, J., 125, 129, 131, 167, 170, 177, 182, 198, 200–201, 204, 209
Einstein, A., ix–x, 9–10, 17–18, 25, 30, 33, 36, 39–43, 47–50, 52, 57, 80, 84, 121, 135, 198, 202, 205, 207
Enlightenment, 20, 59, 73, 99, 103, 199
Epistemic/Epistemology 9–10, 17, 23, 25, 27, 29–31, 33–34, 35, 37–38, 40–43, 46–48, 50, 52, 57, 60–61, 63, 75, 86, 92–93, 95, 96–98, 100–102, 104–6, 115, 117, 122, 157, 177, 204, 206, 208
Eschatological/Eschatology, 52, 103, 115, 146, 151, 153–55, 156, 206
Eternal/Eternally, 10, 15, 30–34, 38–39, 45, 52, 54, 70, 75, 79, 99, 115–16, 125, 127–29, 131, 133, 143, 145, 147, 153–54, 156, 161, 166–67, 169, 172, 176, 178, 182, 186–87, 190
Ethics/Ethical 11, 28, 125, 129, 198, 212
Evangelical, 6, 8, 10, 15–16, 27–31, 33–34, 43, 48, 53, 60, 76, 87, 91–94, 99, 101, 103, 108, 110–11, 114–16, 126, 134–35, 137, 142–43, 148, 152, 163, 174, 176, 181–83, 196, 198–201, 203, 206, 209, 211–12, 215
Evangelicalism, 98, 101, 107, 115, 117, 202, 205
Evil, 102, 126, 141, 150, 166, 170, 174, 199
Evolution, 64, 68, 86, 141, 197–99
Exorcist, 20

Faith/Faithful/Faithfully/Faithfulness, xi, 4, 10, 12, 14, 16, 19, 21, 23, 27–28, 30, 33–34, 38, 40, 43–44, 46, 49, 53–55, 56–60, 64, 70–72, 75, 78, 83–86, 91–92, 96–97, 100, 102, 104–6, 108, 110–15, 117, 125–26, 133–34, 139, 148, 151–54, 161, 171, 176, 193, 195–96, 198, 205–6, 210–12, 214–15
Fall, 65, 71, 77–78, 95, 102–3, 146, 149, 153–55, 167–68, 171–75, 180, 182, 198, 210
Father (God), 16, 21, 28–34, 45–46, 55, 67, 71, 75–76, 78, 83, 108, 111, 129, 133, 143–49, 151, 154–57, 162, 165–66, 169, 172, 174, 177–78, 180, 183, 186–187
Fellowship, 3, 5, 12–13, 82, 114, 145, 151, 154, 156, 197, 216

Index of Names and Subjects | 223

Fergusson, D., 64, 86, 198
Flesh, 34, 45–46, 125, 131, 157, 161–62, 165, 169, 171–76, 178–80, 182, 184–87, 196, 216
Forde, G. O., 138, 198
Forgiven/forgiveness 20, 126, 135, 166
Franke, J. R., 93, 198
freedom, 53–54, 79, 99, 124, 147, 151, 174, 177, 205

Gascoigne, J., 41, 198
Gelwick, R., 56, 198
Gentiles, 67, 104, 166, 202
Gilkey, L., 36, 198
Gloede, G., 66, 198
Glory/glorification, 34, 69–70, 129, 138, 144–45, 147, 149, 151–53, 170, 182, 201, 203, 208
Gnostic, 135, 176
Gospel, 3–4, 6, 8, 20, 24, 27–30, 35–36, 45, 59–60, 73, 82–83, 100, 102, 107, 121, 127, 137–38, 152, 159, 161–63, 183, 199, 204, 206, 208–11
Grace, 24, 34, 58, 67–68, 71, 73–74, 103, 108, 117, 134, 138, 145–48, 152, 168, 170, 182, 188, 191, 195, 201, 218
Grenz, S. J., 92, 94, 98, 115, 144, 147, 198
Grillmeier, A., 163–64, 181, 198
Grudem, W., 93, 199
Guilt/Guilty, 126, 150, 160, 171, 173, 176, 179, 183, 185–86, 168, 190
Gunton, C. E., 59, 81, 99–101, 104, 113–14, 144, 160, 162–63, 167, 169, 188–91, 199, 208

Habets, M., xiii, 10, 13, 15, 28, 51, 53, 60, 67, 73, 103, 107, 122, 124, 129, 146, 149, 183, 191, 193, 199–200
Hardy, D. W., 4, 47, 200
Hart, T. A., 5, 110, 136, 169, 184, 197, 200–201
Hastings, W. R., 170, 200

Hawking, S. W., 68, 200
Heal/Healed/Healing, 129, 152, 161, 167, 176–77, 179, 183–84, 186, 197
Heaven/heavens, 39, 69, 85–86, 88, 146–47, 151, 154, 174, 177, 183, 201, 205
Hebblethwaite, B., 4, 21, 55, 200, 212
Hell, 159, 179, 181, 188, 209
Hellwig, M., 159, 200
Henry, C. F. H., 59–60, 91–104, 117, 196, 199–200, 202, 215
Heron, A. I. C., 5–6, 15, 66, 78, 201
Hesselink, I. J., 6–7, 24, 97, 101, 201
Hitler, A., 72
Holder, R. D., 72, 75, 85–86, 88, 201, 204
Holmes, S. R., 170, 182, 201
Holy/Holiness 13, 16–17, 21, 28–34, 46, 55, 60, 67, 70, 75, 85, 89, 92, 98, 103, 107–9, 111–16, 123–24, 126, 132–33, 144–47, 154, 156–57, 159, 161, 167–70, 172, 176–78, 180–81, 185–87, 189–90, 196, 200, 204, 206, 208, 215
Honor, 13–15, 64, 78, 86, 99, 198, 201, 210–11
Howe, G., 36, 201
Hoyningen-Huene, P., 49, 201
Hughes, P. E., 152, 174, 201
Hunsinger, G., 65, 88, 108, 126–27, 201

Idol/Idolatrous/Idolatry, 72–73, 86
Irving, E., 160, 163, 167, 169–71, 173, 175–78, 184–86, 188–91, 199, 202, 204, 209

Jaki, S. L., 68, 202
Jesus, 11–12, 15, 19–20, 25, 27, 29–32, 34, 39, 42–46, 54, 60, 65, 71–72, 75, 82–83, 86, 95–97, 100, 107, 109–12, 115, 116, 125–29, 131, 133–35, 138, 142–43, 145–47, 150, 154–56, 159–66, 168–73, 175–77, 180–81,

183–91, 197–98, 200, 203, 205–6, 210–11
Jew(s), 58, 104
Judgment, 99, 102, 128, 180, 185, 186
Justice, 151, 190
Justification, 18, 68, 162, 186, 203

Kantian, 40, 71
Kapic, K. M., 163–64, 171, 218, 202
Keating, J. F., 53, 202
Kelly, J. N. D., 163–64, 171, 202
Kernohan, R. D., 16, 202
Kingdom, 130, 142, 148, 153, 183, 205–6, 214
Kögler, H. H., 151, 202
Kreitzmann, N., 67, 202
Kruger, C. B., 185–86, 202
Kuhn, T. S., 17, 49, 201–2, 207, 209

Labyrinth, 149, 208
Lane, A. N. S., 47, 202
Law, 8, 44, 96, 104, 146, 176, 185, 211
Leplin, J., 50, 202
Leung, M. M., 98, 202
Levering, M., 114, 203
Lewis, C. S., 129, 166, 200, 203, 206
Light, 21, 24, 45, 53, 55, 59, 65, 70, 72, 74, 85, 88, 95, 111, 114–15, 122–32, 137, 143, 149, 159, 171, 175, 177–79, 181, 185, 198, 202, 208–9, 211, 214–15
Locke, J., 39, 58, 63, 100
Lord/Lordship 34, 68, 129, 145, 147, 151, 154, 161, 173, 177, 188–89, 203, 205
Lossky, V., 66, 125, 131–32, 134, 150, 203
Louth, A., 36–37, 136–37, 203
Love, 5, 7, 27, 53–54, 82, 127, 132, 136, 145–47, 150–53, 161, 170, 177, 181

Macierowski, E. M., 54, 203
Mackenzie, I., 5–6, 203

MacLeod, D., 4, 66, 83, 103, 160–61, 186, 188–89, 203, 212, 215
Mannermaa, T., 186, 203
Mantzaridis, G. I., 124, 132–33, 204
Marley, A. G., 4, 10, 25, 27, 204
Marx, K., 151
Mascall, E. L., 35–36, 52, 204
Maury, P., 66, 204
Maxwell, J. C., ix, 9, 17, 25, 33, 40, 47–49, 54, 135, 204
McCall, T., 100, 104, 117, 204
McClymont, M. J., 125, 131, 204
McCormack, B. L., x, 167, 180, 185, 188, 190, 204
McDowell, J. C., 72, 75, 204
McFarlane, G. W. P., 167, 170, 204
McGrath, A., 9, 3–5, 7–8, 11–12, 36, 41–42, 47, 49–50, 52, 56, 63, 68–70, 81, 84–85, 105, 115, 148, 150, 204
McIntyre, J., 165, 204
McKenzie, R. H., 188, 205
McMaken, W. T., 82, 205
Messiah, 177, 198
Michelangelo, 101
Ministry, 3, 5–6, 14, 19, 78, 137, 152, 160, 184, 201, 208, 210
Mitchell, R. G., 50, 205
Molendijk, A. L., 45, 205
Molnar, P. D., ix, 16, 69, 81–82, 85–86, 96, 99, 124, 197, 205
Moltmann, J., 142, 205
Moral, 116, 133, 145, 150, 159, 166, 168, 172, 179, 181, 183, 188, 209
Morris, L., 177, 189, 205–6
Morrison, T. V., 25, 28, 38, 40–41, 51, 65–66, 206
Mostert, C., 52, 206
Muller, R. A., 169, 176, 206
Munchin, D., 96, 105–6, 206
Myers, B., 27, 88, 124, 126, 130, 202, 206, 209, 215

Nebelsick, H., 36, 206
Neidhardt, W. J., 30, 39, 206

Index of Names and Subjects | 225

Newbigin, L., 59, 206
Newton, I., 38–39, 108, 151

Ontology, 26, 29–32, 34, 40–42, 47, 52, 55, 58, 73, 76, 88, 93, 97, 101–2, 105, 108, 128, 137–38, 146, 163, 169, 184, 188
Owen, J., 163, 166–70, 173, 176–77, 190–91, 199, 206, 208

Palamas, G., 123–25, 131–33, 159, 177, 179, 204, 208
Palma, R. J., 36–37, 49, 55, 79, 206
Pannenberg, W., 45, 52, 142–44, 153–57, 206, 208
Parker, T. H. L., 65, 207
Pascal mystery, 130, 213–14
Pentecostal, 160, 169, 209
Peters, T., 81, 207
Pettersen, A., 162, 207
Physics, 17–18, 30, 52, 80, 125, 208, 214
Plato, 38–39, 136, 203
Poirier, M. W., 49, 207
Polanyi, M., ix, xi, 9–10, 25, 27–28, 30, 33, 37–38, 40, 42–43, 47, 49–50, 55–60, 88, 97–98, 106, 113–14, 121, 195, 198, 207, 209–12
Polikarov, A., 50, 207
Prayer, 131, 164, 191, 207
Predestination, 7
Prenter, R., 71, 207
Puritan, 15

Rabbi, 20
Rahner, K., 10, 132, 138, 207
Reconciliation, 5, 16, 27, 30, 48–49, 72, 103, 107, 126, 136, 143, 151, 154, 163, 173–74, 176, 178, 181–84, 188, 197, 201, 212
Redding, G., 164, 207
Redeem/ Redemption, iii, 20, 44, 67, 72–73, 133, 142–43, 146, 148–57, 160, 165, 171, 175–76, 179, 181–83, 184–88, 196

Redeemer, 77–78, 83, 112, 133, 176
Rehnman, S., 15, 66, 207
Repentance, 95
Resurrection, 45, 57–58, 64, 75–76, 80, 101–3, 108–10, 112, 115, 122, 129, 138, 146, 150–51, 153–54, 161, 169, 180–81, 184, 187, 212
Richardson, K., 109, 123, 131–33, 135, 139, 207
Ridderbos, H., 175, 235
Righteous/righteousness 102, 174, 187
Rodger, S., 165, 208
Rogich, D. M., 159, 177, 179, 208
Russell, R. J., 52, 208

Sacraments, 137, 152, 210
Sacred, 36, 83, 198
Sacrifice/sacrificial 83, 184, 186, 188
Salvation, 30, 70, 102–3, 107, 125, 131–32, 136, 148–49, 162, 167, 172, 177, 180, 183–85, 188, 190, 197, 204
Sanctification, 103, 168, 180
Sanctified, 70, 103, 167, 176, 184, 187, 189
Satan, 172
Savior/Saviour 5, 27, 83, 146, 163, 166, 179
Schreiner, S., 149, 208
Schwöbel, C., 160, 163, 167, 208
Screwtape, 129, 203
Serpent, 83, 169
Sholz, H., 45, 205, 208
Shults, F. L., 64, 86, 144, 198, 208
Shuster, M., 117, 208
Sin, 20, 71, 78, 83, 87, 126, 150, 153, 160, 165–66, 168, 171–77, 179–80, 182–87, 189–90; sinfulness, xiii, 93, 116, 128, 159–61, 165–66, 169, 171–73, 175–76, 178–82, 185–86, 188, 196, 216; sinless, 160, 165–66, 169–70, 172–73, 175–80, 178, 180, 185–87, 189, 197; sinner, 93, 126, 186

Son, 4–7, 21, 28–35, 45–46, 55, 57, 70–71, 75–76, 78, 89, 108, 124–25, 127–29, 132–33, 143–48, 153–57, 159, 161, 163–64, 163–70, 175–80, 184–86, 190, 196, 202; Sonship, 155
Sorabji, R. K., 54, 208
Soul, 38, 125, 132, 136, 161–62, 164, 168–70, 181–83, 198
Spence, A., 163–64, 167–68, 191, 208
Spirit, 16–17, 21, 28–35, 46, 55, 67, 70, 75–76, 83, 85, 88–89, 93, 103, 108–9, 114–15, 117, 121–22, 124–25, 129, 131, 133–34, 136, 138, 142, 144–48, 155–57, 161, 166–70, 172, 175, 177, 180–81, 185–86, 189–90, 196–98, 200, 202, 204–6
Spirituality, 9, 38, 79, 124, 130, 132, 135–37, 159, 168, 177, 179, 201, 208
Spjuth, R., 50–51, 63, 153, 208
Stăniloae, D., 23, 144, 195, 208
Stein, J., 3, 18, 208
Strachan, C. G., 160, 169, 202, 209
Strobel, K., 125, 129, 209
Strug, C., 49, 209
Sudduth, M., 64, 66, 70, 163–64, 209
Suffering, 53, 80, 87, 150, 155, 159, 162, 164, 183, 202, 216
Supernatural, 67, 92, 125, 198

Tamburello, D. E., 69, 71, 136, 209
Tanner, K. E., 65, 124, 156, 178, 197, 209
Telos, 148, 150–51, 153–54
Temptation, 84, 87, 159, 172, 176–77, 182; tempted, 53, 170, 176
Thiemann, R., 28, 100, 104, 117, 204, 209
Thorson, W. R., 57, 60, 209
Tradition, xi, 9–10, 14, 16, 23–24, 38, 45, 48, 51, 54, 64–67, 70, 80–81, 92–93, 98, 101, 109, 122–24, 126, 130–33, 135–38, 141, 153, 160, 163–64, 166–67, 171–72, 178–81, 185–86, 190–91, 193, 195, 197–98, 203–4, 207, 210–11
Transfiguration, 112, 131
Trinitarian, xiii, 3–4, 20, 8–9, 13–16, 21, 24, 27–29, 31, 33, 41, 53, 55, 59, 64–66, 81, 83, 88, 91–92, 99, 109, 122–24, 126, 132–35, 137–39, 144–45, 147–48, 152–57, 161, 167, 169–70, 190, 196–97, 199, 201, 207–9, 215
Trinity, xi, 4, 13, 16, 21, 27–29, 31–34, 46, 65, 67, 75, 84, 96, 99, 124, 132, 136, 138, 142, 144, 156, 181, 196, 201–2, 205, 207–8, 216
Triunity, 25
Trueman, C., 101, 215
Truth, iv, 4, 15, 20, 25–28, 29, 31, 34, 36, 44, 47, 50–51, 54–55, 59–60, 65, 67, 71, 74, 82, 84–86, 88, 92–98, 101–9, 111–17, 121, 124, 128, 135, 137, 168, 171, 179, 193, 195, 197, 199–200, 205–6, 208, 215; truthfulness, 108

Universalism, 20, 159, 179, 181, 188, 191, 209
Universe, 14, 20, 28, 37–38, 40–41, 43, 47, 50–53, 55–58, 63, 66, 68–71, 75, 79, 81, 84–85, 88, 114, 127, 142–43, 145–47, 149–50, 153–54, 195, 197, 204, 207, 216

Vanhoozer, K. J., 111, 117, 215

Walvoord, J. F., 177, 215
War, 3, 6, 11, 72, 99, 196
Ware, K., 130–31, 215
Webster, J., 65–66, 103, 108, 112, 114, 156, 201, 209, 215
Weightman, C., 14, 28, 41, 50, 56–58, 66, 71, 81, 195, 216
Weinandy, T. G., ix, 53, 161–65, 169, 171–73, 179, 182, 216

Wiles, M., 161, 164, 177–78, 183–184, 216
Willis, E. D., 69, 216
Wisdom, 69, 77, 104, 146, 169
Worship, 21, 27, 29, 34, 55, 77, 132, 151, 182–84

Wrath, 53, 185
Wright, N. T., 51–52, 161, 189, 203, 216

Yeung, J. H.-K., 25, 49, 63, 135, 138–39, 216

www.ingramcontent.com/pod-product-compliance
Lightning Source LLC
Chambersburg PA
CBHW071906290426
44110CB00013B/1294